7/98

Witchcraft, Lycanthropy, Drugs, and Disease

WITHDRAWN

D1275007

American University Studies

Series XI
Anthropology and Sociology

Vol. 70

PETER LANG
New York • Washington, D.C./Baltimore
Bern • Frankfurt am Main • Berlin • Vienna • Paris

H. Sidky

Witchcraft, Lycanthropy, Drugs, and Disease

An Anthropological Study of the European Witch-Hunts

PETER LANG
New York • Washington, D.C./Baltimore
Bern • Frankfurt am Main • Berlin • Vienna • Paris

Library of Congress Cataloging-in-Publication Data

Sidky, H.
Witchcraft, lycanthropy, drugs, and disease:
an anthropological study of the European witch-hunts/ H. Sidky.
p. cm. — (American university studies. Series XI,
Anthropology and sociology; vol. 70)
Includes bibliographical references and index.
1. Witchcraft—Europe—History. 2. Trials (Witchcraft)—Europe—History.
3. Demoniac possession—Europe—History. 4. Hallucinogenic drugs and
religious experience—Europe—History. 5.Werewolves—Europe—History.
I. Title. II. Series.
GR530.S53   133.4'3'09409031—dc20   96-18078
ISBN 0-8204-3354-3
ISSN 0740-0489

Die Deutsche Bibliothek-CIP-Einheitsaufnahme

Sidky, H.:
Witchcraft, lycanthropy, drugs, and disease: an anthropological study
of the European witch hunts/ H. Sidky. –New York; Washington,
D.C./Baltimore; Bern; Frankfurt am Main; Berlin; Vienna; Paris: Lang.
(American university studies: Ser. 11, Anthropology and sociology; Vol. 70)
ISBN 0-8204-3354-3
NE: American university studies/ 11

Cover design by Wendy Lee.

Acknowledgments

Grateful acknowledgment is made to the following for permission to reprint previously published materials:

"De Laguna's commentaries on Hallucinogenic Drugs and Witchcraft in Dioscorides' *Materia Medica*" by Theodore Rothman, in *Bulletin of the History of Medicine* 46. Copyright © 1972 by Johns Hopkins University Press.

This work owes a great deal, in all stages of production, to the constant and proficient efforts of Jennifer Dowling. She has my sincere thanks.

I would also like to thank the expert staff of the High End Learning Lab of the College of Arts and Sciences, Miami University, for their kind and patient assistance during the preparation of the manuscript.

I wish to acknowledge my debt to my teachers, Dr. Anthony Walker, Dr. Erika Bourguignon, and Dr. Richard Moore, anthropologists who have had a profound influence on my thinking, theoretical perspectives, and scholarly interests (although they may not agree with the views expressed in the present study).

Finally, I am indebted to Dr. John Messenger, my friend and mentor, who over the last decade has been a unwavering source of support, advice, encouragement, and inspiration. This book is dedicated to him with great affection and gratitude.

Table of Contents

Table of Figures

Figures

Maps

Preface

Long before the political mass murders of the present century, western Europe experienced another kind of holocaust—the witch-hunts of the sixteenth and seventeenth centuries. The witch-persecutions lasted for over two hundred years, longer than any modern counterpart, when thousands of people were brutally tortured, maimed, and roasted alive; millions more were terrorized and intimidated. The crimes of the accused included flying through the air, changing into animals, dancing with demons, and worshipping the Devil.

The brutal execution of human beings for such implausible offenses might seem incomprehensible to those living in the twentieth century, however, the European witch-hunts bear too grim a resemblance to the large-scale political atrocities and judicial mass murders of our own time to be dismissed or treated as an isolated historical aberration. Nor can the presence of underground religions or secret societies account for the magnitude and duration of the witch-persecutions, although a number of writers have asserted that witches were members of non-Christian or anti-Christian sects on the losing side of a battle for religious hegemony. Attempts to extrapolate the existence of "witch cults" or "satanic sects" from contemporary pamphlets and trial records have ended in fantasy, trivialization, and obscurantism.

Equally untenable is the argument that people believed in witchcraft, therefore witchcraft was real, and we need look no further for answers. This worn-out mentalist approach, which treats thoughts and ideas as independent variables, mystifies cultural and historical processes by disregarding the concrete sociopolitical determinants of the witch-persecutions.

The present work focuses on the process of witch-persecution, rather than on popular witchcraft beliefs. I am more concerned with how and why those in control of the judicial machinery and vehicles of propaganda focused, channeled, and manipulated diffuse anxieties about harmful magic and witchcraft, rather than with peasant mentalities or elementary village crudulities.

Throughout this study, I quote extensively from authoritative fifteenth-, sixteenth-, and seventeenth-century treatises on witchcraft, presenting the arguments in the words of their authors. For the sake of the general readers, who may not have access to the original sources, I have endeavored to make almost exclusive use of easily available sources in English. To ensure the continuity of the text, theoretical and methodological issues that may be of interest to the specialists are dealt with in the introduction and in the notes provided at the end of each chapter. Definitions of unfamiliar terms and concepts as well as supplementary information are also to be found in the endnotes.

Since the completion of this book, a number of pertinent studies have been published which could not be incorporated into the discussion or the bibliography. This is a shortcoming for which I must apologize in advance.

A Note on Quotations

In order to facilitate readability and comprehension I have changed the original spelling and capitalization of the sources quoted.

Introduction

Since the publication of Professor Trevor-Roper's famous (and now highly criticized) article, "The European Witch-Craze of the Sixteenth and Seventeenth Centuries," in 1967, "witchcraft studies" has become a respectable academic subject. The ostensible task specialists in this area have assigned themselves is "to diagnose" the thoughts, beliefs, and sentiments of the people being studied. They wish "to penetrate beyond the trials to the reality of popular beliefs," and to attain the "inside view." Highly critical of the nineteenth- and early twentieth-century "rationalist historians"—who saw the witch-hunts as the product of superstition or the abuse of power—modern writers have attempted to purge their methodologies of "ethnocentric biases" by approaching the subject from the point of view of the "actors" themselves.

The witch-hunts are therefore no longer seen as being explicable in terms of the activities of princes, preachers, and the vicious witch-finders who deliberately fostered fear, hysteria, violence, and mass murder. Equally untenable, from the point of view of these scholars, are works emphasizing the central role of judicial torture and the oppressive legal procedures that produced witches where none existed before, and manufactured evidence of crimes that were never committed. Suggestions that fraud, imposture, greed, and abuse of power were important in sparking and sustaining persecutions, evoke indignant rejections as "1940s thinking." Conclusions based on the terrifying similarities between the atrocities of the witch-hunting officials in early modern Europe and the persecutions and political mass murders of our own century are rebuked as banal, pedestrian, and ethnocentric.

Scholars touting mentalist perspectives (i.e., approaches which focus on phenomenological realities located inside the crania of actors)[1] appear to have appropriated the scholarly study of European witchcraft for themselves. However, the points noted above raise an important question: are mentalist approaches suitable for the task at hand? To answer this question it is necessary to critically examine the ontological assumptions and epistemological principals[2] underlying mentalist research perspectives.[3]

The coterie of writers dominating witchcraft studies define culture in terms of mental phenomena and consider the understanding of human behavior to be predicated upon an understanding of thoughts, beliefs, meanings, and the symbolic forms in which they are expressed. The question that arises immediately is: how can we know, with certainty, what really went on inside the heads of people who have long since gone to their graves? The answer, of course, is that we cannot. Attempts at getting the "inside view" are objectionable from the outset, both on the grounds that such endeavors are impossible because the evidence is fragmentary, and because the accounts and records—documents written by the promoters and engineers of the witch-hunts—are unsuited for such a purpose. Given the incomplete and biased nature of the evidence, a mentalist approach necessarily entails numerous unwarranted assumptions and conjectures about what people did, or did not, think and feel.

The objections raised above, however, are not deemed insuperable by mentalist researchers, and attempts "to hear the voices of the accused through the cracks of the interrogator's questions" have not been slow in forthcoming. In this process, the tangible and concrete have been abandoned in favor of the ephemeral and esoteric, while obscurantism has been advanced and praised as methodological innovation.

There is, however, a more fundamental issue to be dealt with here. Do approaches seeking the "insider's view"—provided that such information is truly accessible—actually yield coherent, parsimonious, objectively-valid, and non-trivial explanations? Not necessarily.

Writers operating under the auspices of mentalist research strategies treat the universe principally as an object of thought.[4]

Mental precepts, which govern behavior, the mentalist argument goes, are based on the transformation of sensory data (knowledge obtained through the senses) and are far removed from the empirical world (i.e., "what exists out there").[5] Objective reality, according to this view, does not exist—the cosmos, universe, world, reality, etc., are constructs of the human mind.[6] This perspective is incompatible with research strategies based on the ontological assumption that there is an objective reality existing outside the observer and that this reality is amenable to rational inquiry. Indeed, mentalist writers programmatically exclude the objective attributes of the human condition from their analyses. These researchers are less concerned with whether or not the beliefs people maintain—in this case witchcraft beliefs—are accurate in empirical or scientific terms, but instead take what people **believe** to be "real" as "real."[7] From this it follows that, in order to comprehend human action and behavior, it is essential to empathize with the people being studied, to get inside their heads, to determine how they formulate their reality, and to make that reality understandable.[8]

Comprehending and rendering the conceptual inner-world of people—the mission of mentalist research—is essentially an interpretive exercise.[9] Explanatory conclusions generated through this procedure are therefore interpretive in nature. An interpretive explanation attempts to make a particular phenomenon understandable by placing it within some meaningful context.[10] Such an approach is useful, to a certain extent, in shedding light on the internal logic of witchcraft and other belief systems. For example, I use E. Evans-Pritchard's now-classic interpretive ethnography of witchcraft beliefs among the Azande for insights into the logical structure of European witch-beliefs. Nevertheless, studies that are exclusively committed to a mentalist stance suffer from a number of serious shortcomings.

Mentalist writers seldom recognize, for example, that renditions of cognitive patterns are fundamentally different from descriptions of actual, behavioral events.[11] Sociocultural phenomena such as magic, witchcraft, religion, kinship, economics, politics, exploitation, warfare, etc., cannot be understood solely in terms of their mental dimensions.[12] Moreover, treating representations of reality shared by a particular group of people (i.e., their inner world) as "real" invariably leads to a confusion between what people say, wish, dream, and believe they do, with what they actually do.[13] In other words, the analyst is in danger of misconstruing what exists objectively with what people think exists, or want to exist, cognitively or emotionally.[14] Research perspectives that fail to make a rigorous distinction between representations of reality and what exists objectively cannot hope to produce tenable explanations.[15]

Finally, the mentalist premise that understanding human action and behavior requires getting inside people's heads (empathy and the insider's view) is unnecessary for an accurate assessment of human action and behavior. As one writer has cogently stated: "Sympathetic identification ... is neither sufficient nor essential to guarantee the discovery of truth in the human studies. It is not sufficient because the mistakes that people make when they think they have identified with others are notorious; it is not essential because it is possible to explain another person's behavior without identifying with him [or her]. It would be something of a nuisance if we tried to be schizophrenic while we studied schizophrenia. I conclude, therefore, that it is false to say that we understand the actions of other human beings 'only because they are known to us from the workings of our own minds.'"[16]

Mentalist writers insist, however, that all cultural phenomena must be interpreted in terms of the "insider's view." Unfortunately, perspectives which focus on, and restrict themselves to, concepts and distinctions that are "real," "culturally meaningful," and "appropriate" solely from the point of view of the "actors" necessarily eschew the legitimacy of scientific accounts of human behavior. This view, taken to its extreme, leads to **epistemological relativism**, the position that all knowledge is equally uncertain, and therefore scientific concepts and knowledge are inapplicable cross-culturally.[17] The intellectual enterprise undertaken to understand sociocultural phenomena is thus diminished to the status of mere aesthetic judgments.[18]

The ontological principals underlying mentalist perspectives necessitate an almost exclusive commitment to the analysis of internal, unobservable, cognitive aspects of human existence. To attain this inner dimension the researcher must employ intuitive insights and imaginative guesswork.[19] Intuition and guesswork, however, are highly subjective procedures that vary from writer to writer, even concerning the same symbol, process, or event. Mentalist research programs seldom provide any precise guidelines to ensure that different researchers studying the same phenomenon and addressing the same question will always adduce the same explanation.[20] The "multivocalic" nature of symbols (i.e., the propensity of symbols to possess different meanings simultaneously)[21] and the multiplicity of complex conceptual structures that must be interpreted thus pose major obstacles for this type of research.

In the ethnographic context, the verification of whether one has achieved an accurate representation of the "inside view" is contingent upon the consent, opinion, and affirmation of one's informants (i.e., the people being studied).[22] Witchcraft studies scholars, of course, do not have the luxury of live informants from whom to elicit confirmation—they must thus rely upon their own intuition when assessing the cogency of their explanations. Unfortunately, it is frequently impossible to intuitively distinguish accurate insights, guesses, and intuitions from inaccurate ones.[23]

How, then, can we evaluate the cogency of mentalist interpretations? This is not an easy task because such explications tend to be immune to verification by any systematic canons of appraisal.[24] Mentalist writers themselves attempt to evade the problems of verification and replication by insisting that their interpretations are to be assessed, not in terms of their empirical validity, but rather in terms of their logical validity, and their capacity to compel assent and appeal to the intellect and imagination.[25]

This, however, raises a further problem: how can we decide which of two or more seemingly equally "compelling" interpretations is correct? The epistemological foundations of mentalist perspectives provide no guidelines to enable us to distinguish a true claim to knowledge from an erroneous one. Explications that cannot be validated, or falsified, one could argue, are vacuous and do not really increase our understanding of the phenomena under study. Mentalist writers themselves, however, are unconcerned with specifying, or are unable to specify, how they know what they know. This is a critical epistemological weakness that renders suspect any claims by these researchers to objectively-valid knowledge.

Among the highly acclaimed studies of the witch-hunts from a mentalist perspective is Keith Thomas' monumental *Religion and the Decline of Magic* (1971).[26] A brief review of this work reveals the innumerable problems inherent in mentalist studies of European witchcraft. Thomas' central argument is that the witch-persecutions stemmed from genuine and widespread popular fears of maleficent magic. Although Thomas deals primarily with witch-beliefs in early modern England, much of what I have to say about his work is equally applicable to the studies of Continental witchcraft that seek explanations in the "mentality of the peasants" and in popular beliefs in *maleficium* (harmful magic). It is not Thomas' scholarship that I question, but rather the ontological premises and epistemological principals of his mentalist perspective. I proceed from a consciously polemic perspective, however, and in doing so, I hope to highlight the theoretical assumptions and epistemological orientation of the present study.

Thomas points out that just as everyone believed in witchcraft, some people believed that they themselves were witches. Such persons were usually women from the lowest and weakest elements of society.[27] They were individuals without family or friends; they were often old, sick, destitute, and dependent on the charity and generosity of uncharitable neighbors. These pathetic creatures lived in a state of desperate frustration arising from their social, political, and economic impotence. Harassed and mistreated by their neighbors who looked upon them as burdens on the community, they felt "genuine hatred" for those around them.[28] They often expressed their hostile feelings by cursing and uttering maledictions, the only form of retaliation (aside from arson) available to people in their social position.[29] Such circumstances, according to Thomas, created "witches."

Hoping to better their condition, Thomas maintains, these wretched individuals may have appealed to the Christian Devil, who tempted them with promises of money, food, and sexual satisfaction. They may have also sought the aid of Satan, he adds, in order to ensure the efficacy of their malevolent spells. In other words, the dynamics of the witch-hunts lay inside the heads of old women who, because of their wicked thoughts, invited persecution and brought death upon themselves.

Tracts written by the European witch-hunters are replete with comparable statements about witches and their motives. Thomas, however, has mistaken what the witch-hunters were saying about their victims as an actual representation of the inner lives of the people of sixteenth and seventeenth century England. He confidently remarks that "there is no reason why we should doubt the reality of such temptations."[30] Resorting to the Devil, he argues, symbolized the witches' alienation from society. Thus, witchcraft and Devil-worship were not total fantasies, they had "subjective reality."[31] As Thomas sees it, these old women who imagined themselves in league with the Devil really were witches. How is he able to establish that these alleged witches were actually enticed by the Devil, or that witchcraft had subjective reality? He does so by intuitive insights, aesthetic judgments, and imaginative guesswork—highly problematic procedures, as we have seen.

Are we to accept that every old beggar woman accused of being a witch bore malice toward her neighbors and, in the hope of unleashing diabolical powers in retaliation for being mistreated, entered into an imaginary alliance with Satan? Thomas seems to think so, although he later admits the tenuous nature of such a conclusion.[32]

Thomas relies on sensationalist pamphlets, information contained in tracts written by unscrupulous witch-hunters, such as Matthew Hopkins and John Stearne,[33] and confessions obtained by force, trickery, false promises, and psychological coercion (see Chapter Five, below). These sources tell us much about the various features of the official demonological propaganda; they are also useful in revealing the procedures employed to terrorize and mutilate innocent people; and they serve as ethnographic documents that detail the savagery of the witch-hunters. However, these documents cannot be relied upon to tell us a great deal about what people accused of witchcraft may have really thought or believed.

Throughout his study, Thomas' intense commitment to mentalist principals leads him to treat wholly imaginary events, e.g., wishing a neighbor's house to burn down, or his child to be stricken by disease, on equal terms with actual empirically-known events, such as an act of arson or murder. Thus, the thousands of people falsely accused of fantastic crimes, although not guilty in fact, were guilty in thought, and for Thomas (and the European witch-hunters) these amount to the same thing.

Fact and fantasy, however, are not the same thing! Indeed, thousands of innocent people would not have been put to death had judges and prosecutors been willing to make a distinction between imaginary and real events. In those few instances when magistrates chose to separate actual events from imaginary ones, the witch-persecutions came to a sudden halt (see Chapter Two, below).

Unfortunately, Thomas, like other mentalist writers (see below), fails to make this vitally important distinction. Thus, in an attempt to attain the "inside view," he inadvertently adopts a position akin to that of the European demonologists and witch-detectors. For example, as Henri Boguet, the obdurate sixteenth-century witch-slayer of Burgundy, declared, "even if witches are guilty of nothing more then their damnable thoughts and intentions, they are nevertheless guilty and should be burned, because the law takes cognisance of intentions in less serious cases, even if nothing concrete has resulted from these intentions."[34] Similarly, the eminent jurist Benedict Carpzov wrote in his notorious *Practica Rerum Criminalium* (1670), the main source book on criminal jurisprudence in Germany, "It makes no difference as to punishment whether witches are present [at the sabbats] personally or in imagination, for they have pact and commerce with the devil and owe him obedience, and moreover, they firmly believe that what they see really happens and their is nothing lacking as to their will."[35]

There are other equally serious problems with Thomas' mentalist treatise. The central premise of *Religion and the Decline of Magic* is that the witch-hunts in England were stimulated by popular fears of maleficent magic, rather than being fueled by the demonological stereotype of Devil-worshipping witches imposed from above by the learned elite, as was the case on the Continent.[36]

Indeed, Thomas maintains, in England the idea of Devil-worship had only a partial influence on the people at large.[37] One may observe, however, that these assertions do not prevent him from using the idea of Devil-worship to establish that witchcraft had "subjective reality."

By assuming that the English persecutions were animated by popular beliefs in *maleficium*—beliefs already centuries old by the time of the witch-hunts—Thomas must somehow explain why the trials took place during the sixteenth century and not earlier. He seems to think that the "demand" for the prosecution of witches did not exist previously.[38] Such a demand arose, Thomas speculates, as a result of a change in "popular opinion" regarding witchcraft.[39]

Public opinion changed, according to Thomas, when Protestant preachers cast doubt on the efficacy of the Catholic Church's "protective magic"—which had kept the threat of sorcery under control during the Middle Ages—and banned recourse to popular folk counter-magic.[40] However, the Church of England did not deny the reality of witchcraft, nor did it guarantee that the faithful would be immune from supernatural assaults.[41] Instead, the new religion placed unprecedented emphasis on the Devil's campaign to weaken men's faith in God by attacking their bodies, destroying their worldly possessions, and forcing them to abandon their faith by resorting to "the abominations of sorcery" (i.e., counter-magic) for protection. Thus deprived of their traditional magical defenses against witchcraft, but at the same time made aware by Church officials of the heightened activities of Satan's earthly representatives, Thomas surmises, people were compelled to take the only course of action open to them: appealing to the courts of law to contend with the pest of witchcraft.[42]

Regrettably, such a total abandonment of traditional religious formulae and folk protective-magic—a condition upon which Thomas' speculations depend—is highly unlikely.[43] Indeed, ideological conversions of entire societies are rarely as complete as Thomas would have us believe. The survival of fragments of pagan customs and charms (in the form of syncretic[44] beliefs and practices) during the Christian era attests to this fact.[45] Thomas himself notes that in England many of the old Catholic magical formulae retained their value during times of emergency.[46]

Only by dismissing powerful concrete forces, such as the stimulus of propaganda and the impetus of the authorities in changing public opinion by deliberately focusing and channeling diffuse anxieties about *maleficium*, can Thomas support his premise that the witch-trials in England stemmed almost entirely from genuine popular fears of maleficent magic. No valid account of the European witchcraft persecutions, however, can legitimately exclude these forces from analytical consideration. Thomas seems to altogether ignore the fact that demonological propaganda, pounded in year after year (both in England and on the Continent), produced an atmosphere of fear and dread largely unconnected with specific misfortunes and calamities, the usual catalysts for intra-village charges of *maleficium*.

As for the laws of the land that made witchcraft a statutory offense during the sixteenth century, Thomas writes[47] as if these made no difference other than making it possible for cases of witchcraft to be brought before magistrates.[48] Moreover, he discounts the significant role of the reformed evangelists, who imported and employed Continental demonology for the purpose of religious propaganda.[49]

Thomas' speculations raise another important question: what about charges motivated by personal hatreds, the desire for profit, or perhaps notoriety, rather than genuine fears of harmful magic? This is a question that witchcraft studies writers cynically dismiss as pedestrian and banal. Thomas' treatment of this issue, however, reveals further difficulties in the mentalist approach.

Thomas admits that accusations were easy to make and difficult to disprove, and were therefore particularly likely to be motivated by malice and imposture. But, after citing numerous instances of fraudulent accusations, e.g., the case of the Bilson Boy and John Darral's staged exorcisms, among others,[50] Thomas dismisses fraud as "an interesting but pathological problem."[51] False and malicious accusations, in other words, were the exception rather than the rule. It is true, Thomas concedes, that some individuals did indeed profit from the credulity of their contemporaries but, he points out, this does not explain how those beliefs came into existence in the first place.[52]

This is not a convincing answer. Beliefs in maleficent magic existed long before the witch-trials and survived long after the last witch was put to death, and an explanation of why such beliefs resulted in arrests and executions during a particular period in time must depend on an analysis of how these ideas were utilized, not how they originated. Fraudulent accusations should not be ruled out as a factor of considerable significance in the persecution of countless innocent people.

Witchcraft studies writers, however, indignantly dismiss such a suggestion because it is incompatible with the ontological foundations of their research perspectives. Their position, we may recall, is that since people believed in witchcraft, witchcraft was therefore real, and answers must be sought in the thoughts, beliefs, attitudes, and sentiments of the people involved in the witch-hunts. In other words, everyone accepted the notion that witchcraft was real, everyone believed that the people on trial really were witches, and the witch-persecutions reflected these genuine popular views. These assumptions, as I shall attempt to demonstrated in the forthcoming chapters, are not entirely supported by the evidence.

Thomas' mentalist perspective also leads him to dismiss the powerful role of printing in the propagation of Continental demonology and witch-hunting in England.[53] Eisenstein, author of *The Printing Press as an Agent of Change* (1979), has criticized Thomas on this issue, pointing out that given the 1486 publication date for the first edition of the *Malleus Maleficarum*, the first most influential text on demonology (see Chapter One, below), and the time needed to import and domesticate its content, there is a plausible correlation between the output of the printing presses, the anti-witchcraft rhetoric of the English authorities, and the timing of the witch-trials in England.[54]

Thomas' attempt to apply his mentalist explanation to the witch-hunts on the Continent, which began well before the Reformation, is wholly unconvincing. He surmises that depreciations of the power of ecclesiastical magic "consummated by Protestantism" resulted in a "change in attitude" on the part of Church leaders. Feeling themselves magically defenseless against the forces of darkness, they resorted to the only possible alternative, the physical extermination of the witches.[55] However, upon embarking on this course of action, Thomas observes, the authorities initially encountered strong popular opposition. Why? Not because the demonology of the Inquisitors and churchmen was alien to the masses. Not because local populations were opposed to the arrest and torture of innocent members of their communities. No, Thomas conjectures, people resisted the Inquisitors because they were terrified of witches and were therefore unwilling to prosecute them.[56] In order to allay such fears, Thomas asserts, the *Malleus Maleficarum* had to emphasize that witches lost their magical abilities once apprehended by the authorities.

This represents a misinterpretation of the evidence. Such an error by an eminent scholar such as Thomas can only be attributed to his exclusive commitment to a mentalist strategy. Thomas neglects to mention that the *Malleus Maleficarum* also stated explicitly in the title page, *Haeresis est maxima opera maleficarum non credere*, "to disbelieve in witchcraft is itself the greatest of heresies." Why did the authors of this sanguinary tome deem it necessary to make such a declaration? Principally because the official demonology had very little popular support. Indeed, it took considerable "pounding in" before a mood of compliance could be instilled among the ordinary people. The statement that witches lost their powers once incarcerated was not intended to reassure potential accusers that they could safely denounce witches in their communities, as Thomas suggests it was. This idea was logically necessary in order to explain why Satan's servants—purported to be masters of black magic and endowed with uncanny powers—turned out, upon arrest, to be powerless old men and women, incapable of saving themselves let alone threatening the whole of Christendom, as the authorities claimed (see Chapter Four, below).

These criticisms should suffice in demonstrating the problems inherent in Thomas' mentalist approach to the study of European witchcraft. The points raised here have a bearing on the speculations of other writers as well. A more recent mentalist work on European witchcraft, which I shall examine next, is Carlo Ginzburg's *Ecstasies: Deciphering the Witches' Sabbath* (1991). In the discussion that follows, I will be concerned principally with epistemological and ontological issues, rather than with Ginzburg's scholarship.

Ginzburg attempts to resuscitate Margaret Murray's idea that the demonological stereotype of diabolical witchcraft was based on a "solid core of facts."[57] This is a subject he carefully and wisely avoided in his earlier work.[58] Ginzburg begins by pointing out that the authorities repeatedly encountered individuals who believed that they did indeed engage in behaviors which matched the official stereotype of heresy (i.e., worshipping pagan deities, engaging in ritual murder infanticide, cannibalism, incestuous sexual intercourse, etc.).[59] There is more here, Ginzburg supposes, than simply the effects of torture, coercion, and leading questions by the good Inquisitors. Ginzburg believes that the defamatory stereotype created by the ecclesiastical and judicial authorities—in order, I might point out, to justify the persecution of targeted individuals and groups—contained elements of truth. Embedded within this stereotype, Ginzburg argues, there exists a "deep and unattainable" layer of beliefs that holds the key to the European witchcraft phenomena.[60]

How does Ginzburg detect this recondite stratum of beliefs? Not through ordinary canons of proof and sociological explanation. He proceeds by deliberately disregarding chronology and cultural and geographical boundaries in order to focus on the "formal affinities" of the testimonies. Through this procedure Ginzburg claims he has determined that the fantastic elements of the demonological stereotype—trances, night flights, metamorphosis, cannibalism, intercourse with supernatural beings—were neither fabrications of the authorities and the learned elite, nor were they based on the subjective reality of psychopaths and hysterics.[61] These beliefs, Ginzburg speculates, comprised an integral aspect of peasant culture and derived from an ancient and widespread shamanistic tradition that originated in the Asiatic steppes.[62]

A brief review of anthropological findings regarding shamanism will show that this is not a plausible thesis. The concept of shamanism embodies two distinct meanings: (I) it refers to the practices of a particular type of religious specialist, the shaman, found cross-culturally; (II) it refers to a specific Asiatic religion centered around a shaman as a cult leader.[63] In the first sense, shamanism refers to a part-time magico-religious specialist, popularly known as "medicine man," who is adept at communicating with the spiritual world and supernatural beings. Such practitioners, who often act as healers and diviners, figure in numerous religions, including Christianity, Judaism, Islam, Buddhism, and Zoroastrianism.[64] Anthropologists use the concept of shamanism to refer to this basic configuration of beliefs and practices that appears cross-culturally among geographically distant societies. However, few anthropologists would suggest any historical connections between the disparate, but generically similar, shamanic practices found around the world. Similarities between certain folk traditions in medieval and early modern Europe (e.g., Ginzburg's so-called fertility cults) and shamanistic practices, which are found cross-culturally, are to be expected.

Shamanism, in the second sense, refers to a body of rites and cult practices associated with a specific religion distributed in Central and Northern Asia. This religion is centered around a practitioner, the shaman (*saman*, or *vaman*, in the Tungus language of Siberia), whose cultist paraphernalia includes a drum, distinctive costume, a specialized mystical language, and special songs that he sings during his performance as curer, diviner, and manager of the psychic equilibrium of his community.[65] Ginzburg attempts to link European witchcraft with this shamanistic religion.

The viability of Ginzburg's thesis depends on sufficient evidence of a historical connection between European witchcraft and Asiatic or Siberian shamanism. The bits and pieces of evidence selectively gleaned by Ginzburg from documents pertaining to witchcraft and lycanthropy trials in Europe (highly questionable sources, as we have seen) is hardly sufficient to establish such a connection. Any similarities between Ginzburg's fertility cults and Asiatic shamanism is adequately accounted for by the generic similarities noted above. Ginzburg's suggestion that European witchcraft represented remnants of an ancient, Asiatic shamanistic tradition is highly conjectural and should be accepted with great reservation.

Returning to Ginzburg's thesis, he maintains that the idea of diabolical witchcraft was created when the shamanistic traditions of the peasant were incorporated into the official stereotype of heresy that depicted religious dissidents as members of a hostile sect of Satan worshippers.[66] Thus, according to Ginzburg, witchcraft existed; it was an integral part of peasant beliefs and practices; and the Inquisitors did not fabricate witchcraft, but simply imposed their own definition upon it.

Ginzburg, like Thomas, bases his conjectures on the subjective accounts and truth claims of particular individuals.[67] I have already pointed out the problems associated with the use of these sources. Moreover, his methodology, although hailed by some as innovative, is disturbingly reminiscent of the nineteenth-century "comparative method" in anthropology, which was wholly demolished by the anthropologist Franz Boas over a half a century ago.[68] This approach consisted of piecing together a composite picture out of disparate customs and traits selected because they corresponded to the researcher's suppositions of how things were.[69]

Finally, one must add that, *Ecstasies*, despite its ostensible innovative methodology, reveals nothing new. That churchmen and inquisitors built their stereotype out of fragments of pagan beliefs and peasant superstitions is well known, as is the fact that many people were familiar with charms, magical formulae, and the tales of Diana's night riders.[70] Moreover, that the stereotype of diabolical witchcraft incorporated calumnies attributed to unorthodox Christian sects (and other groups targeted politically for extermination, such as the Templar Knights), is also not in doubt.[71] Ginzburg's efforts to uncover the "hidden" core of beliefs embedded in the demonological stereotype leads him, predictably, to confuse empirically-known events with the outlandish fantasies and prevarications of the witch-hunters—the familiar mentalist failure to distinguish between representations of reality and what exists objectively.

Ginzburg's approach is objectionable not only because of his mentalist commitments, but also on the grounds that by disregarding chronology and cultural boundaries one can use ethnographic, cross-cultural, and historical data to support or, alternatively, to refute almost any position. After all, did not Margaret Murray, author of the ever popular *The Witch-Cult in Western Europe* (1921), who employed similar procedures (James Frazer's "cut-and-paste," "armchair anthropology"[72]), invent an entire religion, priests, sacrificial rites, and all?[73] It seems that Ginzburg has artificially imposed a systematic relationship on disparate fragments of folk beliefs and practices in the same fashion that European demonologists wove unconnected elements of peasant lore in order to manufacture the non-existent diabolic religion of witches.

By shifting the analytical focus from the activities of judges and prosecutors to the beliefs, sentiments, "dream worlds," and "shamanistic excursions" of those charged with the crime of witchcraft, Ginzburg and other mentalist writers trivialize the atrocities of those responsible for the conflagrations which consumed the lives of thousands of innocent people. Governments culpable for the systematic and wholesale slaughter of their citizens are forgotten, while "fairy cults," shamanistic seances, and the scattered folklore of peasant superstition and elementary village credulities are given analytical priority. Such an approach is questionable not only on theoretical and methodological grounds, but perhaps on ethical ones as well.

Ginzburg, however, is not hindered in the least by such theoretical and methodological considerations. Regrettably, like explanations forwarded by other writers committed exclusively to the analysis of cognitive dimensions of human life, Ginzburg's speculations are immune to verification by any explicit canons of appraisal. Explications that cannot be verified or falsified are vacuous, as I have already stressed, and do not contribute to our pursuit of objectively-valid knowledge.

Further discussions of these issues would take us far from our objectives. I now turn to the theoretical assumptions and epistemological orientation of the present study. This work is concerned with the events, entities, and relationships which, regardless of whether or not they have "subjective reality" for the individuals in question, affect and explain human action and behavior. I attempt to separate wholly imaginary events (atmospheric transportations, dreams, sexual encounters with supernatural beings, contractual agreements with the Prince of Darkness, etc.) from empirically-known phenomena (the effects of hot pincers and boiling oil on the human physiology, forced confessions, sensational show trials, exemplary punishments, and the sociological functions of torture rooms and executioner blocks). Rather than seek hidden realities in the rhetoric of the witch-hunters, as mentalist writers are prone to do, I treat demonology as an ideological device used by princes and preachers to befuddle people by obfuscating the true, earthly sources of the troubles attributed to the malice of witches. I stress the role of intimidation, the force of torture, and the use of officially-sponsored propaganda in sparking and sustaining horrendous and repeated attacks by those in power upon innocent and helpless citizens.

By referring to the actual, objective attributes of the human condition such an approach has the virtue, or at least the potential, of generating causal explanations that can be validated, or falsified, through empirical procedures.[74] Although causal explanations and interpretive explanations are not necessarily mutually exclusive, research strategies that generate causal explanations are usually incommensurable with approaches which generate interpretive explanations. The two perspectives not only pose different questions, they specify different means of solution.[75] Much of what I have to say, therefore, is at variance with the basic assumptions, ideas, and methodological and theoretical perspectives of the coterie of mentalist writers who presently dominate the scholarly study of European witchcraft.

Throughout this study, analytical attention is centered specifically on three aspects of the witch-persecutions: the acts of violence, coercion, and terrorism perpetrated by the promoters and engineers of the witch-hunts; the material circumstances that inspired such actions; and, finally, the ideological means through which the violence associated with witch-hunting was justified and rationalized.

My approach is anthropological, although the present study differs from works that have attempted to interpret the European witch-hunts by comparison with ethnographic findings among contemporary non-Western societies where witch-beliefs exist. Anthropological field research has undeniably yielded many insights into the intricate social mechanisms involved in accusations of witchcraft, and I have utilized such findings wherever appropriate (see Chapter Two, below). But as far as the European witch-trials are concerned, modern ethnographic studies are only of limited use. In Europe, the pattern of witchcraft accusations and witch-hunting was not confined to the types of village-level social formations which have been the subject of modern ethnographic studies of witchcraft. This, however, does not preclude analysis based on cross-cultural anthropological findings regarding the political, coercive, and ideological practices characteristic of stratified social formations. Indeed, this is the approach I have taken. I treat the European witch-persecutions as a sociocultural phenomenon comparable in nature and characteristics to the horrifying persecutions and mass murders of people accused of "thought crimes" in the torture states of our own time. [76]

The explanations forwarded in this study depart considerably from those presented in some of the more conventional treatises on the subject. The merits of this work, if any, lie both in the range of topics covered, and in the types of explanations forwarded for phenomena ordinarily attributed to mysterious, unfathomable causes emanating from the nether regions of the human mind.

Notes

1. Under the rubric of mentalism, I include cognitivism (componential analysis, ethnoscience) structuralism, symbolic anthropology, phenomenology, and psychological anthropology. I also classify as mentalist the works of a variety of researchers operating under the paradigm of "cultural determinism," which is based on (and does not go beyond) the assumption that culture (defined as a set of rules and ideas) determines behavior.
2. Ontology refers to assumptions about the nature of "reality" and epistemology which addresses the question, "How do we know what we know?," refers to the foundations of claims to knowledge.
3. For the sake of the non-specialists, I deal with this extremely complex theoretical issue only in general terms. I have attempted to confine the discussion only to the most relevant and influential works within the discipline of anthropology. My list of mentalist works is therefore far from comprehensive. See Lett (1987), Harris (1979), Werner (1973), and Spiro (1986) for a more detailed discussion.
4. Lett (1987:124). See, for example, Levi-Strauss (1966:3), whose works have inspired a variety of mentalist strategies.
5. Spradley (1972:34–35).
6. For example, Douglas (1970), Schutz (1967), and Spradley (1972:34–35).

7. Dolgin, et al. (1977:5).
8. Lett (1987:113). See, for example, Geertz (1973:10), (1977), whose works have also influenced a number of mentalist researchers.
9. Lett (1987:115). See the comments by Geertz (1973:10; 1977:492).
10. Hatch (1973:336–337).
11. Harris (1975a:159).
12. Harris (1979:285).
13. Harris (1975a:163).
14. Harris (1975a:163).
15. Harris (1975a:163).
16. Frankel (1960:99).
17. For example, Schutz (1967) and Douglas (1970). See Spiro (1986) for a detailed critique.
18. See Spiro (1986) and Harris (1976) for a more detailed discussion.
19. Lett (1987:101, 113). Examples from among the highly influential and much emulated mentalists works that rely on interpretations based on intuition and imagination include, among others, Geertz (1973:20; 1977:492), Levi-Strauss (1963:23), Goodenough (1956), Douglas (1966; 1970).
20. Lett (1987:102).
21. Turner (1969).
22. Harris (1975a:159–160; 1979:32). It must be noted, however, that even when it is possible to elicit such confirmation from the "native informant," knowledge of "native rules" and "codes" cannot account for phenomena such as war, poverty, political repression and persecution, etc. (Harris 1979:285). Code, in other words, does not determine conduct (Geertz 1973:18; Lett 1987:116).
23. Lett (1987:18–19).
24. Lett (1987:105); Werner (1973:295–299). Geertz (1973:24) uses this argument to criticize "ethnoscience," or componential analysis (see Goodenough 1956), an anthropological paradigm devoted to the investigation of the emic dimensions of culture, although his own approach suffers from the same shortcoming (cf. Lett 1987:117).
25. Lett (1987:163); Honigmann (1976:322).
26. Critics have questioned the legitimacy of Thomas' use of anthropological data on African witch-beliefs to interpret European witchcraft (see Rowland 1990; Burke 1990). I am concerned with the shortcomings of Thomas' mentalist approach, problems which his work shares with other mentalist studies.
27. Thomas (1985:620).
28. Thomas (1985:624).
29. Thomas (1985:634). The idea that rural poverty drove people to resort to witchcraft as a means of obtaining revenge was posited years ago by Jules Michelet (1862).
30. Thomas (1985:621).
31. Thomas (1985:623).
32. Thomas (1985:624,625,627).
33. Notestein (1911:164–205).
34. Boguet (1929 [1602]:155).
35. Carpzov (1670); Lea (1939:840).

36. Thomas (1985:543, 546, 548).
37. Thomas (1985:543, 546, 548).
38. Thomas (1985:548).
39. Thomas (1985:551).
40. Thomas (1985:589, 594).
41. Thomas (1985:589, 590–591).
42. Thomas (1985: 594).
43. See, for example, Wallace's (1966:76–77, 78, 84, 254–55) general discussion.
44. "Syncretism" refers to the process by which new and old cultural traits are fused together (cf. H. G. Barnett 1953:49, 54). This phenomenon is well documented in the ethnographic context. See, for example, Madsen (1967) and Tonkinson (1974).
45. See Walzel (1974) for examples from the European context.
46. Thomas (1985:589).
47. Thomas (1985:548–556).
48. Trevor-Roper (1988:65); Cohn (1975:160–163).
49. Notestein (1911:10–18, 46); Trevor-Roper (1988:65).
50. See Robbins (1981:48–49, 118) and Notestein's (1911:73–92) chapter on English exorcists.
51. Thomas (1985:646).
52. Thomas (1985:646).
53. Thomas (1985:523).
54. Eisenstein (1979:436–438). The invention of the printing press (circa 1448–1454) served as one of the witch-hunters' most powerful allies. Gutenberg's moveable-type printing press contributed to the increased production of books on witchcraft: the first was Alphonsus de Spina's *Fortalicium Fidei*, printed in 1467. In addition, the early presses produced large numbers of *teufelsbücher* (books about the Devil), pamphlets, and chapbooks describing cases of demonic possession, famous exorcisms, and notable executions of witches and werewolves. Printing thus facilitated the flow of demonological ideas across the broad spectrum of society (see Burr 1943b:178; J. B. Russell 1972:234). Although some writers have remarked that printing played only a peripheral role in spreading demonological theories, which would have been disseminated by word of mouth or by hand written manuscripts (Scarre 1987:18), historical evidence does not support this assertion (see Burr 1943b). With the printing press came the mechanical means for promulgating ideas more widely than previously possible, and these included the belief in diabolical witchcraft. Indeed, printing not only advertised to Europe the new epidemic of witchcraft, but it also contributed to the codification of demonology (Eisenstein 1979:436). For example, the two periods of the publication of the *Malleus Maleficarum*, 1486–1520, when it was published 15 times, and 1574–1669, when it was printed 19 times, correspond to two episodes of severe witch-persecutions. Printing influenced other aspects of European witchcraft as well. Walker has shown in his *Unclean Spirits* (1981:20), for instance, that printed accounts of exorcisms played a principal role in both stimulating and shaping the characteristics of other cases of demonic possession attributed to witchcraft. Thomas (1985:574) himself calls attention to a similar phenomenon in cases of demonic possession in England. Finally, coinciding with the large-scale witch-trials

in Germany during the second half of the sixteenth century was the publication of vast amounts of literature on the Devil and his servants, which Midelfort (1972:70) says, both reflected and fostered a new fear of the Devil. On the other hand, in his book *Irish Witchcraft and Demonology* Seymour (1973 [1913]:12) has called attention to the fact that in Ireland the absence of printed materials concerning witchcraft greatly hindered the spread of the prevailing demonological theories and witch-hunting in that country.

55. Thomas (1985:588, 594).
56. Thomas (1985:595).
57. Ginzburg (1991:8–11).
58. For example, Ginzburg (1983).
59. See, for example, Ginzburg (1991:7, 76, 94–97, 109, 303).
60. See Ginzburg (1991: chapters 2 and 3).
61. Ginzburg (1991:15).
62. See Ginzburg (1991:182–184, 207–225).
63. Krader (1963: 130).
64. Krader (1963:130); Sidky (1990, 1994).
65. Krader (1963:130–131).
66. See Ginzburg (1991:79–81, 92–94). The stereotype of Sabbat witchcraft, according to Ginzburg (1991:296) was created through the fusion of two distinct elements: the theory of conspiracy of a hostile sect elaborated by Inquisitors and secular judges in the context of the crises of the fourteenth century, especially the Black Death; and elements of shamanistic origins, such as magic flight and metamorphosis, rooted in folk culture.
67. See Ginzburg (1991:154–156).
68. Boas (1938:1–6). See also Wallace's (1966:252–255) critique of this approach.
69. Honigmann (1976:116).
70. Trevor-Roper (1988:40–41, 51); Cohn (1975:103–110); Thomas (1985:614).
71. See M. Barber (1978:182); Trevor-Roper (1988:52–53, 112–115); Burr (1943b); A. Murray (1976:67–68).
72. Sir James Frazer, author of the renowned *The Golden Bough* (1890), whose work and methodology greatly influenced Margaret Murray, supported his grandiose, but highly speculative, explanations by selectively culling reports and accounts written by travelers, missionaries, and other casual observers. He himself never conducted any first-hand field research (cf. Beattie 1964:7; Hays 1964:120–121; Honigmann 1976:116).
73. For example, Cohn (1970; 1975).
74. cf. Lett (1987:91–92).
75. Lett (1987:115).
76. The similarities are indeed astonishing. See Cohn (1967) and Reitlinger (1953) for Nazi Germany; Beck (1951) for the former Soviet Union; Staub (1989) for Argentina; Etcheson (1984) for Cambodia; and Cardozo (1970) for McCarthy's witch-hunt in the United States in the 1950s.

Chapter One

The European Witch-Craze

At the close of the Middle Ages, the people of western Europe were led to believe that they were the target of a vast occult conspiracy of witches orchestrated by the Devil. Many were convinced that Satan himself walked the earth, bringing disaster and destruction. Secular and ecclesiastical authorities, along with leading jurists, theologians, and philosophers, all confirmed the reality of the threat. According to a contemporary chronicler: "All who have afforded us some signs of the approach of [the] Antichrist agree that the increase of sorcery and witchcraft is to distinguish the melancholy period of his advent; and was ever [an] age so afflicted as ours? The seats destined for criminals in our courts of justice are blackened with persons accused of this guilt. There are not judges enough to try them. Our dungeons are gorged with them. No day passes that we do not render our tribunals bloody by the dooms which we pronounce, or in which we do not return to our homes discountenanced and terrified at the horrible confessions which we have heard. And the devil is accounted so good a master, that we cannot commit so great a number of his slaves to the flames but what there shall arise from their ashes a sufficient number to supply their place."[1]

The Church joined with civil authorities to battle the occult threat. Anti-witchcraft legislation was enacted, and across Europe systematic campaigns to eradicate the satanic conspiracy were put into motion. Wherever witches were found—and they were found everywhere—they were arrested, tortured, legally convicted, and burned. Every new confession diligently set down on paper by

Map 1.1 Lands of the witch-hunts during the 16th and 17th centuries.

horrified Inquisitors revealed new, as yet unknown atrocities committed by witches. Each witch racked and scourged revealed long lists of diabolical accomplices. Those named revealed, in turn, under torture, still more co-conspirators in the satanic plot. The innumerable denunciations, confessions, and executions all confirmed that the demonic insurrection was of unimaginable proportions.

The greatest minds of the age devoted themselves to the study of this perplexing diabolical phenomenon. Each new dissertation elaborated additional and more horrible details about Satan and his minions. The doctors of religion who examined the evidence supplied by the stouthearted Inquisitors, the combatants at the front-lines of the holy war, were unanimous in their conclusions: the Devil and his legions of darkness were about to overrun the earth. Every country, city, town, and village, it seemed, had been affected by the wickedness of witchcraft that was creeping like a cancer and spreading infection. Why else would magistrates and Inquisitors find witches wherever they cared to look? The pious and learned experts specializing in the growing science of demonology,[2] the European witch-doctors,[3] had but one remedy: immediate and merciless extermination. Thus, for nearly three hundred years, European authorities conducted an unrelenting war against their own citizens suspected of complicity in Satan's sinister plot.

As landmark developments in the Church's official position on witchcraft, historians generally cite the manifesto of Pope Innocent VIII, the *Summis Desiderantes* (December 5, 1484) and the publication of the *Malleus Maleficarum* (1486) [The Hammer of Witches], by the Dominican Inquisitors Heinrich Kramer and Jakob Sprenger. The "witch bull" of Innocent VIII—issued in response to public opposition encountered by Inquisitors attempting to prosecute people for witchcraft—proclaimed that Europe was being abominated by the malignity and infectiousness of witchcraft, and endorsed the authority of Kramer and Sprenger to take legal action against witches in Germany. The directive also advised secular and ecclesiastical authorities not to impede the pious doctors in their efforts to eradicate witches.[4]

Kramer and Sprenger included Innocent VIII's manifesto in their manual and were thus instrumental in disseminating the

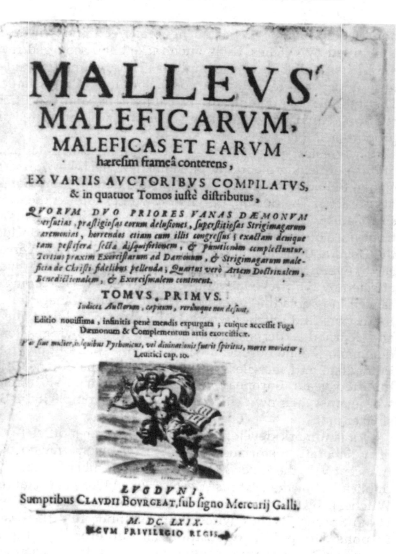

Figure 1.1 Frontispiece from Heinrich Institoris' *Malleus Maleficarum*, the encyclopedia of demonology. By permission of The British Library, London.

Church's official position regarding witchcraft. The inclusion of the bull, in turn, enabled the self-styled "witch-hammerers" to declare papal endorsement for the demonological theories espoused in their treatise.

The book written by these two infamous detectors-of-evil proclaimed to the whole of Europe the reality of the diabolical conspiracy and urged secular authorities to actively assist in the extirpation of the vile heresy. It also provided detailed legal and procedural guidelines for judges and prosecutors on the apprehension, interrogation, torture, and conviction of witches.[5] The *Malleus Maleficarum* quickly became the standard reference on demonology and witch-hunting. From 1486 to 1520 it went through fifteen editions, and was printed nineteen additional times between 1574 and 1669. This sanguinary work was to greatly influence all subsequent developments in the field of demonology, as well as to inspire later witch-hunters, Catholic and Protestant alike.[6]

The publication of the *Malleus Maleficarum*, as one modern scholar has observed, imparted great force and substance to the papal mandate.[7] Its appearance marked the beginning of large-scale, chain-reaction trials referred to by some historians as the "European witch-craze," which gained momentum towards the close of the fifteenth century. During these bloody and violent episodes, scores of witches were committed to the flames in order "to appease God" and "offer solace to the innocent."

At the turn of the sixteenth century, witch-trials and executions escalated with unprecedented ferocity, and "burning courts" were established in city after city for the sole purpose of effectively dispatching great numbers of the evil-doers. The executions continued at varying rates throughout the 1500s, but by the end of the century Europe's witch-hunters were more alarmed than ever before. Pierre de Lancre, a leading French trial-judge and witch-slayer, was convinced that Pays de Labourd, the Basque-speaking area adjoining the Spanish Frontier, had fallen into the Devil's hands and that all of its 30,000 inhabitants, including the priests, had embraced Satan as their lord and master.[8] Nicholas Remy and Henri Boguet, two other famous magistrates and ruthless witch-hammerers, claimed to be facing comparable situations in Lorraine and Franche-Comté.

Figure 1.2 A broadsheet depicting a witch burned at Schiltach, near Rottweil, in 1533. Courtesy of the Department of Prints and Drawings, Zentralbibliothek, Zürich.

By the first decade of the seventeenth century, the witch-hunts reached an unimaginable crescendo. As the historian Lea remarked: "Protestant and Catholic rivalled each other in the madness of the hour. Witches were no longer burned in ones or twos, but in scores and hundreds."[9] Village after village was decimated; in others only one or two people escaped the fury of the witch-hunters.[10] All the while, intellectuals lamented, not for the victims of the witch-hunts, but for rulers forced to obliterate thousands of their "demonized" citizens.

"Germany," wrote Boguet in his *Discours des sorciers* (1602), "is almost entirely occupied with building fires for [witches]. Switzerland has been compelled to wipe out many of her villages on their account. Travellers in Lorraine may see thousands and thousands of stakes to which witches are bound. We in Burgundy are no more exempt than other lands; for in many parts of our country we see that the execution of witches is a common occurrence. Returning again to our neighbours, Savoy has not escaped this pest; for every day she sends us countless [numbers] of persons possessed by demons which, on being exorcised, say that they have been sent by witches into the bodies of these poor wretches: moreover, most of the witches whom we have burned here come originally from Savoy.... I say nothing of other more remote lands. No, no; there are witches by the thousands everywhere, multiplying upon the earth even as worms in a garden. And this is a shame to the Magistrates whose duty it is to punish felons and criminals; for if we had no more than the direct command of God to put them to death as being His bitterest enemies, why should we endure them any longer, and thus disobey the Majesty of the Most High?"[11]

At this critical moment in the crisis, when Christendom seemed to be on the verge of collapse, Satan's minions were being discovered everywhere, among all classes, and in high offices.[12] The hysterical witch-hammerers, astonished at the plethora of witches that fell into their hands daily, clamored for greater zeal, fire, and death and destruction for the Devil's servants. By 1630 the witch-persecutions had turned into a large-scale holocaust, during which judges, lawyers, priests, university professors, rich and poor were burned alongside old women for the crime of witchcraft.[13]

The Chancellor of the Prince-Bishop of Würzburg (Germany) described the horrendous persecution of witches there in 1629: "the affair of the witches ... has started up afresh, and no words can do justice to it. Ah, the woe and misery of it—there are still four hundred in the city, high and low, of every rank and sex, nay, even clerics, so strongly accused that they may be arrested at any hour. It is true that, of the people of my Gracious Prince here, some out of all offices and faculties must be executed: clerics, electoral councilors and doctors, city officials, court assessors....

There are law students to be arrested. The Prince-Bishop has over forty students who are soon to be pastors; among them thirteen or fourteen are said to be witches. A few days ago a Dean was arrested; two others who were summoned have fled. The notary of our Church consistory, a very learned man, was yesterday arrested and put to the torture. In a word, a third part of the city is surely involved. The richest, most attractive, most prominent, of the clergy are already executed. A week ago a maiden of nineteen was executed, of whom it is everywhere said that she was the fairest of the whole city, and was held by everybody a girl of singular modesty and purity. She will be followed by seven or eight others of the best and most attractive persons.... And thus many are put to death for renouncing God and being at the witch-dances, against whom nobody has ever else spoken a word. To conclude this wretched matter, there are children of three and four years, to the number of three hundred, who are said to have had intercourse with the Devil. I have seen put to death children of seven, promising students of ten, twelve, fourteen, and fifteen. Of the nobles—but I cannot and must not write more of this misery. There are persons of yet higher rank, whom you know, and would marvel to hear of, nay, would scarcely believe it; let justice be done."[14]

Faced with such a diabolical epidemic, judges and Inquisitors could not possibly keep detailed accounts of the trials. For many victims of the witch-hunts the only epitaph in the court records was the phrase *convicta et combusta*, "convicted and burned."

Not everyone, however, agreed to the wholesale slaughter. Even during the height of the persecutions, when fear and terror gripped much of Europe, there were skeptics and critics, a few courageous men such as Johann Weyer,[15] Reginald Scot, Johann Meyfarth, Friedrich von Spee, and Cornelius Loos, who vehemently denounced the atrocities of the remorseless witch-hammerers and demonologists.

But the majority remained silent. Why? Was there widespread popular support for the bloody enterprise promoted by the hammerers of witches? Was all of Europe wholeheartedly behind the state-sponsored witch extermination programs? No, not quite. Indeed, as one illustrious witch-slayer lamented, "The *Malleus* [*Maleficarum*] asserts that to deny witchcraft is heretical; but those who do so are so numerous and ignorant, it is impossible to inflict upon them the death penalty of heresy, so the rigor of justice is to be tempered."[16] There were no public outcries primarily because few wished to share the same fate as the witches. According to a contemporary eyewitness: "If anyone dares to raise his voice in defence of the innocent, however, upright and honorable he may be, at once there is an outcry against him. He fears for his wife, his children, his friends and for himself and seeks to save his body and theirs from the jailer, the executioner, the headsman and the flames."[17] With the majority thus intimidated into silence, the learned doctors were free to arrest, torture, behead, and burn at the steak with impunity.

Calculating exactly how many people were executed is exceedingly difficult, as many executions were not recorded, and the records of many that were have not survived.[18] Estimates range from as low as 100,000 to as high as one million.[19] Nevertheless, even if the lowest estimate is correct, the figure is still staggering once we realize that these unfortunate people were subjected to insufferable tortures, methodically mutilated, and burnt at the stake for crimes of which they manifestly could not have been guilty. While the total number of victims may never be known, what is certain is that many more were persecuted and millions were terrified and intimidated.[20]

European Witchcraft and Demonology

Demonologists described witches as the vilest, most poverty stricken, abject, and hateful of the human race. Satan, they explained, makes them feeble and mean in soul and body; he takes away their intelligence, spoils their sense, cripples them, makes their gaze wandering and oblique, their countenance repugnant, their mouth awry, their breath stinking, their face death-colored.[21] It is impossible to conceive of anything uglier, poorer, or more miserable than the witches. Looks, however, are deceiving, the witch-hammerers proclaimed, for these seemingly weak and helpless creatures in reality possessed unlimited magical powers to inflict infinite evils and calamities upon man and beast.

Figure 1.3 Three witches. People accused of witchcraft belonged to the weakest elements of society; usually they were females who outnumbered males by a ratio of three to one. From a pamphlet entitled *The Witchcraft of Margaret and Philipa Flower* (1619).

In an overwhelming number of cases the accused belonged to the socially marginal, impoverished, and weakest elements of society; usually they were females who, among those indicted for witchcraft, outnumbered males by a ratio of three to one. The pious doctors were quite aware of this disparity between the number of male and female witches. "As for the reason why women are more frequently concerned in this craft than men," one demon specialist explained, "it is partly occasioned by their frailty, as Eve was thought the fitter subject for the Devil to work upon, and partly because they are more inclined to revenge."[22] Satan chose women as his instruments more often, wrote another demonologist, because they are more obstinate and given to evil and commit more execrable things, such as strangling infants, offering them to the Devil and making foul ointments out of their fat, things which male witches seldom or never do.[23]

By no means, however, were all those convicted and burned old and defenseless women. On the Continent, the legal application of torture meant that anyone, man or woman, young or old, could be accused, arrested, tortured, forced to name accomplices, and executed.

Witches were dangerous, according to demonologists, because of their ability to cause harm to others by virtue of occult or magical powers, referred to as *maleficium*. As Satan's instruments for the perdition of mankind, witches were thought to possess limitless powers to cause harm and destruction. They could fly through the air, change themselves into wolves and other animals, pass through locked doors and solid walls, control other people's thoughts and emotions, and "bewitch" or kill humans and animals with a mere gaze. These infernal creatures frequently raised tempests, hailstorms, floods, and lightning; they damaged crops and destroyed harvests, and caused sterility in animals and impotence in men. They could produce flies, locusts, serpents, frogs, lice, worms, fleas, toads, mice, and other such creatures and send them into the harvests. In addition, it was believed, witches conjured up demons, precipitated demonic possession, renounced God, made pacts with and worshipped the Devil, and devoted their own offspring to Satan during their hideous nocturnal rites.

Witches were also notorious for their unnatural craving and lust for human flesh. "Our witches have slain many infants," one demonologist reported, "as appears everywhere in their trials; what is still more abhorrent to nature, they cut out their hearts and eat them."[24] They tear living infants to pieces, wrote another demon specialist, and drink their blood to rejuvenate themselves, or else they roast them and eagerly devour them during their obscene rituals.[25]

The pious doctors spared none of the lurid details when describing the horrifying cravings of these man-eating monsters. One demonologist reported that in Lausanne, Switzerland, witches cooked and ate their own children, while in the Canton of Berne at least thirteen infants belonging to others were devoured in this manner. The witches arrested for these scabrous crimes divulged the horrifying details of their activities: "We set our

De Lanijs et phitōicis mu-
lieribus ad illustrissimū pziei
pem dominum Sigismundum archiducem austrie tractatus
pulcherrimus p Ulricum molitoris de Constantia studij sa-
pientis decretorum doctorem. Curieq̃ Constantiensis causa-
rum patronum ad honorem clementis principis sueq̃ sub cele-
situdinis emendatione conscriptus.

Figure 1.4 Witches performing weather-magic through simple
maleficium. After the title page of Ulrich Molitor's *De Lamiis et
Phitonicis Mulierbus* (1489).

Figure 1.5 Obtaining human flesh. In this woodcut two witches are shown exhuming a cadaver (left), a group of witches butchering an infant (center), and another witch stealing a body from the gallows (background). From Francesco Maria Guazzo's *Compendium Maleficarum* (1626 edition). Courtesy of the Special Collections Library, Duke University.

snares chiefly for unbaptized children, and even for those that have been baptized, especially when they have not been protected by the sign of the Cross and prayers ... and with our spells we kill them in their cradles or even when they are sleeping by their parents' side, in such a way that they afterwards are thought to have been [smothered] or to have died of some other natural death. Then we secretly take them from their graves, and cook them in a cauldron, until the whole flesh comes away from the bones to make a soup which may be drunk. Of the more solid matter we make an unguent which is of virtue to help us in our arts and pleasures and our transportations; and with the liquid we fill a flask or skin, whoever drinks from which, with the addition of a few other ceremonies, immediately acquires much knowledge and becomes a leader of our sect."[26] Thus, by killing and eating the flesh of Christian children, demonographers attested, witches acquired their magical abilities, especially the power to fly through the air, a feat they accomplished by means of an ointment made from the fatty residue of their cannibalistic meals.

Aside from devouring infants, witches were thought to regularly consume the putrid flesh of human corpses, which they secretly exhumed from cemeteries in order to serve up during their hideous nocturnal banquets. The witches' lust for gore, it seems, had no bounds.

Sabbats and the Pact with Satan

Originally, *maleficium*, which alludes to simple acts of sorcery, such as blasting crops, killing cattle, causing sickness, etc., did not involve the notion of a diabolical pact; this idea was attached to it during the latter part of the fourteenth and early part of the fifteenth centuries.[27]

Maleficent magic is performed through the utilization of philtres, love-potions, the manipulation of wax images, and the casting of charms and spells according to what anthropologists have termed the laws of *contagion* and *imitation*.[28] Contagious magic operates on the principle that two objects in contact remain so in a supernatural sense even when apart, and the magical manipulation of the one will produce similar effects on the other. Thus, obtaining articles of clothing belonging to an enemy and subjecting them to prescribed procedures will produce the desired effects on the person to whom the clothing belongs. Imitative magic, on the other hand, is founded on the precept that "like produces like:" mutilating a wax image of an enemy with a needle, for example, will cause the person the effigy represents to sicken or die.

Both procedures function automatically and do not necessarily involve the invocation of demons or supernatural beings. In medieval and post-medieval Europe, some people, motivated by revenge, malice, a desire to obtain another person's property, etc., may have performed maleficent magic,[29] but such vulgar sorcery was never practiced as a collective enterprise involving Devil-worship or pacts with evil spirits. The concept of pact served both to explicitly link sorcery to demonic agencies and the Devil, and to explain how witches acquired their lethal supernatural powers to cause the large-scale disasters imputed to them by the authorities.

In this discussion I will use the word *maleficium* to refer to simple sorcery (the sorts of practices designated as witchcraft in the ethnographic context, see Chapter Two, below), and I employ the expressions "diabolical witchcraft," or "Sabbat witchcraft," to denote injurious magic deriving its efficacy from compacts with the Christian Devil, i.e., the lethal theory of witchcraft that animated the large-scale witch-persecutions.

Magic does not operate without the pact, doctors of religion explained. A pact is a promise by the man to Satan and by Satan to the man. The man pledges obedience and negation of the divine precepts and sacraments; the Devil promises to empower him with occult, preternatural, or supernatural abilities. But for bestowing such magical powers, the witch-hammerers avouched, Satan demands to be worshipped as God. Witchcraft was therefore seen as a demonic religion, a cult of evil, an abomination created by Satan for the spiritual and physical ruination of Christendom.

The theoretical foundation of pacts with the Devil rests on the passage in Luke 4:7, in which Satan tempts Christ, saying, "If thou therefore wilt worship me all shall be thine" (also Isaiah 28:15, which reads, "For you have said: We have entered into a league with death; we have made a covenant with hell"). Witches made a pact with and worshipped Satan, professors of religion argued, to acquire riches and all their hearts' desires.[30] Indeed, witchcraft flourished, according to one demon specialist, because men hoped to acquire by it what they most desired—love, beauty, wealth, greatness, and knowledge.

According to the *Errores Gazariorum*, a treatise written by an anonymous Inquisitor in Savoy around 1450, witches were compelled to seal the compact with the Devil by signing a contract in their own blood. A pact could be made anywhere, and at any time of day or night, but usually it was sealed during the witches' sinister assemblies, known as Sabbats. Sorcerers and witches always held their meetings at night, mainly in forests, hidden caves, ruined castles, or any other desolate places. They congregated in such locations to avoid capture by the authorities and because "the devil since his fall has been dark and obscure, hating light, performing works of darkness in the obscurest places and times."[31] But in some instances, demonographers reported, witches held their obscene rites inside churches.

Figure 1.6 The Witches' Sabbat (left); and the fate of those accused of attending these imaginary banquets (right). From a Swiss manuscript dated 1514 (Ms F23, p. 399). Courtesy of the Department of Manuscripts, Zentralbibliothek, Zürich.

Nearly all accounts state that the Devil appeared before his disciples during the Sabbats, either as a black cat, a goat, a giant toad, or a human dressed in black. When the demonic being arrived, his devotees paid him homage by kissing his posterior, an act the demon specialists termed *osculum infame*, "the obscene kiss." Following the ritual formality of homage, the Devil preached a sermon, telling his devotees not to go to church, nor to make confessions to priests, and urged new recruits to encourage still others to join his legions of darkness. Then, Satan sat on his throne like a king, surrounded by his hideous hordes of demons, and received pledges from his newly-recruited disciples.

Boguet described the sealing of a pact as follows: "At this point Satan forms a league with his followers against Heaven, and plots the ruin of the human race. He makes these wretched creatures repeat their renunciation of God, Chrism [anointing oil] and Baptism, and renew the solemn oath they have taken never to speak of God, the Virgin Mary, or the Saints except in the way of mockery and derision: he makes them abandon their share in Paradise and promise that they will, on the contrary, for ever hold to him as their sole master and always be faithful to him. He then urges them to do all the harm that they can, to afflict their neighbours with illness, to kill their cattle, and to avenge themselves upon their enemies, saying to them: 'Avenge yourselves, or you shall die.' Also he makes them promise to waste and spoil the fruits of the earth, and gives them a certain powder or ointment for that purpose—or so, at least, he persuades them to believe. Also he makes them take a solemn oath not to lay information against each other, and not to reveal anything that is done amongst them."[32]

After the newly recruited witches swore allegiance to the monstrous king of the demons, he marked or branded their bodies with his talons, producing an insensitive scar, the *stigma diabolicum*, the "Devil's mark."[33] "Satan marks them thus," Boguet explained, "to show them that they are in the future to become his slaves...."[34] The *stigma diabolicum* was different from the "witch's

Figure 1.7 The activities at the Witches' Sabbat. From Francesco Maria Guazzo's *Compendium Maleficarum* (1626 edition). Courtesy of the Special Collections Library, Duke University.

mark," which refers to the presence of an extra nipple (*polythelia*), a mole, or wart, allegedly used by a witch to nurse her demon-familiar. The presence of an insensitive scar was often sufficient to confirm a prisoner's guilt and serve as cause for the authorities to use torture (see Chapter Five, below).

Figure 1.8 The Devil branding a new recruit. From Francesco Maria Guazzo's *Compendium Maleficarum* (1626 edition). Courtesy of the Special Collections Library, Duke University.

A central aspect of the Sabbat activities was the performance of ritual blasphemy—the ceremonial desecration of the Church's sacred objects as part of religious services. Witches also used holy objects to perform black magic. According to the *Malleus*

Maleficarum "in all their methods of working injury they [devils] nearly always instruct witches to make their instruments of witchcraft by means of the Sacraments or sacramental things of the Church, or some holy thing consecrated to God: as when they sometimes place a waxen image under the Altar-cloth, or draw a thread through the Holy Chrism, or use some other consecrated things in such a way."[35]

During the Sabbat, witches also made magical unguents that enabled them to fly through the air and attend their nocturnal gatherings hundreds of miles away. The night skies over western Europe during the sixteenth and seventeenth centuries, it would appear, were congested with these demonic air travelers. In France and England witches achieved their atmospheric transportation astride brooms; in Italy and Spain they rode on the back of the Devil, or a demon in the shape of a goat. The witches' flights, or *transvection*, could be either corporeal visits, or spiritual excursions, and often a witch used both methods.[36]

Dining and dancing followed the Devil's sermon, often lasting into the late hours of the night. The sinister festivities concluded with the witches having sexual intercourse with the Devil, or demons, in the form of *incubi* and *succubi*. An *incubus* had sexual intercourse with a female witch, while a *succubus* copulated with a male witch.

The good friars and pious doctors expressed an unusual interest in the witches' carnal relations with demonic beings. The theologian Ludovico Sinistrari, a consultant to the Supreme Tribunal of the Inquisition of Rome and Vicar-General to the Archbishop of Avignon, devoted an entire treatise to the subject. He tells us that, "each [witch] has assigned to himself a [demon] called *Magistellus* or Little Master, with whom he retires aside for carnal satisfaction; the said [demon] assuming the shape of a woman if the initiated person be a man, the shape of a man, sometimes a satyr, sometimes a buck-goat, if it be a woman who has been received a witch."[37]

Alternatively, witches had sexual relations with the Devil himself. According to *Newes from Scotland* (1591), a pamphlet describing the high-profile cases that inaugurated the first great Scottish witch-hunt: "when the Devil did receive them for his

Figure 1.9 Transvection. From Martin le Franc's *Le Champion des Dames* (c. 1451). Cabinet des estampes, fonds français 12476, f. 150 v. By permission of Bibliothèque Nationale, Paris.

Figure 1.10 Demoniality. After a page from Ulrich Molitor's *De Lamiis et Phitonicis Mulierbus* (1489).

servants, and that they vowed themselves to him, then he would carnally use them, albeit to their little pleasure, in respect of his cold nature: and would do the like at sundry other times."[38] Sinistrari stressed the gravity of such sexual union with demons or the Devil: "The intercourse of witches with demons, from its accompanying circumstances, apostasy from the faith, the worship of the Devil, and so many other abominations ... is the greatest of all sins which can be committed by man; and, considering the hideous enormity against religion which is presupposed by coition with the Devil, demoniality [copulation with demons] is assuredly the most grievous of all offenses."[39]

There was great debate among scholars and theologians regarding the witches' sexual intercourse with the Devil and demons, its implications, and whether offspring could be generated in this manner. As to the latter question, sixteenth-century Catholic scholars argued that if demons were unable to generate offspring how could one explain the birth of Martin Luther?[40] One account stated that the Devil, disguised as a jewel merchant, had arrived in the town of Wittenberg and asked a citizen to give him lodging, as he feared his jewels would be stolen in the local inn. That night the Devil seduced his host's daughter, and thus Luther was conceived. With aid from the demon, the boy Luther advanced rapidly in school and became a monk. But when he did not gain the favor of the Pope and the Cardinals, he attacked the Church out of malice.[41]

Aside from its use in sectarian religious propaganda, the idea of demonic offspring had other ramifications. For instance, in 1519, Nicholas Savin, the Inquisitor of Metz, brought charges of witchcraft against a woman whose mother had been burned as a witch. Savin argued that, as the daughter of a witch, the accused woman was obviously either the offspring of an *incubus*, or was at least devoted to Satan at birth, and thus deserved to die.[42]

The logical consequence of the belief in the diabolical conspiracy of witches—a belief which authorities did their utmost to propagate—was that all the ills and misfortunes that befell society, such as epidemics, wars, crop failure, famines, and economic slumps were attributed to the machinations of witches. As Reginald Scot pointed out in his *Discoverie of Witchcraft* (1584): "if any adversity, grief, sickness, loss of children, corn, cattle, or

Figure 1.11 The Sabbat panorama. During the late sixteenth and early seventeenth centuries the idea of the diabolical conspiracy of witches grew to a plot of astonishing proportions and demonologists reported the presence of hundreds of thousands of witches attending Sabbats throughout Europe. The horror generated by these tales animate the witch-persecutions. From Pierre de Lancre's *Tableau de l'inconstance des mauvais anges et démons* (1612). By permission of Special Collections and Archives, Milton S. Eishenhower Library, The Johns Hopkins University.

liberties happens to them; by and by they exclaim upon witches … a clap of thunder, or a gale of wind is no sooner heard, but either they run to ring bells,[43] or cry out to burn witches ...."[44] Such mishaps, demonologists said, could only be remedied by ferreting out the baleful agents of Satan who abominated the world, forcing them to name their accomplices, and dispatching them to the stake. If not eradicated, officials warned, witches could ultimately overthrow Christendom and convert the earth into the kingdom of Satan. Jean Bodin, the great Renaissance political philosopher and noted witch-destroyer, warned in his *De la démonomanie des sorciers* (1580): "Those ... who let the witches escape, or who do not punish them with the utmost rigor, may rest assured that they will be abandoned by God to the mercy of witches. And the country which shall tolerate this will be scourged with pestilences, famines, and wars; and those which shall take vengeance on the witches will be blessed by him and will make his anger to cease."[45]

In the deft hands and fertile imagination of the late sixteenth and early seventeenth century Catholic and Protestant demonologists, the idea of the satanic conspiracy of witches grew to a plot of astonishing proportions. The war against the legions of darkness, it appears, was not going well on all fronts. Witches were being burned by the scores and hundreds—to no avail, for the ranks of Satan's armies were swelling daily with new recruits. As Remy, the witch-slayer of Lorraine, pointed out in his *Daemonolatria* (1595), "all those taken up for witchcraft are unanimous in their assertion that the Sabbats are attended by great numbers."[46] One report claimed the presence of as many as 100,000 witches attending the Sabbat—some were apparitions, but many flesh and blood human beings.[47] In France, a witch by the name of Trois-Eschelles testified before King Charles IX, the royal physician, and other high officials that the number of witches in that country ranged anywhere from thirty thousand to three hundred thousand,[48] and that his own accomplices numbered over twelve hundred.[49] Boguet estimated that Europe alone harbored 1800,000 witches, an evil army more formidable and more dangerous than any hitherto encountered in history.[50]

The horror generated by the nerve-wracking tales of dark deeds, heinous crimes, and cosmic conspiracies, eloquently described by demonographers and widely disseminated by the official propaganda machinery, served to animate the European witch-craze. A question of importance for scholars interested in the problem of European witchcraft has been whether these allegations had any factual basis. This is a subject to which we shall turn in the following chapter.

Notes

1. In Mackay (1932 [1841]:479).
2. The term "demonology" refers strictly to the theoretical study of witchcraft undertaken by European intellectuals, and not to the beliefs and practices of demon worshippers, or "demonolatry."
3. This term was first used in the European context by Trevor-Roper (1988:19) as a convenient label to describe the scholars, lay and clerical, who in their writings formulated, elaborated, and propagated anti-witchcraft propaganda. I include in this category magistrates, Inquisitors, and others directly involved in the extermination of witches.
4. Thurston (1912:676).
5. The *Malleus Maleficarum*, although written by Inquisitors, was intended for secular and ecclesiastical courts, not the tribunals of the Inquisition. The latter had ceased to conduct witch-trials outside Italy, Spain, and Portugal after the 1530s. Witchcraft trials in France, Germany, and elsewhere in Central Europe during the sixteenth and seventeenth centuries were conducted primarily by secular and ecclesiastical courts using inquisitorial procedures (see Tedeschi 1990; Henningsen et al. 1986).
6. Davies (1947:4); Baroja (1990:31).
7. Trevor-Roper (1988:25).
8. Henningsen (1980:23–25); Baroja (1964:157–160).
9. Lea (1887:549).
10. Lea (1939:1075).
11. Boguet (1929 [1602]:xxxiii–xxxiv). Boguet is referring to Exodus 22:18, "Thou shalt not suffer a witch to live."
12. Trevor-Roper (1988:18).
13. Trevor-Roper (1988:19).
14. In Burr (1897:28–29).
15. Johann Weyer was among the first to object publicly to the witch-persecutions. Weyer alone could openly voice his opinion, because he held the post of personal physician to Duke William of Cleves, a powerful nobleman who, for a time, did not permit witch-hunting within his domain. Although Weyer acknowledged the powers of Satan in his books, *De Praestigiis* (1568) and *De Lamiis* (1577), he nevertheless argued that witches possessed no supernatural abilities, but were simply melancholic, senile old women, confused by illusions from the Devil. Instead of the prosecution of witches, Weyer called for the stern punishment of magicians, practitioners of the occult arts who voluntarily entered into commerce with demons. Weyer 's post protected him from retaliation; such was not the case with other critics of witch-hunting.
16. Del Rio (1599); Lea (1939:642).
17. Meyfarth (1635); Lea (1939:733).
18. See Davies (1947:4); Levack (1987:19).

19. See Cohn (1970:12). These estimates are guesswork at best. Bossenbrook (1961:198) gives the figure of one million put to death in Germany alone. Kors and Peters (1972:13) place the number of executions in Europe between 50,000 to 500,000. Quaife (1987:79) and Robbins (1981:180) estimate that 200,000 witches were executed. Monter (1977:130) places the total at 100,000. Levack (1987:19–22) estimates that the total number of witch prosecutions throughout Europe was roughly 110,000, with 60,000 executed. Earlier estimates placing the total number of executions in the hundreds of thousands or millions were inflated, according to Levack (1987:19), "both by the claims of the witch-hunters themselves, who often boasted about how many witches they had burned, and by subsequent writers, who for different reasons wished to emphasize the gravity of the process they were discussing." The views of Mr. Levack and other "witchcraft studies" scholars, which are also subject to prevailing ideologies, represent the conservative trend in the social sciences of the 1980s, a phenomenon closely tied to the demise of liberalism, and the rise of neo-conservative politics.
20. Russell (1987:415).
21. Brandt (1662); Lea (1939:867).
22. Boulton (1715:15).
23. Michaelis (1587:60–63). See Larner (1987:84–88) for a discussion of witch-hunting as an expression of cultural misogyny. Thomas (1985:678–679) and MacFarlane (1970:161) attribute the victimization of women to their economic vulnerability; Klaits (1985:48–85) stresses sexual fears; Midelfort (1972:184–185) suggests the fear of "loose" women; Wiltenburgh (1992:23) notes cultural misogyny. Ross (1995) links the timing of this widespread "explosion" of misogyny to the spread of syphilis during the sixteenth century. See also the volume edited by Levack (1992).
24. Binsfeld (1623:541–542); Lea (1939:593).
25. See Lea (1939:916).
26. Kramer and Sprenger (1971 [1486]:100–101).
27. See Peters (1978:158).
28. See Frazer (1922:12–55).
29. See Jones (1972).
30. Burr (1939:xxviii).
31. Damhouder (1601): Lea (1939:757).
32. Boguet (1929 [1602]:59–60).
33. Remy (1930 [1595]:8).
34. Boguet (1929 [1602]:128).
35. Kramer and Sprenger (1971 [1486]:115–116).
36. Kramer and Sprenger (1971 [1486]:100).
37. Sinistrari (1927 [c. 1690]:11).
38. *Newes from Scotland* (1591:18).
39. Sinistrari (1927 [c.1690]:87).
40. Trevor-Roper (1959:58).
41. Lea (1939:506).
42. Lea (1961:836).
43. Bells were thought to prevent witches from using weather magic to damage crops.
44. Scot (1584:1–2).

45. Burr (1897:5). Bodin's *Démonomanie des sorciers* (1580) was one of the most influential demonological texts ever published. It served as a handbook for secular courts engaged in prosecuting witches (Baxter 1977a:78). Bodin stated that the campaign against witchcraft was in actuality a war against Satan himself (Burr 1943a:148). Since the Devil could not be arrested and tried in court, Bodin argued, Satan's pernicious emissaries on earth—the witches—could and had to be brought to justice. Furthermore, Bodin declared that those who said that witchcraft was an illusion, and who thus impeded the cosmic war against Lucifer, were most certainly witches themselves (Lea 1939:555; Thorndike 1941:527).
46. Remy (1930 [1595]:56).
47. Lea (1939:1297).
48. Boguet (1929 [1602]:xxxii).
49. Mackay 1932 [1841]:483); Lea (1939:567).
50. Boguet (1929 [1602]:xxxii, xxiv).

Chapter Two

Witch-Sects and Flying Cannibals: Fact or Fantasy?

European demonologists claimed that witchcraft was a religion, a vile diabolical sect whose adherents worshipped Satan. The Devil's sect, according to Inquisitors such as Nicholas Jacquier and Silvestro Mozzolino, first appeared in the Alps in 1404, and thereafter spread with astonishing swiftness across much of Europe. Careful and detailed investigation by modern scholars, however, has failed to turn up a shred of evidence in support of this assertion.[1] Nevertheless, the idea of witchcraft as a sectarian organization has generated considerable discussion and debate, and, as one historian has observed, almost every possible explanation, ranging from total credulity to complete skepticism, has been forwarded.[2]

Margaret Murray's ideas, espoused in an article entitled "Organisations of Witches in Great Britain (1917)," and later elaborated in her book *The Witch-Cult in Western Europe* (1921), still remain quite popular. After carefully scrutinizing demonological treatises, Murray concluded that witches did indeed exist, but rather than being Devil-worshippers, as ecclesiastical authorities maintained, they belonged to a surviving pagan religion. The zealous friars and Inquisitors were indeed combating an organized religious sect, according to Murray, but they were simply incorrect about the nature of the organization they were trying to suppress.

The witch-cult, whose principal deity was a horned god with two faces, supposedly dated to pre-Christian times and was the

Figure 2.1   A coven of witches in the company of demons worshipping the Devil during the Sabbat rites. From Paul Christian's *Histoire de la Magie* (1870).

ancient religion of western Europe and Britain.[3] The witches, according to Murray, possessed a widespread, clandestine organization based on covens—groups comprising twelve witches headed by a priest.[4] Murray herself was able to identify a meager total of eighteen covens, distributed in Germany, France, England, and Scotland.[5] Members of these religious associations, Murray believed, assembled at various times in joyful festivals in order to conduct rituals for promoting fertility, an abundance of crops, and the well-being of members of the sect.[6]

The witches' religion, in Murray's view, was not just a minor sect but was practiced by the majority of the people under a "veneer of Christianity," and retained its dominant position in western Europe through the seventeenth century. Only when Christianity had finally attracted a wide base of support, during the Renaissance, she argued, was the ecclesiastical establishment able launch a campaign of suppression against its deeply entrenched rival, resulting in the large-scale witch-hunts of the sixteenth and seventeenth centuries.

In often convoluted arguments, Murray attempted to show that the demonological conception of the Sabbat derived from biased and distorted accounts of the fertility rituals of the witches' religion. One example worth discussing is the reason she gave for the acts of cannibalism during the Sabbats. Witches ate the flesh of infants, Murray observed, not out of a lust for gore, as demonologists believed, but as part of a magical rite based on the principle that eating the flesh of a child too young to speak would bind the tongue, and thus prevent members of the sect from testifying before Christian judges.[7]

Murray did not consider, however, that being accused of cannibalism and actually being a cannibal are not the same thing. Indeed, as the anthropologist William Arens has shown in his book *The Man Eating Myth* (1979), there is little concrete historical or ethnographic proof that humans partake in ritual cannibalism (see below). There is ample and solid evidence, on the other hand, that accusations of cannibalism have often served to defame and dehumanize targeted groups.

In medieval and early modern Europe, the cannibal theme played a central role in the definition of malevolence and ultimate human depravity.[8] In ancient times, Roman officials used the charge of cannibalism in a similar fashion to portray the Christians as human-eating monsters, thus justifying the persecution and slaughter of members of this faith. Yet, despite the allegations by Roman authorities, there is no reason to assume that these charges were true. Likewise, there is no reason for accepting the validity of similar accusations made by the witch-hammerers. Murray, however, consistently failed to question the trustworthiness of her sources, choosing instead to focus on how the alleged enormities of accused witches reflected the rites and rituals of the so-called witch-cult.

Thus, the monstrous witches portrayed in the grim demonological tomes were replaced in Murray's work by a group of fun-loving nature worshippers, wrongly equated with evil and suppressed by the officers of the rival Christian faith. Murray even argued that the term Sabbat derived from the word s`ebattre, which means "to frolic," rather than from the Hebrew shabbat.[9]

Murray's contention, however, is not borne out by historical evidence. The word Sabbat did indeed have its etymological roots in the Hebrew shabbat and was applied to the witches' night-time conclaves through the association of Jews with sorcery and Devil-worship by thirteenth-century mendicant friars and Inquisitors.[10] This image derived partially from the anti-Jewish polemics of The New Testament, for example, Revelations 2:9 and 3:9, where the term "synagogue of Satan" is employed, and in part from the idea that Jews rejected Christ as the "Messiah" and thus allied themselves with the Devil.[11] This false and malicious stereotype influenced the subsequent conceptualization both of Christian heretics and witches.[12] In the early treatises on witchcraft, such as the Errores Gazariorum (1450), the word synagogue was employed, and the term Sabbat first appears in connection with the witches' night-time gatherings around 1458.[13]

Murray's position regarding witch-covens similarly fails to withstand a critical review. Among the best evidence Murray cited as proof that witch-covens did indeed exist was the infamous case of the North Berwick witches in Scotland.[14] The events, discussed partly in the pamphlet Newes from Scotland (1591), commenced when a servant girl by the name of Geillis Duncane was suspected of witchcraft by her employer, tortured, handed over to the authorities, and subjected to further torment with the thumbscrews. Her tongue thus loosened, Geillis confessed her guilt and disclosed a long list of accomplices, which included a woman named Agnis Sampson, a schoolteacher named John Fian, and nearly seventy others.

Agnis Sampson was arrested and thrown in prison where, under agonizing torture and sexual abuse, she revealed the details of an astonishing and insidious conspiracy by the Devil and a local coven of witches to murder King James VI of Scotland (James I of England in 1603). The monarch himself, appalled at the ghastly details of the plot, took an active part in the inquisition, and personally supervised the interrogation and torture of several of the accused witches.[15] Because a number of other writers have also cited this case as evidence that organized witch-covens did indeed exist,[16] it may be useful to examine it in some detail.

According to *Newes from Scotland* (1591), "[Agnis Sampson] confessed that upon Allhallows Eve last, she was accompanied ... with a great many other witches, to the number of two hundred: and that all together went by sea each one in a riddle or sieve, and went in the same very substantially with flagons of wine making merry and drinking by the way ... to the Church of North Barrick in Lowthian, and that after they had landed, took hands on the land and danced back-to-back ... the Devil being then at North Barrick Church attended their coming in the habit or likeness of a man, and seeing that they tarried over long, he at their coming enjoined them all to a penance, which was, that they should kiss his buttocks, in sign of duty to him: which being put on the pulpit bare, every one did as he had enjoined them: and having made his ungodly exhortations, wherein he did greatly inveighed against the King of Scotland, he received their oaths for their good and true service towards him.... At which time the witches demanded of the Devil why he did bear such hatred to the King, who answered, by reason the King is the greatest enemy he has in the world: all which their confessions and depositions are still extant upon record."[17]

Agnis Sampson also revealed startling details about dark deeds of sorcery directed at the King: "she confessed that at the time when his Majesty was in Denmark, she being accompanied with the parties before specially named, took a cat and christened it, and afterwards bound to each part of that cat, the chiefest parts

Figure 2.2 King James VI presiding over the interrogation and torture of the North Berwick witches. The failure of the much publicized diabolical conspiracy against the monarch served to affirm the divine nature of James' sovereignty. From *Newes from Scotland* (1591). Reprinted with the permission of His Grace the Archbishop of Canterbury and the Trustees of Lambeth Palace Library, London.

of a dead man, and several joints of his body, and that in the night following the said cat was conveyed into the midst of the sea by all these witches sailing in their riddles or sieves as is aforesaid, and so left the said cat right before the Town of Lieth in Scotland: this done there did arise such a tempest in the sea, as a greater hath not been seen: which tempest was the cause of the perishing

Figure 2.3 The deeds of the North Berwick witches: the sorceries of Dr. Fian (top); witches raising a storm to wreck a ship (center); the company of witches listening to Satan's sermon, while Fian, "the clerk of the Sabbat," records the proceedings (lower left); members of the diabolical coven drinking wine and celebrating (lower right). From *Newes from Scotland* (1591). Reprinted with the permission of His Grace the Archbishop of Canterbury and the Trustees of Lambeth Palace Library, London.

of a boat or vessel coming over from the town of Burnt Island to the town of Lieth, wherein was sundry jewels and rich gifts, which should have been presented to the now Queen of Scotland, at her Majesty's coming to Lieth."[18]

Finally, Sampson declared that, "the said christened cat was the cause that the King's Majesty's ship at his coming forth of Denmark, had a contrary wind to the rest of his ships, then being in his company, which thing was most strange and true, as the King's Majesty acknowledges, for when the rest of the ships had a fair and good wind, then was the wind contrary and altogether against his Majesty: and further the said witch declared, that his Majesty had never come safely from the Sea, if his faith had not prevailed above their intentions."[19]

The legal proceedings—trials for treason and sorcery—lasted from November 1590 to May 1591 and involved one hundred people, an unknown number of whom were executed.[20] During the much publicized affair, it was revealed that the prisoners belonged to a coven of witches headed by James' cousin, Francis Stewart Hepburn, the Earl of Bothwell—the person posing as the "devil" at North Berwick, according to Murray[21]—who happened to be a hated and dangerous rival of the King.[22] Bothwell was accused of treason and sorcery and eliciting the aid of the Devil to murder James VI.[23] The authorities proclaimed, however, that the King escaped unharmed and was, in fact, in no personal danger while interrogating these witches, because the Almighty defended and protected the monarch.[24] The failure of the diabolical conspiracy was thus used to affirm the divine nature of James' hitherto wavering magistracy.[25]

Accusing a dangerous and hated political enemy of witchcraft proved to be an extremely effective strategy. Following the exposure of the details of the heinous plot, and the Earl's dealings with the Devil, public opinion turned against him, and he was eventually forced to flee the country in 1595.[26] Many of Bothwell's alleged diabolical accomplices were burned alive at the King's insistence.[27]

However one looks at it, accusations made in conjunction with obvious political and personal motives, confessions extorted under brutal torture, and testimony with fantastic features (sailing on the sea in sieves, causing storms by drowning cats, etc.) can hardly be taken as proof of real occurrences. Indeed, as one eminent historian has said in this regard, "stories which contain manifestly impossible elements ought not be accepted as evidence for physical events."[28] Writers who consider the North Berwick case as proof that witch-covens did indeed exist, also ignore substantial historical evidence suggesting that the ideas of a clandestine diabolical organization and nocturnal anti-Christian proceedings conducted in churches were not elements of an ancient local tradition, but were introduced into Scotland by James himself, who had been exposed to Continental demonology while in Denmark to fetch his bride.[29]

Despite rejection by most serious scholars,[30] popular audiences, as well as some anthropologists and psychiatrists,[31] have uncritically accepted Murray's thesis. Her work has also inspired twentieth-century "witch-covens" that have sprung up across the United States and Europe,[32] whose members attempt to cope with the alienating conditions of industrial society by wearing imaginative costumes and performing contrived and fanciful rituals.[33]

The only body of evidence that appears to support Murray's argument that witchcraft was linked with a "fertility religion" is to be found in Carlo Ginzburg's work, *The Night Battles: Witchcraft and Agrarian Cults in the Sixteenth and Seventeenth Centuries* (1983). Ginzburg describes a set of fertility beliefs in the Friuli region of northern Italy, centered on individuals who called themselves the *benandanti*, "doers of good." Ginzburg's study, based on an analysis of documents in the archives of the Venetian Inquisition, suggests that this fantasy, which survived until the end of the sixteenth century, was rooted in a pre-Christian fertility religion associated with the pagan goddess Diana (also known as Holda, or Herodias).

The *benandanti* were thought to have the ability to contact the world of the dead and to exercise control over the powers of nature for the benefit of society. In their role as protectors of agricultural fertility, they entered into catatonic states, during which they envisioned themselves armed with fennel stalks and astride cats, goats, and horses, engaging in fierce nocturnal forays with witches. Victory over the witches during these dream-state battles assured a good harvest, whereas defeat meant crop failure.

The *benandanti*, Ginzburg maintains, were therefore indisputably connected to fertility beliefs, a fact that confirms a "kernel of truth" in Murray's theories.[34] The "doers of good" retained their anti-witchcraft stance until around the year 1610. Shortly afterward, they came under persecution by the Inquisition, and were identified as witches. As a result the local beliefs underwent a profound transformation, and by 1640 the *benandanti* themselves were acknowledging that they were in fact "witches."[35]

The historian Russell thinks that the *benandanti* prove that "witchcraft existed, that it was largely the product of elements of folk belief and practices, and that the role of the Inquisition was not to invent witchcraft, but to impose on others its own definition of witchcraft."[36] However, there is no evidence that these *benandanti* ever met one another in person, or that they belonged to an actual organization. The *benandanti* night-battles were fought in dream-states. In other words, Ginzburg is describing trance phenomena, or spiritual excursions, not actual events.

Ginzburg himself takes issue with Russell's interpretation and points out that "the documents have no bearing on the question of the physical reality of the witches' congregations."[37] Ginzburg reiterates the same points in his more recent study, *Ecstasies* (1991), which I have already discussed.[38]

What then are we to make of the *benandanti* materials? Instead of an actual witch-sect, critics have observed, Ginzburg has uncovered a local version of the tale of Diana's night riders, an element of folklore regarding the pagan goddess of Classical times, which until the sixteenth century many, especially those within the Church, believed to be wholly imaginary.[39]

Ginzburg's conclusion, that under the force of persecution the *benandanti* came to believe that they were indeed witches,[40] illustrates how impinging demonological propaganda molded public opinion. This does not mean, as Russell maintains it does, that there was a witch-sect in the Friuli, or that Inquisitors needed evidence of beliefs akin to those of the *benandanti* in order to persecute people as witches. In the majority of witchcraft trials, as we shall see, torture and leading questions created the evidence, in the form of detailed and elaborate confessions, used to convict and burn people as witches. Upon close examination, therefore,

Ginzburg's findings fail to substantiate Murray's conception of witchcraft as a pagan fertility religion.

Unless one is ready to accept the fantastic allegations made by European demonologists,[41] there exists little external evidence to support the idea of witchcraft as a clandestine religion. The absence of such evidence is confirmed by the investigations of the learned Alonso Salazar y Frias, a ranking official of the Spanish Inquisition during the seventeenth century, whose meticulous firsthand examination of close to two thousand cases of witchcraft in Logroño (May 1611 to January 1612) failed to reveal a shred of evidence that such a covert organization did in fact exist.[42] As Salazar argued, "The real question is: are we to believe that witchcraft occurred in a given situation simply because of what the witches claim? It is clear that the witches are not to be believed, and that the judges should not pass sentence on anyone, unless the case can be proven by external and objective evidence sufficient to convince everyone who hears it. However, who can accept the following: that a person can frequently fly through the air and travel a hundred leagues in an hour; that a woman can get out through a space not big enough for a fly; that a person can make himself invisible; that he can be in a river or a sea and not get wet, or that he can be in bed and at the *aquelarre* [Sabbat] at the same time ... and that a witch can turn herself into any shape she fancies, be it housefly or raven? Indeed, these claims go beyond all human reason and many even pass the limits permitted the Devil."[43]

Salazar's conclusion was categorical: "Considering the above with all the Christian attention in my power, I have not found even indications from which to infer that a single act of witchcraft has really occurred, whether as to going to the *aquelarres*, being present at them, inflicting injuries, or other of the asserted facts."[44] It was largely because of Salazar's conclusions, which were adopted by the Inquisition and incorporated into its guidelines regarding witchcraft, that Spain escaped the witch-craze and the horrible conflagrations sweeping across the rest of Europe.

Ethnographic Studies of Witchcraft

Further light may be shed on the issue of the reality of the witches' religion by an examination of modern ethnographic findings about witchcraft. Anthropologists conducting field research in village- and band-level societies have discovered beliefs in malicious, night-flying, anthropophagic females remarkably similar to the European conception of witches. However, very few instances of someone actually practicing witchcraft have been documented.[45]

Lyle Steadman, who conducted anthropological fieldwork among the Hewa people in New Guinea, discovered that the Hewa, who also believe in the existence of cannibalistic female witches, regularly accuse women of witchcraft, and many of those accused are murdered. Annually, the total number of deaths resulting from such incidents amounts to as much as one percent of the entire population (no small number, demographically speaking). Yet Steadman found that the accused are executed for imaginary acts; no one actually engages in the practices, or commits the crimes for which they are killed.[46]

Beidleman reports comparable beliefs in imaginary night-witches among the Ukaguru in Tanzania.[47] Middleton, who conducted research among the Lugbara of Uganda, writes that Lugbara witches walk at night, transform into leopards, wild cats, or snakes, and often, while their bodies remain in their huts asleep, their spirits roam about in order to cause harm, illness, and death.[48]

These ethnographic examples of witchcraft bear a striking resemblance to the European variety. Yet, the witches familiar to anthropologists are creatures of a nightmare world; they do not exist in the real one. As Middleton tells us, "Witches do not exist in actuality, but are only figures of belief."[49] Witchcraft has the same status among the Dinka.[50] Finally, the eminent social anthropologist Evans-Pritchard, whose work *Witchcraft, Oracles and Magic Among the Azande* (1937) remains a classic in the field, made the observation that "the act of witchcraft is a psychic act."[51]

If witchcraft is a figure of belief, as many anthropologists suggest, how and why are such ideas maintained? Ethnographic investigation indicates that the concept of witchcraft can fulfill certain sociological functions. First, the concern over witchcraft seems to be related to socioeconomic distress and political disruptions.[52] Disasters, cultural dislocations, and other society-wide calamities can, under some circumstances, be accounted for by ascribing them to the malice of witches. This personifies the woes of the community by laying blame on specific individuals or groups. Ferreting out and punishing these pretended malefactors and public enemies may temporarily alleviate built-up tensions and anxieties. Thus, witchcraft and witch-hunting can act as explanation and remedy for situations beyond human control. This is well illustrated by the horrendous witch-hunts which took place at Trier, Germany (1582–1586), where disasters such as bad weather, crop failure, plagues of mice, snails, and grasshoppers, and the activities of Protestant and Spanish mercenaries cutting off supply lines, were attributed to witches who, according to a contemporary chronicler, were able to wreak cruel woes on mortals, kill cattle, ruin harvests, and to stir up other horrible things.[53]

Second, in small-scale social formations, where there is intimate interaction among members of the community, misfortunes that fall outside individual human control are thought of in personal terms, and a man seeks personal reasons why a misfortune has befallen him. In such a case bewitchment supplies the answer.[54] Attributing to witches unavoidable misfortunes, such as a death in the family, beer going sour, or a milk-cow going dry—events against which a person is normally powerless—can in some cases allay built-up apprehensions by shifting the blame to flesh-and-blood culprits against whom countermeasures can be taken.[55]

Finally, because witches, defined as malicious and inhuman creatures, exemplify the epitome of antisocial behavior, the fear of being suspected or accused of witchcraft discourages unfriendly and belligerent tendencies. Hence, in small-scale societies which lack central authority, witchcraft can act as a means of social control.[56]

Functionally, the European notion of *maleficium*—in contrast to the idea of witchcraft as a diabolical religion—is very similar to the ethnographic examples of witchcraft beliefs just described. As early as the sixth and seventh centuries, mishaps and misfortunes

arising within the context of everyday village-life were now and
then translated into charges of *maleficium*, and occasional
retaliatory actions by individuals or mobs led to the killing of an
unfortunate suspect. But such acts were performed illegally and
often without official approval.[57]

Figure 2.4 Large-scale witch persecutions took place only where
the stereotype of diabolical witchcraft was fostered by the
authorities. A broadsheet depicting the fiery death of three
female witches and two men at Derneburgh in the Harz region,
October 1555, with eyewitness reports that the Devil snatched
one of the women from the fire. Courtesy of the Department of
Prints and Drawings, Zentralbibliothek, Zürich.

Beliefs associated with *maleficium* seem to have persisted unchanged down to the fifteenth and sixteenth centuries,[58] and still survive in some parts of Europe.[59] Nevertheless, these notions by themselves do not, and indeed did not, lead to large-scale witch-persecutions. As a number of historical studies have shown, diffuse popular beliefs in witchcraft and a witch-craze (i.e., an organized large-scale persecution) are entirely different phenomena.[60]

There were two indispensable prerequisites for large-scale witch-hunting in Europe: action had to be instigated by the authorities, operating according to a theory of witchcraft vastly different from popular notions regarding *maleficium*; and legal avenues to deal with occult crimes of this nature had to be made available. The governing classes provided both requirements. In point of fact, the demonological theory of Sabbat witchcraft (i.e., witchcraft as a satanic religion) contrived by the elite was so irrelevant to the popular beliefs regarding *maleficium* that it failed to become incorporated in a permanent tradition; frequently it was forgotten during intervals between witch-hunts, and people had to be reeducated before new mass-persecutions could be inaugurated.[61] Large-scale witch-hunts occurred only where the idea of diabolical witchcraft was fostered by those in control of the coercive and legal machinery.[62]

Cannibalism and European Witchcraft

My criticism of Murray's explanation for the role of cannibalism during the Sabbat rites has elicited the following obtuse comment from a "scholar" of European witchcraft: "The Aztecs surely did practice cannibalism." The evidence that the Aztecs were man-eaters is circumstantial and highly suspect. However, it makes no difference in the context of the present discussion whether the Aztecs did or did not eat people. My contention is that there is no external and objective evidence that people in late-medieval and early modern Europe practiced ritual cannibalism.

The erudite popularizers of the myth of the witches' diabolical conspiracy, Nider, Peter of Berne, Kramer and Sprenger, Del Rio, Torreblanca, Remy, and Bodin, all had their

Figure 2.5 Two witches roasting a child, while a third witch is about to place an infant into a boiling cauldron to be cooked. Cannibalism was an important feature of European witchcraft. From Francesco Maria Guazzo's *Compendium Maleficarum* (1626). Courtesy of the Special Collections Library, Duke University.

favorite cannibal tales, which they repeated *ad nauseam*. But many of their contemporaries were aware of the absurd nature of such allegations. As Dr. Meyfarth (1635), professor of Holy Writ at the University of Erfurt, pointed out, it is impossible that dead and buried children should be eaten and yet still be found untouched in their graves.[63] He also cited reports by physicians who observed that the consumption of putrid carcasses, the main course during the Sabbat repast, could cause illness and death. Scholars such as Meyfarth approached the problem by differentiating between facts and hearsay evidence.

There are sufficient grounds for use to conclude that the charges of cannibalism brought against people suspected of witchcraft were nothing more than politically-inspired slander. Those who would argue to the contrary must accept demonological propaganda—a set of officially certified non-facts and untruths fabricated through the combined intellectual efforts of master calumniators—as authentic descriptions of actual incidents.

The nightmarish tales of the witches' orgies of blood, gore, and people-eating—scenes almost too horrible to contemplate—were widely circulated in late-medieval and early modern Europe. But this anthropophagy fixation was not confined to that particular time period. Europeans have always displayed a morbid preoccupation with cannibalism, accepting almost any yarn about the people-eating proclivities of savages in distant places, as the anthropologist Evans-Pritchard noted years ago.

Dr. Arens, who has carefully reviewed the available sources, has expressed doubts that cannibalism actually existed as an accepted custom for any time or place. In other words, he argues, there is very little evidence that the consumption of human flesh has ever been a **socially-approved** cultural practice.[64] This excludes acts of emergency (survival) cannibalism, such as in the case of the Donner Pass parties, or the plane crash in the Andes,[65] which represent desperate measures by people facing certain death by starvation.

Arens' position flies in the face of conventional wisdom by calling into question an idea that has been treated as an unchallenged fact of human behavior. He contends simply that cannibalism is by definition an observable phenomenon and therefore the evidence for its existence should be derived from observation by reliable sources. Indeed, I would add, the idea that people eat people is an extraordinary claim and, as the famous saying goes, "extraordinary claims requires extraordinary evidence."[66] Such evidence is in dire short supply, as Arens has clearly demonstrated. After examining the most popular and best-documented examples of cannibalistic societies, such as the Tupinamba, the Aztecs (anthropology's so-called "Cannibal Kingdom"), various groups in Africa and New Guinea (the traditional man-eaters' stomping grounds), as well as examples from the archaeological record, Arens points to the near absence of reliable documentation, trustworthy sources, or concrete evidence. While rumors, suspicions, allegations, ethnocentric conjectures,[67] and deliberate lies abound in the extensive literature on people-eating, there is not a single adequate documentation of anthropophagy as a custom in any form for any society.[68]

Arens concludes that the belief in the cannibalistic nature of others is a myth,[69] rather than a literal description of actual occurrences, and transmits important cultural messages for those who maintain it. While ritual anthropophagy is certainly a theoretical possibility, he adds, the idea is more often used to denigrate targeted groups by depicting their monstrous nature.[70]

This is precisely how the notion of people-eating was used by the Inquisition during the brutal suppression of medieval heretics, such as the Cathari.[71] The charge of cannibalism was also employed in a similar fashion by the witch-burners during the sixteenth and seventeenth centuries. It is perhaps no coincidence that the European monks and friars engaged in the dreary war against Devil-worshipping cannibal witches on the home front were also the ones to discover "Cannibal Kingdoms" in such places as Mesoamerica, home of history's most celebrated people-eaters.[72]

Modern scholars who tenaciously cling to, and furiously defend, the supposition that cannibalism is, or was, a part of the human behavioral repertoire, have criticized Arens for his insistence on objective evidence.[73] In fact, Arens' wholly sensible call for more rigorous standards of proof (which is not unlike Salazar's insistence that the magistrates follow acceptable standards of proof) has sent many anthropologists into fits of hysterical indignation. Such a response by scholars from a discipline that extols strict adherence to scientific methods and canons of proof is perplexing indeed. To deny cannibalism esteemed colleagues declare, is ethnocentric and disavows the central precept of the field, which admits all possible variations of human behavior. For example, the writer of a recent textbook, after testifying to his own steadfast belief in the existence of people-eating societies, accuses Arens of displaying the views of a European liberal who thinks humans are inherently perfectible, and hence incapable of such barbaric acts.[74] This writer goes on to point to the horrendous acts of human cruelty in the twentieth-century to support his remark. Acts of human cruelty and cannibalism, however, are altogether different phenomena. The author of another textbook, ironically during a discussion of scientific paradigms and the scientific method, flatly states that Arens is wrong on the facts.[75]

What is the latest evidence that such writers flaunt as confirmation of the orthodox view? An often cited work is Gajdusek's study of *kuru*, a brain disease among the Fore people of Papua New Guinea. *Kuru* is allegedly contracted by the consumption of raw human brains infected by a slow virus. This study, conducted by an authority who won the Nobel Prize in Medicine, we are told, shows convincingly that the Fore are cannibals.[76] This is not new evidence. Arens has examined Gajdusek's data and has revealed that the connection between *kuru* and cannibalism is based on conjecture rather than concrete evidence. Indeed, a more plausible explanation links *kuru* to the handling of infected dead kin and affines in mortuary practices, without cannibalism.[77]

Another line of evidence often cited in support of the orthodox view are archaeological discoveries of human bones that have "cut marks," taken as evidence that the flesh had been "systematically stripped from the bones to make fillets," or have been cracked, "as if to extract the marrow for food."[78] There is nothing new here either. Moreover, such data do not necessarily support the orthodox position. If we do not jettison scientific standards and ignore the customary canons of proof, and if we suppress our *a priori* notions that humans eat, or ate, each other on a regular basis, a plausible explanation might be that the archaeologist has uncovered evidence of survival cannibalism, an isolated instance of man-eating, a last resort against starvation. Can we use such evidence to stamp the label of cannibal on whole populations and cultures? Does such evidence prove that cannibalism is, or was, a widely accepted part of human cultural repertoire? Is it reasonable to assume on the basis of these data that European witches ate human flesh? Certainly not.

Another question to consider is this: if cannibalism is, or was, so widespread, why are we always presented with circumstantial evidence for its existence? The answer is that it is difficult to produce concrete evidence when such evidence is in short supply.

The reaction to Arens' call for critical thinking and rigorous standards of proof is surprisingly reminiscent of the controversy during the sixteenth and seventeenth centuries regarding the reality of the Sabbats and the witches' ability to fly. A few examples should illustrate my point. One modern defender of the orthodox view writes: "Accounts too numerous and too consistent with each other to have been made up support the fact that cannibalism is (or was) an authentic human custom."[79] He then goes on with a specific example, the case of cannibalism among the Fore: "When this region of Papua New Guinea came under Australian rule in the 1940s, the authorities prohibited cannibalism. During this period many alleged cannibals faced trial in Australian courts. In these proceedings the evidence and testimony convinced judges that cannibalism had in fact occurred."[80]

Now let us compare these comments with those of Jean Bodin, the great Renaissance intellect, eminent scholar, "the father of political science," and notorious witch-hammerer: "[the proof of night-flying witches] is by demonstration and obvious truth coming from human and divine laws, by so many stories from all the peoples of the earth, by so many confessions partly voluntary and partly forced, by so many judgments, convictions, condemnations and executions made for three thousand years in every country of the world."[81] Let us also consider what the sanguinary Peter Binsfeld, slayer of witches and intractable champion of orthodoxy, had to say regarding those who doubted the reality of witches' atmospheric transportation: "It is incredible that the conscience of jurists should be so bound by the authority of this council [the *Canon Episcopi* which said that nigh-flying is an illusion], when theologians and others whose business it is to decide upon matters of the faith find no difficulty in it. Do not all doctors whose business it is to judge the sense of Scripture approve and believe in bodily transportation? So popes, cardinals, theologians, doctors, Italians, Spanish and Germans believe. So also right-thinking jurists whose names are above. It is the height of temerity to prefer one's own judgment, led by fragile and apparent reason, to such a cloud of witnesses. This testimony is supported by the most certain experiences, which is confirmed by the common voice of the people."[82]

If these arguments sound remarkably alike, it is because in both cases the defenders of orthodoxy have to supply proof for something that does not and did not exist. Thus, appeal is made to hearsay evidence and authority, rather than concrete proof, common sense, or reason.

The belief that cannibalism is, or was, rampant among humans across the globe is an extraordinary misrepresentation, which in fact is based on unsubstantiated impressions, rumors, prejudice, ethnocentrism, propaganda, and deliberate lies. It is believed by almost everyone, because they have heard it so often. They have heard it from experts in the field who have fallen victim to their own cultural myth. Indeed, researchers accustomed to making the most careful and critical judgments in other matters, are willing to accept any sort of statement about people-eaters. This lack of critical sense is especially reprehensible in eminent scholars whose repetition of such accounts has done so much to secure the unwarranted acceptance of this prejudicial and ethnocentric fable as a fact of human behavior.

The allegation by European demonologists that witches were avid eaters of human flesh—and for which writers such as Murray have conceive clever explanations—were nothing more than attempts to portray the monstrous nature of the people being targeted for persecution. Thus, even if tomorrow an intrepid ethnographer were to stumble across an anomalous population of "man-eating savages" in some remote corner of the earth and is able to film them "in the act," this will not alter the general conclusion that the idea of cannibal witches in Europe was a myth with no relationship to historical reality.

The witch-hammerers cleverly employed the symbols of homicide, cannibalism, incest, and Devil-worship to define witchcraft as a revolting abomination, the ultimate in human perversion and wickedness. With such a myth to justify their cause, the learned witch-doctors set about their bloody business with impunity, incarcerating, mutilating, and slaughtering pretended miscreants wherever they could be found.

Notes

1. See Macfarlane (1970:10); Thomas (1985:614–617); Cohn (1970, 1975:107–125).
2. Klaits (1985:8).
3. Murray (1917:228). The god of the witches was male, but there was a female form, Diana.
4. Murray (1971 [1921]:190).
5. Robbins (1981:116).
6. Murray (1971 [1921]:115).
7. Murray (1917:256). This idea was forwarded by, among other witch-hammerers, the Jesuit Peter Binsfeld, Suffragan Bishop of Trier.
8. Arens (1979:95).
9. Murray (1971 [1921]:97).
10. Cohen (1982:244).
11. Peters (1978:12); Cohen (1982:146–147); Ben-Sasson (1976:481–483).
12. Peters (1978:12); P. Brown (1972:141–142); Cohen (1982:244); Newall (1973:111–115).
13. Robbins (1981:281–282, 415); J. B. Russell (1972:17).
14. Murray (1971 [1921]:50–59).
15. This experience led James VI to write a treatise on the subject of witchcraft, entitled *Daemonologie,* lending great authority to demonology.
16. Rose (1962:141–142); Seligmann (1948:248–249); Summers (1971 [1948]:v–vi).
17. *Newes from Scotland* (1591:13–14).
18. *Newes from Scotland* (1591:16–17).
19. *Newes from Scotland* (1591:17).
20. Pitcairn (1833:209–213, 230–241); Larner (1987:10).
21. Murray (1917–18:310–321).
22. Stafford (1953:103–104).
23. Pitcairn (1833:172–182).
24. Roughead (1919:205).
25. S. Clark (1977:166).
26. Stafford (1953:114).
27. Roughead (1919:226).
28. Cohn (1975:124).
29. S. Clark (1977:157); Larner (1987:10, 13).
30. Cohn (1975:109–116, 129); Mair (1970:226, 229); Thomas (1985:614–615); Burr (1939).
31. For example, Harner (1973:146–147); Howells (1962:105); Prince (1974:119, note 10).

32. Parrinder (1973:126); Davidson (1978:48); Cohn (1975:110).
33. Moody (1971:284–286); Luhrmann (1989).
34. Ginzburg (1983:xiii, xix).
35. Ginzburg (1983:xv).
36. J. B. Russell (1972:42).
37. Ginzburg (1983:xiv).
38. Ginzburg (1991:9–10).
39. Lea (1961:806).
40. Ginzburg's (1983:96, 107, 112).
41. A variant of the idea of witchcraft as a sectarian organization was forwarded by Montague Summers, an eccentric priest who believed in the Devil and diabolical forces and consequently subscribed fully to the position advocated by sixteenth- and seventeenth-century demonologists (e.g., Summers 1987 [1926]:4, 12–16, 163). Much of his work is too preposterous to take seriously. It is interesting to note, however, that Summers relied on essentially the same sources as did Murray, such as propaganda pamphlets, trial records, and demonological treatises, particularly Pierre de Lancre's *Tableau de l'inconstance des mauvais anges* (1612) [Description of the Inconstancy of Evil Angels]. He similarly glossed over the bizarre and implausible portions of testimony to make the point that the Sabbat was a real event, attended by flesh-and-blood Devil-worshippers, and not an implausible fantasy, an impression one gets from reading the original documents (Cohn 1975:121). In any case, Summers' credulous and obscurantist interpretation of European witchcraft contributes nothing to our understanding of history.
42. Henningsen (1980:393).
43. In Henningsen (1980:350).
44. In Kors and Peters (1972:340). Salazar was not alone in this opinion. Similar conclusions had been reached by Pedro de Valencia (April, 1611), commissioned by the Inquisitor General to investigate cases of witchcraft prior to Salazar's mission (Kamen 1985:213).
45. Wallace (1966:116).
46. Steadman (1975); Steadman and Merbs (1982).
47. Beidleman (1963:62–63).
48. Middleton (1967:59).
49. Middleton (1967:59); Nadel (1952); Krige (1970:239).
50. Lienhardt (1951).
51. Evans-Pritchard (1937:21, 33–34).
52. Nadel (1952:18–29); Redfield (1941:330–331).
53. Robbins (1981:202).
54. Wilson (1951:313).
55. Krige (1970).
56. Wallace (1966:180).
57. The Church, then secure in its sociopolitical foundations and upholding the theory of immanent justice—that God eradicates evil directly—did not deem it necessary to take physical measures against sorcerers and witches (Peters 1978:11; Davies 1947:2–3). The Church at this time had adopted a general explanation for misfortune that laid blame directly on demonic agencies, bypassing the human agents of evil (witches and sorcerers) altogether (P. Brown 1972:131–132).

58. Cohn (1975:155).
59. Baroja (1964:227–241); Henningsen (1980:12–13); Monter (1976:191–192); Risso and Böker (1968).
60. Robbins (1981:218); Trevor-Roper (1988:12); Henningsen (1980:391).
61. Henningsen (1980:390–391); Midelfort (1981:29).
62. Cohn (1970:13); Levack (1987:36); Midelfort (1972:19, 89).
63. Meyfarth (1635); Lea (1939:739).
64. I am concerned only with the consumption of human flesh obtained through the deliberate slaughter of victims. This excludes the consumption of a minuscule amount of ash residue following the cremation of a dead kinsman, a mortuary practice apparently found among the Yanomamo of Venezuela (see Chagnon 1983:106). It must be stressed, however, that the Yanomamo, like many other indigenous peoples labeled as people-eaters by Western scholars, are not cannibals and the thought of eating human flesh is abhorrent to them.
65. Read (1993); Mills (1946).
66. This saying belongs to Professor Carl Sagan (1981:73).
67. See Pandian (1985:92–93).
68. Arens (1979:21).
69. See Pandian's (1985:92–93) discussion of the myth of the "cannibal other."
70. Arens (1979:182).
71. The charge of cannibalism was also directed against the heretical Manicheans, Montanists, Paulicians, the heretics of Orleans (executed in 1022), the Waldensians, and the Fraticelli, among others.
72. The following passage, written by Fray Diego Durán, a sixteenth-century Dominican friar, describes how Aztec priests prepared magical ointments. The text, with the exception of a few words, could well have come from one of the standard sixteenth-century demonological texts on witchcraft: "They took ... poisonous animals and burned them in the divine brazier which stood in the temple. After these had been burned, the ashes were placed within certain mortars, together with a great deal of tobacco.... This herb, then, was placed in the mortars together with scorpions, live spiders, and centipedes, and there they were ground producing a diabolical, stinking, deadly ointment. After these had been crushed, a ground seed called *ololiuqui* [morning glory] was added, which the natives apply to their bodies and drink to see visions. It is a drink which has inebriating effects. To all this were added hairy black worms, their hair filled with venom, injuring those who touch them. Everything was mixed with soot and was poured in bowls and gourds. Then it was placed before the god as divine food. *How can one doubt that the men smeared with this pitch became wizards or demons, capable of seeing and speaking to the devil himself, since the ointment had been prepared for that purpose?*" (Durán 1971:115–116, italics mine). The influence of European demonology on Durán's account is quite clear. See Arens (1979:63–66) for comments on the unreliability of Durán's information on Aztec cannibalism.
73. For example, Brady (1982).
74. Moore (1992:14).
75. Gross (1992:56).
76. Gross (1992:55).
77. Steadman and Merbs (1982).

78. Gross (1992:56).
79. Gross (1992:55).
80. Gross (1992:55).
81. In Monter (1969:51).
82. Binsfeld (1623:317).

Chapter Three

The Black Death: Prelude to the Witch-Persecutions

It was a society obsessed with the fear of the Devil which took up the wholesale massacre of people for complicity in Satan's conspiracy to destroy the world, and this obsession can be traced to the social, economic, and psychological dislocations arising from the incessant outbreaks of the plague. This chapter begins with an examination of European society's encounter with one of the most extraordinary events in its history—the mid-fourteenth century visitation of the plague.

The Black Death, as the first outbreak of the plague is called, was a "virgin soil" epidemic. This term refers to the onset of a virulent disease among a population with no previous exposure to the infective agent.[1] Cross-cultural and historical data demonstrate that during virgin soil epidemics vast numbers of people quickly become infected, and casualty figures are often astronomical: one quarter to one third of those afflicted die.[2] In terms of mortality, the Black Death was undoubtedly the greatest disaster to befall western Europe in the last thousand years—surpassing the two World Wars of the present century.[3] Aside from being an unparalleled human calamity, the mid-fourteenth century plague epidemic was a decisive factor in the subsequent economic, sociopolitical, and religious development of medieval Europe.[4]

Few works have systematically examined the bearing of the plague on the preoccupation with witchcraft and the idea of a large-scale diabolical conspiracy of witches. Historians have generally rejected such a causal relationship.[5] Yet, the resemblance between the persecutions of people accused of spreading the plague and those accused of witchcraft, the fact that both witchcraft and plague-spreading were believed to be accomplished at the instigation of the Devil, and the correspondence between the large-scale witch-hunts and the plague pandemic (lasting roughly from 1348 to 1664) demand serious analytical consideration.

Shortly before the onset of initial plague epidemic, Europe experienced a widespread famine which lasted from 1315 to 1317. The ensuing casualties, numbering in the hundreds of thousands, are said to have surpassed any previous calamity of its kind.[6] Typhoid fever broke out immediately after the famine, taking thousands of more lives. The etiological picture was further complicated by recurring epidemics of ergotism, a disease of plant origin, with bizarre symptomatology.[7] Additional famines followed in the years 1321, 1333, 1334, 1337–42, and 1345–47.[8] Europe had hardly recovered from the effects of the latest famine when the Continent was hit by waves of the plague.

The plague is an infectious disease caused by the *Yersinia pestis* bacilli which live in the digestive tracts of rat fleas (*Xenopsylla cheopis* and *Cortophylus fasciatus*). The bacilli can be endemic to rodent populations. Rodents are able to tolerate a small quantity of the microorganisms in their bloodstream, and can therefore act as reservoirs where the pathogen can survive for lengthy intervals. Periodically, but for as yet unknown reasons, the bacilli multiply rapidly and block a valvular-like structure (the proventriculus) at the entrance of the flea's stomach. When the flea next tries to feed, it must regurgitate to clear its digestive tract, thus injecting the lethal bacilli into its host's body, and causing an eruption of the disease among the rodents.[9] When such an animal epidemic breaks out, killing the rats, their fleas must seek alternate hosts—preferably other rodents—although humans may serve as temporary habitations.[10] People bitten by these infected parasites subsequently contract the fatal illness.

The presence or establishment of the *Yersinia pestis* bacilli within rodent populations (which act as reservoirs for the disease) determines the pattern of future plague epidemics among humans.[11] In the absence of such a reservoir for the bacilli, afflicted humans simply die off, taking the contagion with them.

The black rats (*Rattus rattus*) that lived in the densely packed homes and unsanitary towns and cities of medieval Europe were an ideal transmission vector for the plague because of their close proximity to humans.[12] These animals, however, did not harbor the disease until shipboard rats, hosts to plague-bearing fleas, arrived from Constantinople in the ports of Messina, Genoa, and Venice in 1347 (Map 3.1).[13]

The contagion, which originated in Asia[14], was thus introduced into Europe. Thereafter, as the disease spread to other cities via commercial channels, the rats and rodents of medieval Europe became hosts to a microorganism that was to significantly alter the course of Western civilization.[15] The establishment of the plague bacilli among rodent populations accounts for the cyclical outbreaks of the plague in medieval Europe (two to three epidemics per generation) for nearly three centuries after the Black Death.[16]

The plague occurs in three forms: bubonic, pneumonic, and septicaemic.[17] All three are caused by the same bacillus, and transmission to humans in the first instance takes place by rat fleas. The characteristic symptoms of the bubonic plague are the enlargement of the lymphatic glands and the black blotches on the skin produced by hemorrhages, from which the disease received its ghastly name.[18] Fifty to sixty percent of those contracting the bubonic plague die. Pneumonic plague results when the bacilli reach an afflicted person's lungs. This is an extremely contagious airborne infection spread by exhaled droplets of sputum, and anywhere from ninety-five to one hundred percent of those who develop this disease perish.[19] Septicaemic plague, a variant of the bubonic form, is always fatal and occurs when the bacilli enter the victim's blood stream so rapidly and in such massive quantities that death occurs before the enlarged buboes or other symptoms appear.[20]

It is estimated that a total of 25,000,000 people—a third of Europe's population at that time—perished during the initial outbreaks of the plague.[21] In Germany, according to one estimate, over a million people died.[22] Italy and England are believed to have lost half their inhabitants.[23] Towns in Provence lost nearly four-fifths of their residents, and many villages were left

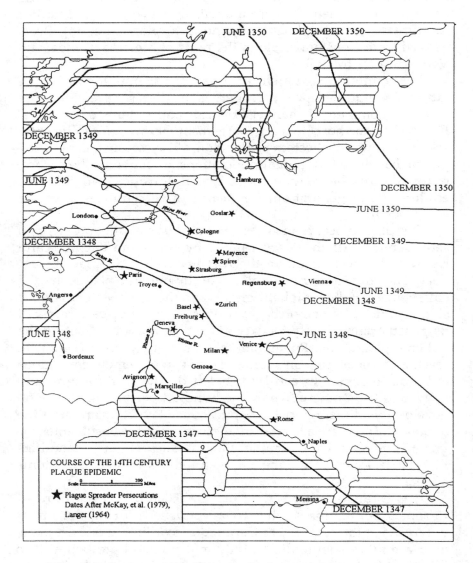

Map 3.1 Course of the plague and the sites of plague-spreader persecutions.

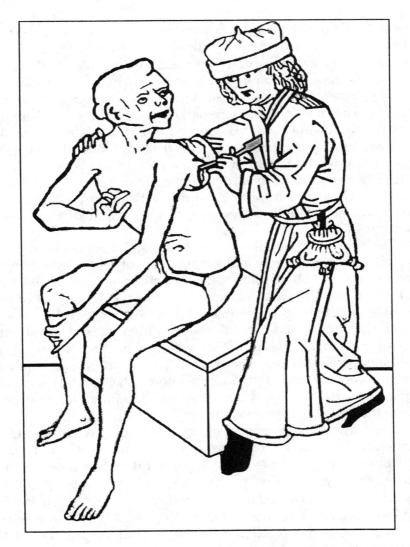

Figure 3.1 A physician lancing the enlarged lymphatic gland of
a plague victim. After a woodcut from Nürnberg (c. 1482).

completely deserted. In 1348 at Avignon, an entire monastery was
swept away, with no one outside its walls aware of the calamity.[24]
A priest who witnessed the general disaster in that city wrote:
"One-half or more ... of the people ... are already dead. Within

the walls of the city there are now more than 7,000 houses shut up; in these no one is living, and all who have inhabited them are departed; the suburbs hardly contain any people at all.... On account of this great mortality there is such fear of death that people do not dare even speak with anyone whose relative has died, because it is frequently remarked that in a family where one dies nearly all the relations follow him, and this is commonly believed among the people.... And it is said that altogether in three months—that is from January 25th to the present (April 27th) 62,000 bodies have been buried in Avignon."[25] According to one historian, two hundred thousand European villages and farmholds were totally depopulated as a result of the plague casualties.[26]

The greatest loss of life occurred among the poor, who died by the thousands in streets and hovels. Others died alone in their homes, the stench of their putrefying corpses often the first indication that they had succumbed to the pestilence. Out of fear for their own lives, people dragged the bodies of their loved ones out to the streets, and each morning traffic was obstructed with the corpses of the previous night's victims. The macabre sounds of the bells tied to the legs of grave-diggers and corpse handlers (usually convicts conscripted for the morbid task), who carted the dead away daily, served as a constant reminder to those still living that death was lingering nearby.

Everywhere the plague raged the death tolls were staggering. Cemeteries became so congested that mass graves had to be dug and bodies laid in rows, one atop the other like merchandise packed in ships, with only a thin layer of earth separating one level from the next.[27] Many more bodies remained unburied for the lack of space. The Pope, Clement VI (1342–1352), then residing in Avignon, consecrated the Rhone so that corpses could be disposed of in the water.

Petrarch (1304–1374), a canon of the cathedral of Parma and an eyewitness to the tragedy in Italy, left an appalling impression of the catastrophe's extent: "the empty houses, the abandoned towns, the squalid country, the fields crowded with the dead, the vast and dreadful solitude over the whole world." The shocked and bewildered Petrarch wondered if anyone living later would believe the magnitude of the disaster when he himself could hardly accept what he saw: "How will posterity believe that there has been a time when without the lightnings of heaven or the fires of earth, without wars or other visible slaughter, not this or that part of the earth, but well-nigh the whole globe, has remained without inhabitants.... Will posterity ever believe these things when we, who see, can scarcely credit them?"[28]

Figure 3.2 Burying the plague victims in a mass grave. Detail from a Flemish Illustration (1352). By permission of Bibliothèque Royale Albert I, Brussels.

The terror of the plague was amplified by the agony of the afflicted, the absence of medical remedies, and the ease of contagion.[29] Victims, one day in the best of health, the next vomiting blood, died a loathsome and horrible death. A contemporary French doctor, describing the symptoms of the disease, wrote: "all the matter which exudes from their bodies lets off an unbearable stench; sweat, excrement, spittle, breath, so fetid as to be overpowering; urine turbid, thick, black or red."[30] Physicians were completely confounded by this strange disease and were unable to offer any solutions.[31] According to the historian Coulton, the plague was a new malady to medieval Europe, and therefore proportionately violent, baffling, and fatal.[32] (Europe had not experienced a plague epidemic since "Justinian's Plague," the first outbreak of a two hundred year pandemic which began in 541 A.D.) In its pneumonic form, the disease was so contagious that the slightest contact often led to infection and death. In numerous instances, priests administering the last rites joined the patients in graves.[33] Some people even believed that a mere glance, or the evil-eye, of the sick could transmit the illness to the healthy.[34]

Giovanni Boccaccio (1313–1375) described the frightful contagiousness of the pestilence in *The Decameron* (written between 1348–1353): "the virulence of the pest was the greater by reason that intercourse was apt to convey it from the sick to the whole, just as fire devours things dry or greasy when they are brought close to it. Nay, the evil went yet farther, for not merely by speech or association with the sick was the malady communicated to the healthy with consequent peril of common death, but any that touched the clothes of the sick or aught else that had been touched or used by them, seemed thereby to contract the disease."[35]

In many areas the epidemic led to a total social breakdown.[36] Administrators, officials, and law-enforcement personnel were either dead or had abandoned their posts for the safety of the countryside. Church officials and clergy had no answers, nor were they themselves spared. Soon churches were left desolate and religion was forgotten. In numerous places the immense numbers of casualties brought local economies to a standstill, and harvests lay ungathered in the fields.[37] Those spared by the pestilence itself faced the terrible prospect of death by starvation. Some people, it was alleged, even resorted to cannibalism.[38]

Reaction to Disaster: The Flagellants

The medical historian Hecker did not exaggerate when he observed that "the mental shock sustained by all nations during the prevalence of the Black Plague, is without parallel and beyond description.[39]" Historical and ethnographic studies have shown that the staggering die-offs associated with virgin soil epidemics are frequently accompanied by extreme socio-psychological responses, as faith in established institutions fade away and values disintegrate.[40]

Often such epidemics lead to scapegoating, physical violence, and recourse to supernatural explanations.[41] Such reactions express the pervasive human impulse to do something in times of extreme stress and upheaval in hopes of reestablishing control over a world gone awry. As one researcher has observed, "When a killing epidemic strikes a society that accepts violence as a way of reacting to crises and believes in life after death—characteristics of many Christian ... societies—the results can be truly hideous."[42] So it was in Europe during the Black Death. In many respects the violence which followed in the wake of the plague foreshadowed the witch-hunts soon to come.

In Germany, such violence at first manifested itself in flagellant cavalcades of penance and self-castigation. The flagellants set out to atone for the sins of Christendom—the cause, many felt, for the visitation of the plague—by mortification of the flesh. "They each carried a scourge of leathern thongs," wrote a chronicler, "which they applied to their limbs, amid sighs and tears, with such violence, that the blood flowed from the wounds. Not only during the day, but even by night, and in the severest winter, they traversed the cities with burning torches and banners, in thousands and tens of thousands, headed by their priests, and prostrated themselves before altars. They proceeded in the same manner in the villages: and the woods and mountains resounded with the voices of those whose cries were raised to God."[43]

As the movement spread through Germany, many joined the incredible processions of self-mutilation. From Germany, flagellants moved eastward into Hungary and Poland, southward into Silesia and Bohemia, and westward, through Flanders, into

France, as far as the city of Troyes.[44] About the same time a group of flagellants calling themselves the Devoti appeared in Italy.

Figure 3.3 Flagellants scourging their bodies with leather whips. From Hartmann Schedel's *Liber Chronicarum* (1493). Courtesy of Kent State University Libraries, Department of Special Collections and Archives.

Flagellantism was the reaction of a society dumfounded by the catastrophic deaths of hundreds of thousands of its members. Every town and city welcomed the self-mutilating mourners, and forthwith, the flagellants became as formidable as either secular or ecclesiastical authorities, occupying churches and marshaling vast popular support.[45] Growing bolder by their popularity, the flagellants proclaimed that God, in a letter delivered to them by an angel, offered "divine grace" to all who joined them. To their list of declarations they also added the ability to perform miracles, exorcise demons, raise the dead, and offer absolution from sins. As the messianic pretensions of flagellant leaders became more obvious, the movement itself grew increasingly anti-clerical. In Germany, flagellants began to attack the religious hierarchy, mock the sacraments, interrupt religious services, and rob churches.[46]

Outraged by such a challenge to their monopoly over the supernatural, clergymen and their secular allies reacted swiftly.[47] Emperor Charles of Germany and the Theological Faculty of the University of Paris turned to the Pope for assistance. When a group of flagellants arrived at Avignon, the Pontiff prohibited their performance, under penalty of excommunication. Secular authorities followed suit. The French monarch promptly banned the flagellants from pushing further into France; the King of Sicily threatened them with the death penalty. All over Europe flagellants were relentlessly persecuted: many were burned at the stake.

The Plague-Spreader Conspiracy

Flagellant processions were not the only reaction to the plague. Fear and confusion, produced by the massive casualties, combined with flagellant fanaticism and long-standing prejudices, to give rise to the allegation that the epidemic was caused by Jews who had poisoned wells.[48] Scapegoats were needed and candidates were thus promptly found.

The violence began in southern France during the summer of 1348, where rumors spread that the Jews had conspired to destroy Christendom and were producing the plague by poisoning wells with magical salves and powders. The horrendous tales of plague-spreading swept like wild-fire across Europe.[49] By autumn that year the popular panic gripped much of Germany: wells were sealed, springs were covered, people were told to use river or rain water, and city gates were shut against strangers.

Many of the accused were brutally tortured into confessing to the monstrous crimes. Nobles and administrators joined in the quest to extirpate the well-poisoners. The few officials who tried to dismiss the allegations brought against innocent Jews were nevertheless forced to submit to the slaughter. With a logic remarkably similar to that of later European witch-hunters, angry mobs cried out that the wells would not have been covered if the charges were false.

Figure 3.4 Fear and prejudice combined to give rise to the false allegation that the plague was caused by Jews who poisoned wells. As a result, thousands of innocent men, women, and children were burned and their properties confiscated. From Hartmann Schedel's *Liber Chronicarum* (1493). Courtesy of Kent State University Libraries, Department of Special Collections and Archives.

In Basel and Fribourg (see Map 3.1) thousands of Jews—men, women and children—were sealed in large wooden structures, made specially for the occasion, and set ablaze.[50] In Strasbourg,

2,000 Jews were torched. In Speyer a large number of Jews committed suicide, while the rest were murdered and their bodies, put into empty wine barrels, were thrown into the Rhine. In Mayence, as in other places, the appearance of the flagellants triggered violence, leaving 12,000 murdered Jews in its wake. Jews in Cologne suffered the same fate. On account of such persecution, many Jewish communities in Germany were totally obliterated.[51] In parishes where there were no Jews, grave-diggers, corpse handlers, lepers, and paupers were rounded up, tortured to confess to smearing "plague poisons," legally condemned, and sentenced to be burned alive.[52] Christians accused of the heinous crimes were thought to be operating under Jewish orders.[53]

In Vienna, Goslar, Regensburg (Ratisbon), Avignon, Paris, and Rome, Jews and Christians alike were put to death as sowers of the plague.[54] In Spain and Italy the charge of plague-spreading brought against the Jews was combined with more familiar and equally false accusations of diabolatry, killing Christians and using their blood in rituals (blood libel), and behaving "just like witches."[55]

The hysteria over *pestis manufacta* (diabolically produced disease) and the brutal massacre of Jews and others blamed for the pestilence, bear many similarities to the subsequent witch-hunts.[56] Because of the plague, wrote the historian Nohl, "the imagination of the people was terribly excited and highly strung and, because they attributed the disease rather to magic than to natural causes, they demanded victims and could only be appeased by the ruthless executions of the pretended miscreants. Full of horror, they heard the confessions of the plague smearers which for the most part originated on the rack. In many places it was asserted that the plague immediately decreased if the heads were cut off the bodies of witches and sorcerers who had already been buried."[57]

As more data were gathered, and all the evidence sifted and scrutinized, it soon became evident that the monstrous plague smearers did not act alone, but were part of an organized conspiracy of unimaginable proportions. Moreover, it was announced that the heinous miscreants, commonly called "*semeurs de peste*," "*engraisseurs*," or "*bouteurs de peste*," were spreading the lethal disease under the directives of Satan himself.

Figure 3.5 The burning of plague-spreaders. The brutal massacre of those blamed for outbreaks of the plague was reminiscent of the later witch-persecutions. After a fourteenth-century woodcut.

It was not long before the good Inquisitors projected their stereotype of heresy[58] onto this newest and most lethal of all anti-Christian conspiracies. The search for scapegoats thus contributed to the creation of a fantastic myth about a hitherto unknown organization of Devil-worshippers, whose members were masters of black magic, able to destroy man or beast alike with their magical powders and unguents. The plague-spreaders, who were accused of diabolism, acting collectively under the directives of

Satan, and conspiring against Christendom, were almost indistinguishable from witches.[59] Only recently have modern writers considered the possibility that the idea of a satanic conspiracy of plague-spreaders may well have engendered subsequent beliefs in a diabolical conspiracy of witches.[60]

The procedures used to prosecute those accused of spreading the plague were strikingly similar (as was the general level of attendant paranoia) to the methods employed by the witch-hammerers. The following incident which took place during the 1630 epidemic in Milan illustrates: on the morning of June 21st, 1630, during the prevalence of the plague, Guglielmo Piazza, commissioner of health of the city, was seen strolling down the street writing from an ink-horn at his belt and wiping his ink-stained fingers on the walls of a house. Some neighborhood women accused him of smearing their houses with plague poisons. They lodged a complaint with the City Council and Piazza was immediately apprehended and put to the torture. The wretched Piazza withstood two applications of torture, but capitulated to the "third degree."

To spare himself from further torments he confessed to all that was required. When threatened with further and more terrible tortures, he revealed the identity of his accomplice, a barber named Giangiacomo Mora. The latter also yielded to the insufferable torments, confessing his guilt. Mora divulged that he had prepared the lethal ointment with foam from the mouths of plague casualties, and said that Piazza, whose post gave him access to dead bodies, had provided him with this essential ingredient. Mora also incriminated Don Juan de Padilla, son of the commandant of the fortress, whom the barber had once treated for syphilis. Count Padilla was ultimately acquitted, but Piazza and Mora were condemned to death.[61]

The inscriptions on the *colonna d'infamia* [column of infamy] erected to forever blast the memory of the two conspirators, detailed their sentence:

> Here, where this plot of ground extends, formerly stood the shop of the barber Giangiacomo Mora, who had conspired with Guglielmo Piazza, Commissary of the Public Health, and with others, while a frightful plague exercised its ravages, by means of deadly ointments spread on all sides, to hurl many citizens to a cruel death. For this, the Senate, having declared them both to be enemies of their country, decreed that,

placed on an elevated car, their flesh should be torn with red-hot pincers, their right hand cut off, and their bones broken; that they should be extended on the wheel, and at the end of six hours be put to death, and burnt. Then, and that there might remain no trace of these guilty men, their possessions should be sold at public sale, their ashes thrown in the river, and to perpetuate the memory of their deed the Senate wills that the house in which the crime was projected shall be razed to the ground, shall never be rebuilt, and that in its place a column shall be erected which shall be called Infamous. Keep afar off, then, afar off, good citizen, lest this accursed ground should pollute you with its infamy. August 1630. [62]

The sentence was carried out to the letter.

As the stereotype of diabolical witchcraft gained currency, witches quickly emerged as the paramount suspects in the supernaturally-directed diabolical germ warfare. For example, in 1542, a famine accompanied by an outbreak of the plague in Geneva led to a massive witch-hunt, covering the entire gamut of evil-doers, Satan-worshippers, sorcerers, and witches. [63] In a letter dated March 27, 1545, Calvin complained bitterly: "Here … God is trying us sorely. A conspiracy of men and women has been discovered, who for a space of three years have spread the plague through the city, by what sorceries I do not know…. Fifteen women have already been burnt. Some of the men have been punished even more severely. Some have committed suicide in prison. Twenty-five are still in custody. Notwithstanding, the conspirators do not cease to smear the locks of doors with their ointments. Behold the perils that beset us."[64]

The jails were filled with men and women who were tried in the cruelest manner. Many were torn with red-hot pincers or subjected to other, newly devised forms of torture. Those who would not confess were walled up in their prison cells to die. Thirty-four people were brutally executed between February 17 and May 15, 1545.[65]

Geneva's plague-spreader persecutions had a significant impact on the prevailing ideas about witchcraft. As one historian has observed, Geneva assumed a leading position in the sphere of witch-persecution.[66] Some regarded it as the principal authority on methods of witch-hunting. Judges from Lyons, Valais, several Swiss cantons, and Savoy wrote to the authorities in Geneva for advice on the treatment of their own witches. Outbreaks of witch-

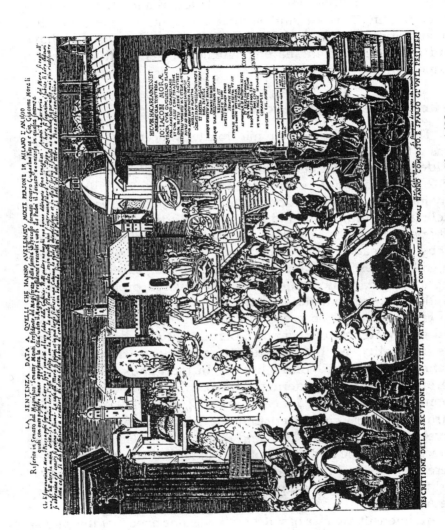

Figure 3.6 Execution of plague-spreaders in Milan, 1630.

mania in Geneva during plague epidemics in 1566, 1567, 1568, 1571, and 1615, and the resultant executions of the *semeurs de peste*, added considerably to the city's reputation as a foremost center of witch-hunting.[67] These and similar incidents suggest that the plague epidemics and plague-spreader persecutions may have had a greater role in shaping witchcraft beliefs than hitherto suspected.

Witch-Hunts after the Great Plague

The period following the mid-fourteenth century Black Death was a time of skepticism, gloom, and uncertainty.[68] The second epidemic of the plague pandemic, *pestis secunda*, struck in 1361–1362, while the third, *pestis tertia*, broke out in 1369, cutting short any interim resurgence of population and economic recovery, and fueling mounting fears and anxieties.[69] By the year 1400 nearly fifty percent of the population of western Europe had been carried off by the dreaded disease. Epidemics erupted again between 1470 and 1480. These incessant flare-ups of the plague set a pattern of depopulation, reduced lifespans, and lowered productivity that would continue up to the sixteenth century.[70]

Historians have observed that the recurrent plague outbreaks, and the awareness of them as a permanent evil, deeply marked the mentality of the fourteenth and fifteenth centuries.[71] Eschatological fears loomed heavily in the minds of many.[72] In Germany and Italy wandering prophets who preached impending doom and destruction appeared in 1472, 1484, 1490, and 1492.[73] Europeans were convinced that the prophecy of the Book of Revelations had come to pass and that the "Four Horsemen of the Apocalypse"—the harbingers of war, famine, death and disease— were upon them. Many lived in constant anticipation of disaster, and there were frequent reports of people seeing the apparition of the Antichrist.[74]

An intensifying fear of witchcraft was one aspect of this age of unprecedented calamities. In the words of one historian: "When we reflect that by the fifteenth century medieval culture was declining; that economic prosperity, political freedom and self-government, chivalry, and public charity were waning; that the fourteenth century had been marked by the terrible Black Death which demoralized society and never ceased its visitations thenceforth during the entire time of the witchcraft delusion, and by the perhaps worse pest of mercenary soldiers who, aided by artillery and firearms, made all wars from the Hundred Years' to the Thirty Years' so cruel, devastating, and financially exhausting—when we consider this, we may incline to regard the witchcraft delusion as in congenial company."[75]

Figure 3.7 The pestilence, carrying a coffin and wielding a javelin, emerging from the jaws of Hell. After a medieval woodcut (c. 1499).

The period after 1375 saw a startling rise in the frequency of witch-trials involving the charge of diabolism,[76] and a corresponding attempt by ecclesiastical and civil authorities to ferret out and purge Satan's earthly delegates—witches and sorcerers—thought responsible for everything that was going wrong.

Notes

1. Crosby (1976:292).
2. Crosby (1986:94, 280).
3. Cohn (1957:130).
4. Siraisi (1982:9).
5. For example, Kors and Peters (1972:22, note 5); Scarre (1987:38).
6. Pirenne (1936:195); J. C. Russell (1966:466).
7. See Matossian (1989:47–58).
8. Coulton (1929:8).
9. McElroy and Townsend (1985:155).
10. Gottfried (1983:6–7).
11. Benenson (1976:503). These fleas can remain alive for over two months away from their rodent host, enabling them to be conveyed over great distances in trade goods (Horrox 1994:7).
12. Carmichael (1986:5); Bean (1982:23–38).
13. Bean (1982:25). From here the disease spread in all directions, including to the Middle East (Dols 1977:56).
14. See McNeill (1976:164–165).
15. Gottfried (1983:163).
16. See Gottfried (1983:8–9,133); Langer (1964:114); Acha and Szyfres (1980:84).
17. Hirst (1953:28–30).
18. Smith (1941:4). The name "Black Death" was coined during the fifteenth century and does not appear in any of the contemporary accounts of the mid-fourteenth-century plague.
19. Gottfried (1983:8); Benenson (1976:504–505).
20. Bean (1982:24–25); Bradley (1977:12).
21. Hecker (1844:30); Helleiner (1980:5–10); Sigerist (1943:115); Durant (1957:64); Acha and Szyfres (1980:84).
22. Hecker (1844:26).
23. Hirst (1953:13).
24. Creighton (1965 [1894]:133).
25. In Gasquet 1977 [1908]:46–47).
26. Sigerist (1943:115).
27. Gasquet (1977 [1908]: 27).
28. In Gasquet (1977 [1908]:33).
29. The bacilli responsible for the medieval outbreak of the plague appears to have been more virulent than nineteenth- and twentieth-century strains.

This may explain the highly contagious nature of the fourteenth-century epidemics (Horrox 1994:8).

30. In Ziegler (1969:20).
31. Langer (1964:115).
32. Coulton (1929:8).
33. Creighton (1965 [1894]:121).
34. Baron (1986:v).
35. Boccaccio (1903:6).
36. Langer (1970:370).
37. Langer (1964:118, 121); Helleiner (1980:10); Hirst (1953:13).
38. Nohl (1969:163). Camporesi (1989:50–52) says that Europeans frequently resorted to cannibalism and necrophagy (the consumption of human corpses) during times of dire necessity, such as sieges, famines, and other crises. However, as people-eating is always hidden, Camporesi points out, we shall never know precisely how many tons of human flesh was consumed. "It is the clandestine quality," he adds, "that renders this consumption non-quantifiable." Camporesi's speculations, of course, are based entirely on hearsay and circumstantial evidence. His remarks nevertheless illustrate the fixation Europeans seem to have for lurid tales of people-eating, as I have already noted in Chapter Two.
39. Hecker (1844:32).
40. See McNeill (1976:205); Langer (1964:121).
41. See Sjoberg (1962:362–365). For the religious response (i.e., call for prayers, processions, pilgrimages, etc.) to the plague see the collection of contemporary narrative accounts compiled and edited by Horrox (1994:111-157).
42. Crosby (1976:298).
43. In Hecker (1844:36).
44. Hecker (1844:35); Lea (1961:449).
45. Hecker (1844:36).
46. Lea (1961:449–451).
47. See Kieckhefer (1979:81–82).
48. Ben-Sasson (1976:486–497). For contemporary accounts of such persecutions see Horrox (1994:207-226).
49. Hirst (1953:18).
50. Hecker (1844:42).
51. Cohen (1982:245).
52. Nohl (1969:179).
53. Guerchberg (1964:208).
54. Abrahams (1985:332–333).
55. See Cohn (1967:25–45); Nohl (1969:187); Ben-Sasson (1976:481–487); Trachtenberg (1987 [1939]:5–10); J. B. Russell (1972:167); Trevor-Roper (1988:36).
56. Hecker (1844:41).
57. Nohl (1969:178–179).
58. Heretics brought before the tribunals of the Inquisition during the Middle Ages were accused of worshipping Satan, infanticide, ritual murder, cannibalism, performing blasphemous parodies of the Sacraments, desecrating the cross and sacramental paraphernalia, and engaging in incestuous and promiscuous sexual intercourse. The symbols of homicide,

cannibalism, incest, and Devil-worship were thus ingeniously used to define heresy as the utmost in human depravity.

In Germany, the ruthless Conrad von Marburg (1231–1233), Pope Gregory IX's specially appointed Inquisitor, employed such charges to indiscriminately seize, torture, and burn scores of people as "Luciferans," who, he maintained, abjured the Christian faith, engaged in obscene rites, and worshipped Lucifer (Kieckhefer 1979:13; Cohn 1975:22, 24–31). However, the satanic sect vanished from the historical records immediately after Conrad was removed from the picture, suggesting that the allegations were a fabrication based on confessions extracted by torture.

The same formula was utilized again, in 1307, during the persecution of the Templar Knights, members of a powerful monastic military order who had attained great prestige and wealth for their role during the Crusades in the Holy Land. The Templars were accused of and, under brutal torture during which a number of them died, confessed to outrageous crimes, such as worshipping demons and the Devil, adoring a satanic cat and kissing it under the tail, desecrating the cross, and practicing sodomy. This catalogue of offenses is remarkably similar to the list of crimes that appeared during the witchcraft trials in the sixteenth and seventeenth centuries (M. Barber 1978:182).

The legal proceedings against the Templars were conducted by the Inquisition under the directives of the financially-troubled French monarch, Philip IV, who intended to obliterate the monastic order and confiscate its enormous landholdings and wealth (Lea 1961:689–699; Kieckhefer 1976:14). Such confiscations were justified by the allegation that the Templars had acquired their wealth by entering into a league with the Devil (M. Barber 1978:182). There is no objective evidence, however, that the Templars were guilty of any of the charges brought against them (M. Barber 1978:243). Indeed, references to diabolical sects completely vanish from the historical records after Philip IV successfully expropriated the Templars' assets in France, making it clear that the idea of a satanic religion was a fiction, substantiated by confessions obtained through the use of suggestive questioning and insufferable tortures (Cohn 1975:31). Nearly one hundred years after the Templars were crushed, the myth of Satan's sect reemerged in connection with witchcraft.

59. See Levack (1987:122, 154).
60. For example, Ginzburg (1991).
61. Haggard (1929:203–205); Fletcher (1898:175–180).
62. Fletcher (1898:175–180).
63. See Monter (1967:73).
64. In Davies (1947:7).
65. Lea (1939:1117).
66. Davies (1947:8).
67. Davies (1947:8); Levack (1987:154).
68. Langer (1964:121); McNeill (1976:169); Gottfried (1983:163).
69. Gottfried (1983:131); Lütge (1971:80); Mitchell (1982:13).
70. Gottfried (1983:133); Thrupp (1966:483); Helleiner (1980:11).
71. Carpentier (1971:36–37).
72. Lerner (1982:78).

73. McGinn (1979:277).
74. Ziegler (1969:274); Thorndike (1936:682–683).
75. Thorndike (1936:686–687).
76. Levack (1987:170–171).

Chapter Four

Demonology: Ideology of Terror

European demonologists sought to validate their assertions in numerous ways. They appealed to the Scriptures, legends from Classical times, travelers' tales regarding witchcraft in other lands, the poetical authority of Homer, Virgil, and Ovid, and confessions compiled during previous persecutions.[1] The reality of witchcraft, as Bodin put it, is demonstrated by the countless stories from around the world, the innumerable confessions, and the untold convictions, condemnations, and executions that have taken place for millennia in every country on earth.[2] The witch-hammerers also appealed to the authority of the Church itself. Francesco Guazzo, a seventeenth-century Italian friar and demonologist, argued in his *Compendium Maleficarum* (1608) [Handbook of Witches] that, "they who assert that all this [Sabbats, night-flying, and Satan worship] is not true, but only a dream or illusion, certainly sin in lack of true reverence to our Mother Church. For the Catholic Church punishes no crime that is not evident and manifest, and counts no one a heretic unless he has been caught in patent heresy. Now for many years the Church has counted witches as heretics and has ordered that they be punished by Inquisitors and handed over to the Secular Courts.... Therefore either the Church is in error, or they who maintai this belief. But he who says that the Church is in error over a matter concerning the faith is Anathema Maranatha."[3]

Demonological axioms were thus presented as incontrovertible truths. To doubt the reality of witchcraft, in other words, was tantamount to heresy. As Joseph Glanvill declared in his *Saducismus Triumphatus* (1689), one of the most influential English works on demonology, when men disbelieve in witches and Satan, "we are beholden to them if they believe either Angel, or Spirit, Resurrection of the Body, or Immortality of Souls. These things hang together in a chain of connection ... and it is but a happy chance if he that has lost one link holds the other."[4] In this chapter I shall focus on the logic of demonology and examine how the sanguinary witch-doctors, men like Bodin, Guazzo, Glanvill, and others, affirmed, bolstered, and perpetuated their ideology of terror.

Some insights into the logical structure of European witch beliefs may be gained by a review of ethnographic findings about witchcraft. I turn again to Evans-Pritchard's classic work on the Azande. This study has revealed that beliefs about witchcraft, although unscientific, are neither irrational nor illogical for those who hold them.[5] If an Azande man is injured by fire, for example, they say it is witchcraft. But, Evans-Pritchard pointed out, we must make a distinction here between fire and its heat, on the one hand, and the fact that a certain person was injured by a particular fire, on the other. Injuries do not result whenever someone uses fire. Why, then, the Azande would ask, was this man burned by this fire, on this occasion? The answer: "witchcraft." Evans-Pritchard added, "Fire is hot, but it is not hot owing to witchcraft, for that is its nature. It is a universal quality of fire to burn, but it is not a universal quality of fire to burn you."[6] Thus, "It is the particular and variable conditions of an event and not the general and universal conditions that witchcraft explains."[7] In other words, the belief in witchcraft represents a theory of causation that applies only to specific situations and under particular circumstances.

Evans-Pritchard's study has, in addition, revealed that witchcraft accusations are not random, but arise where there are ill-feelings between an accuser and an accused.[8] In certain respects Azande witchcraft is similar to the European notion of *maleficium* (harm by supernatural means directed against person or property), before the conception of witchcraft as a diabolical enterprise. *Maleficium* explained why a misfortune happened; furthermore, it enabled the victim to cast the blame for his or her misfortune on a flesh-and-blood perpetrator. In Europe such accusations often arose in the context of personal animosities and village hatreds. Later on, Inquisitors and magistrates, operating according to demonological premises, were able to capitalize on such ill-feelings by prosecuting cases of *maleficium* as diabolical witchcraft.[9]

Such findings contradict psychiatric assessments which cast witches in the role of misdiagnosed mental patients, psychotics, and hysterics, and strive to explain the witch-hunts in terms of the psychopathology of the individuals targeted for persecution. This position, first made popular by Zilboorg's *The Medical Man and the Witch During the Renaissance* (1935),[10] has been advanced more recently in Vieth's *Hysteria: The History of a Disease* (1965) and Masters' *Eros and Evil: The Sexual Psychopathology of Witchcraft* (1966). George Mora, a medical historian, writing in the same tradition, states that the age of the witch-hunts "was a period in history when irrationality had an accepted place in the realm of human experience."[11] But explanations which lay blame on the victims' sick minds, or human irrationalities, overlook the socio-political determinants of the witch-hunts, and thus obfuscate the issue rather than contribute to an understanding of this particular historical period.[12]

Among the Azande a witch-hunt is both a public demonstration against witches and a communal confirmation of the menace posed by witchcraft. The Azande use divination, professional witch-finders, and public seances to discover the identity of witches and counteract their maleficent influence. These procedures also serve to sustain the belief in witchcraft. Similarly, in Europe, accusations of witchcraft, the divination of the torture chambers, anti-witchcraft laws (e.g., Charles V's *Constitutio Criminalis Carolina* [1532], and Canon Law), public executions, and the availability of channels for counteracting witchcraft (i.e., courts, appealing to Inquisitors, exorcists, etc.) all served to sustain and propagate the belief in witchcraft.

The anti-witch campaigns undertaken by European authorities were themselves instrumental in imposing the myth of the witches' conspiracy on the public.[13] For example, the witch-hunts occurring in Pays de Labourd between the years 1610 to 1614 were preceded by official directives ordering priests and religious functionaries to teach local people about witchcraft and its dangers.[14] Similarly, in Nassau, Germany, in 1628, the authorities established "witch-committees" in the villages with instructions to preach against the evils of witchcraft. As a result, between the years 1629 and 1632 large numbers of people were imprisoned and put to death for this horrible crime.[15] The spectacle of publicly executing witches and werewolves, sometimes seen by audiences of many thousands, functioned both to spread the fear of witchcraft as well as to empirically confirm demonological assertions.

Figure 4.1 The Pappenheimer family on the way to execution in Munich, in 1600, during a sensational show trial designed to deter resistance and lawlessness. The anti-witchcraft campaigns of the authorities were instrumental in inculcating the official stereotype of diabolical witchcraft. From Michael Kunze's *Highroad to the Stake: A Tale of Witchcraft*. Copyright © 1987. Courtesy of the University of Chicago Press.

Evans-Pritchard's study disclosed other features of Azande witchcraft beliefs that have clear parallels with European witchcraft, including the use of ritual procedures to detect a witch. The Azande use the poison oracle, in which a certain quantity of *benge* (a magically potent botanical poison) is fed to a live chicken, while questions are posed regarding the guilt of a suspect. Answers are determined on the basis of whether the fowl lives or dies from the action of the poison. Evans-Pritchard observed that although the poison oracle is put into operation by following exact ritualistic procedures and rules, the test is nevertheless open to manipulation by the operator.

Figure 4.2 Divination of the torture chamber, initiated by the ritual blessing of the instruments of pain. From Hermann Löher's *Hochnötige unterthänige wemütige Klage der frommen Unschultigen* (1676), Rare Bd. Ms. 37 (Witchcraft Collection, 4621). By permission of the Rare and Manuscript Collections Department, Cornell University Library.

In Europe, torture chambers were places where suspected witches were "searched with the torture"[16] to determine their guilt and the identity of their accomplices. The process of search by torture also operated according to specific procedures, including the ritual blessing of the instruments to ensure their efficacy, and, like the Azande poison oracle, were open to manipulation by the technicians, motivated either by a desire for profit or the need to extort a confession at all costs.[17] As one contemporary observer wrote: "Then there are the liberties and wickedness of the executioners, who in some places control the torture instead of silently doing what they are ordered. They question, urge, and insist with terrible threats, if the accused does not confess; they augment the torture till it is insufferable. Thus some are praised because not a single one of their victims is not forced to confess, and these are called in when others have failed.... Some executioners, when preparing the accused for torture, will tell them what accomplices to denounce and warn them not to refuse; they will also tell them what others have said about them, so that they will know what details to confess, and thus make all accord. Thus the protocols are made to agree and the evidence of guilt is perfect."[18]

Azande witchcraft beliefs, Evans-Pritchard[19] has shown, are structured in vague terms so that empirical experience does not contradict them.[20] Similarly, the logical structure of demonology ensured that almost any contradiction noted or objection raised by critics could be explained away as the "subtlety of the devil," who could and often did interfere with the process of ordinary cause and effect. William Perkins, the influential Puritan English demonologist, wrote in his *Discourse of Witchcraft* (1609) that the Devil was able to do this: "First, by corrupting the humor of the eye, which is the next instrument of sight. Secondly, by altering the air, which is the means by which the object or species is carried to the eye. Thirdly, by altering and changing the object, that is, the thing seen, or whereon a man looks."[21]

Take for example the charge of night-flying, often brought against suspected witches in Europe. If witnesses were produced to testify that the accused was at home, asleep the entire night, the rejoinder was that, "the devil can and does place a false body in the bed to deceive the husband while the witch has gone to the

Sabbat; and in order that the husband may not suspect that she is absent, he either causes him to fall into a heavy sleep, or substitutes a likeness of his wife so that the husband on awaking may think that it is indeed his wife."[22] Alternatively, it was maintained that, "[witches] are most often actually transported by the devil, and that sometimes they go on foot: and when they wish to be transported bodily they anoint themselves ... with an ointment made from the fat of infants' bodies; but when they wish to attend the Sabbat only in a dream, they lie down on their left side: but when they prefer to keep awake, and yet see what is done at the Sabbat as if they were present at it, then by some devils' work they send a thick vapor from their mouths, in which they can see all that is done as if in a mirror."[23]

In any case, whether someone was said to have attended the Sabbats in person, or vicariously through dreams, the final verdict was the same. Demonological arguments on this issue became so complicated, with "causes" so needlessly multiplied, that a skeptical sixteenth-century humanist lawyer, Andreas Alciati of Milan, asked, "Why not rather presume the demon to be with his demons and the woman with her husband? Why invent a real body in a fictitious sabbat and a fantastic one in a real bed?"[24]

Similarly, when faced with the question of producing evidence that a certain person had entered into a contract with the Prince of Darkness, demonographers claimed: "Infernal Contracts are not supposed to be made in the presence of witnesses; being as has been said, against the law of God and Man; so that the Devil out of a seeming regard to the safety and immunity of his prostitute may omit the Ceremony of Tests; the black pupil acting with greater security when she apprehends none knows of, or is privy to the confederation."[25]

Likewise, to the argument that a certain suspect was a good Christian who observed all religious rituals and hence could not be a witch, the *Errores Gazariorum* (c. 1450) asserted that, "it is proved by the confessions of those burned that the members of the sect [i.e., sect of witches] to conceal their errors, are regular in attendance at mass, confess often, and frequently take communion."[26] As one eyewitness decried: "rumors fly about Anna, a poor but discreet woman. The council consult together. Is Anna in good or bad repute? If bad, she is a witch; if in good, she is undoubtedly a witch, for witches always seek to be well thought of. She is arrested; they ask if she is frightened or not; if yes, she is a witch; if not, she is certainly a witch, for witches always represent themselves as innocent. The people clap their hands and rejoice, the preachers thunder from the pulpit."[27] Similarly, another contemporary observer pointed out, "if a woman is especially regular in public worship, it is argued that it is the worst witches who make the greatest show of piety—and, if she is neglectful, it is the same. So with morals—an irreprehensible life is an *indicium* [evidence] and so is a flagitious one. According to the absurd judgments of these judges everything is an excuse for torture and condemnation. As an old poet says, physicians and judges can slay with impunity."[28] Careful scrutiny of demonological treatises reveals that their arguments cover every possibility, with guilt a foregone conclusion.

Reginald Scot, the perspicacious sixteenth-century opponent of witch-hunting, called attention to a number of logical defects in the arguments forwarded by the promoters and engineers of the witch-persecutions. Scot observed, for instance, that demonologists attributed to witches and the Devil that which could be explained in terms of natural causes: "Seeing therefore that some other things might naturally be the occasion and cause of such calamities as witches are supposed to bring; let not us that profess the Gospel and knowledge of Christ, be bewitched to believe that they do such things, as are in nature impossible, and in sense and reason incredible. If they say it is done through the devil's help, who can work miracles; why do not thieves bring their business to pass miraculously, with whom the devil is as conversant as with the other? Such mischiefs as are imputed to witches, happen where no witches are; yea and continue when witches are hanged and burnt: why then should we attribute such effects to that cause, which being taken away, happen nevertheless?"[29] But, Boguet and other witch mongers put objections of this sort to rest with the rejoinder that "demons never work except through second and natural causes."[30]

There were two logical inconsistencies in the demonological theory of witchcraft, however, that could not be explained away so easily: why the Devil was given a free hand in the world to torment devout Christians; and why witches were unable to save themselves by magical means, or simply to fly away, and thus avoid apprehension by the authorities. In addressing the first dilemma, the *Malleus Maleficarum* stated that witches commit their fiendish deeds only "when the Justice of God permits such things to be."[31] (The more commonly used phrase was *Deo permittente*, "with God's permission.") Bodin argued that each act of witchcraft was possible only with God's permission, "who takes his revenge on his enemies through his enemies."[32] And according to Richard Boulton, the staunch English defender of demonology: "As for the persons whom God permits to be afflicted thus, and to be under the power of witchcraft, they are of three kind, viz. either such as God thinks fit should be punished for their horrid sins; or sometimes the godly, to awaken them out of ... great sins or infirmities, or to try their patience as Job's was, it being in God's power to suffer any punishments to be inflicted as he pleases. And as God may permit some persons to be more under their power than others, so those often are most subject to the power of witchcraft, that are of a weak and infirmed mind, being weak in faith, whereas those who through faith in God defy their power, he will not suffer the Devil their master to hurt them that trust in him."[33] But if witchcraft was perpetrated with God's permission, why punish witches? Demonologists had no satisfying rejoinder other than reciting Exodus 22:18, "Thou shalt not suffer a witch to live."

As to the second problem, that of the witches' inability to save themselves, professors of religion maintained that once a witch was revealed, Satan abandoned him, thereby withdrawing his powers to do harm. The reason for this, the doctors explained, was that from the moment witches were apprehended, the Devil's supreme desire was to see them executed, thereby ensuring the damnation of their souls. "But for this, indeed," Lea cynically remarked, "it might have been difficult to find men hardy enough to seize, imprison, try, and execute these delegates of Satan, whose slightest ill-will was so dangerous."[34]

Demonographers contended, moreover, that once witches were imprisoned, Satan not only robbed them of their magical powers, but he immediately set out to destroy them.[35] He did this, according to Remy, "either by basely persuading his disciples to

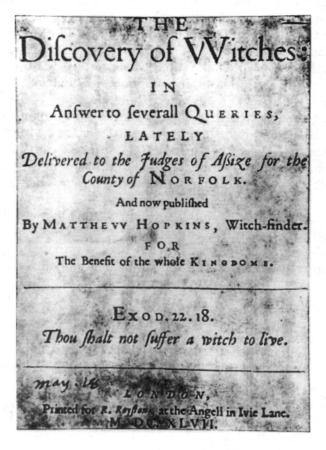

Figure 4.3   Title page of Matthew Hopkins' *The Discovery of Witches* (1647). Exodus 22: 18 proved extremely useful to witch-finders such as Hopkins. By permission of The Pepys Library, Magdalene College, Cambridge.

hang themselves, or else himself actually twists their necks or beats them to death, or kills them in some other way, unless God restrains him."[36] This, of course, was a very convenient explanation for the fact that many prisoners died at the hands of the torture technicians (see Chapter Five, below). According to the *Malleus Maleficarum*, "after they [the witches] have admitted their crimes, they try to commit suicide by strangling or hanging themselves. And they are induced to do this by the Enemy [Satan], lest they should obtain pardon from God through sacramental confession."[37]

Remy provided the example of Didier Finance, of St.-Die, condemned of parricide, as well as sorcery, and sentenced in July 1581, by the College of the *Duumvirs* of Nancy, to be tortured with red-hot tongs and then burned alive: "Whether he was informed of this by his Demon, as we shall later show to have happened to certain others, or whether it was foreseen by his own conscience of so terrible a crime, he determined to escape this sentence by seeking his own death. Therefore he took a knife which had carelessly been left in the bread chest by one of the jailers, thrust it down his throat as far as he could, and so died."[38]

Guazzo related a similar incident involving a fifty-year-old woman: "After she had undergone every torture and had obstinately denied all her crimes, she cut her throat in prison. So the devil, having accused her of witchcraft through the mouth of a possessed woman, killed her."[39] Father Guazzo also explained the circumstances surrounding the suicide of another prisoner, a ninety-year-old friar awaiting execution for witchcraft: "A demon appeared to him and tempted him so that on Sunday morning, the 25th September of the year 1605, now passed, he cut his own throat with his knife, and although the wound was not serious enough to cause instant death, yet the demon, in that very act of desperation, seized violently on to his soul and carried it to hell. I saw the man dead, and still warm, lying on the straw; and as he had led the life of a beast, so he lay on the provender of beasts. For so did Divine Justice dispose, which rewards every man according to his works; and God willed that he, who had for ninety years lived as a follower of Satan, should also end his life at the hands of Satan."[40]

There were few circumstances for which the demon experts lacked suitable and convenient explanations. If a prisoner died under torture, it was caused by the treachery of Satan, not the severity of his human tormentors, for the law clearly stated that it was illegal to kill prisoners under torture. If not the work of the Devil, how else could such an event be explained? Similarly, if an accused witch was abused, raped, or molested in some way, these crimes were committed by neither the torturers nor the jail guards, but the Evil One. Another case discussed by Remy illustrates: "Thus, although Catharina Latomia of Marche, at Haraucourt, Feb. 1587, was not yet of an age to suffer a man, he [Satan] twice raped her in prison, being moved with hatred for her because he saw that she intended to confess her crime; and she very nearly died from the injuries she received by that coition."[41]

Even torture and mutilation were depicted as benevolent measures necessary for the salvation of those duped by the "Father of Lies." As Remy emphasized, "the first light of liberty dawns on their misery on that day when the Judge uses violence, terrorism and torture against them; and they earnestly beg not to be discharged from prison and again be delivered into the bondage of that Tyrant; for their only hope of salvation was to be taken quickly as possible to their death while they were penitent and sorry for their sins. And they entreat the Judge to punish in the same way all others who come up for trial and confess their crime; for by no other means can they put an end to their evil-doing and witchcraft, however, much they may wish to."[42]

Witches wanted to die, the demon doctors proclaimed, and putting them to death was an act of compassion by the authorities who worked so diligently for their salvation, despite the fact that these abominable creatures had dedicated themselves to the archenemy of the Almighty. The interest of the Church in these proceedings, the authorities affirmed, was to save souls, not to seek the death of those found guilty of witchcraft: *ecclesia non sitit sanguinem*, "the Church thirsts not for blood."[43] As a formality, a standard request for mercy was issued every time a prisoner was "relaxed" to the secular arm for punishment: "We ask, and that with urgency, the secular court to moderate its sentence so that effusion of blood and peril of death may be avoided."[44] That a judge would abstain from passing the death sentence, knowing full well that clemency would surely lead to accusations against himself, is difficult to imagine.[45] As Del Rio stated in his *Disquisitiones Magicae* (1599), the book which displaced the *Malleus Maleficarum* as the encyclopedia of demonology: "As sorcerers are mostly heretics, those who knowingly defend them, even without defending their errors, render themselves very suspect and are to be investigated and are to be punished, as well as advocates and notaries who defend them in court."[46] Likewise, the sanguinary Bodin raged, "The judge who does not put to death a convicted witch should be put to death himself."[47]

Remy justified the execution of witches, even repentant ones: "what madness it would be to condone in them a crime with which they must be contaminated for as long as they live, to the greatest despite of God and men! Indeed it would be like allowing mad dogs to live, although everyone knows that they are incurable, simply because it was through no fault of their own that they became mad."[48] Similarly, Bodin declared: "Now, it is not within the power of princes to pardon such a crime which the law of God punishes with the penalty of death—such are the crimes of witches. Moreover, princes do gravely insult God in pardoning such horrible crimes committed directly against his majesty, seeing that the pettiest prince avenges with death insults against himself."[49]

Remy argued that the very fate of Christendom depended on the eradication of witchcraft: "Woe also to those who would palliate the odium of so horrible and execrable a crime, and would diminish its punishment on the plea of fear, age, sex, imprudence, and the like, which no sane man would dare to consider as grounds for mercy in even less abominable crimes! For what is this, if it is not ... openly to tempt God? It is, indeed, blasphemy ... for Judges to deal leniently with those who are liable to the just punishment of Heaven. This is to delay the coming of His Kingdom; for nothing can so firmly establish it as the routing, overthrow and destruction of all His enemies, together with Satan, who is their Captain. When the wicked [are] slain ... Christ is received: when an abomination is destroyed, sanctity is hallowed."[50]

The ultimate argument forwarded by the witch-doctors clamoring for swift and merciless death for the witches was presented in the *Malleus Maleficarum*, which stated that if those imprisoned and executed were not really witches and Satan's servants, then God would not have permitted them to fall into the hands of the authorities to be burned.[51] The *Malleus* declared emphatically that "it has never hitherto been known to have happened that an innocent person has been defamed by the devil to such an extent that he was condemned to death for this particular crime."[52] Thus, the pious and learned experts—scholars such as Del Rio, Bodin, Remy, and others—who were themselves far removed from the horrors and squalor of the prisons, deliberately turned their backs on the gang-rapes, mutilations, amputations, and homicides taking place in the torture rooms, solaced by the thought that God would not permit the innocent to suffer.

Contemporary critics vehemently disagreed with the demonological position. The Jesuit Adam Tanner (1629) wrote: "… this axiom is false. God permitted the martyrdom of innumerable pious Christians in the early Church. He permits wars and massacres. The witches confess to killing many innocents, even their own kindred. Prudent and learned men who have served as confessors admit that they are so perplexed that they know not what to believe."[53] Likewise, Father Spee argued: "Is it credible that God would permit the innocent to be involved? Some hold that God would not permit the innocent to be involved with the mass of guilty. Binsfeld and Del Rio use this argument. This is not to be admitted, as it relieves judges and princes from responsibility. Besides it is not true, as is evident from the martyrs whom he allowed to perish."[54]

Such arguments were of no avail, however, for the witch-hammerers ruled the day. Demonological axioms were upheld by means of the coercive apparatus at the disposal of the authorities and served to legitimize acts of repression, torture, brutality, and terrorism.

Notes

1. Burr (1943b:167); Anglo (1977a:10; 1977b:122).
2. In Monter (1969:51).
3. Guazzo (1929 [1608]:39).
4. Glanvill (1689:67).
5. Evans-Pritchard (1935, 1970).
6. Evans-Pritchard (1937:69).
7. Evans-Pritchard (1937:69).
8. Evans-Pritchard (1937:1).
9. Trevor-Roper (1988:18).
10. Zilboorg (1935:153).
11. Mora (1967:15).
12. Szasz (1967:204–220); Parrinder (1973:136; 1958).
13. Lea (1961:832).
14. Levack (1987:53).
15. Lea (1939:1086).
16. Remy (1930 [1595]:164).
17. Lea (1939:1086).
18. Spee (1631); Lea (1939:706).
19. Evans-Pritchard (1937:20).
20. See Gluckman (1955:275).
21. Perkins (1609:653).
22. Guazzo (1929 [1608]:33).
23. Guazzo (1929 [1608]:39).
24. In Robbins (1982:514).
25. Bovet (1684:47–48).
26. Lea (1939:275).
27. Meyfarth (1635); Lea (1939:737).
28. Oldekop (1654); Lea (1939:858).
29. Scot (1584:14).
30. Boguet (1929 [1602]:xlii–xliii).
31. Kramer and Sprenger (1971 [1486]:99).
32. In Monter (1969:54).
33. Boulton (1715:17).
34. Lea (1961:813).
35. Boguet (1929 [1602]:131).
36. Remy (1930 [1595]:166).
37. Kramer and Sprenger (1971 [1486]:224).
38. Remy (1930 [1595]:163).
39. Guazzo (1929 [1608]:56).
40. Guazzo (1929 [1608]:57).
41. Remy (1930 [1595]:166).
42. Remy (1930 [1595]:167).

43. Carus (1900:324).
44. In Robbins (1981:271).
45. See Burr (1943a:150).
46. Del Rio (1599); Burr (1897: 14–18).
47. Bodin (1580); Lea (1939:573).
48. Remy (1930 [1595]:185).
49. Burr (1897:5).
50. Remy (1930 [1595]:188).
51. Kramer and Sprenger (1971 [1486]: 136); see Anglo (1977a:28).
52. Kramer and Sprenger (1971 [1486]:136).
53. Tanner (1629); Lea (1939:649).
54. Spee (1631); Lea (1939:700).

Chapter Five

Torture: The Proof of All Proofs

When prosecuting people accused of witchcraft and sorcery the authorities were confronted with the problem of producing evidence: acts of witchcraft took place unseen, at night, or in faraway places. For this reason, Bodin advised that, "one accused of being a witch ought never be fully acquitted and set free unless the calumny of the accuser is clearer than the sun, inasmuch as the proof of such crimes is so obscure and so difficult that not one witch in a million would be accused or punished if the procedure were governed by the ordinary rules."[1]

Witchcraft was considered *crimen exceptum* [an exceptional crime], a crime so horrendous that it was excluded from the customary process of law. All legal safeguards were denied the suspect, and the broadest latitude of evidence was permitted: children of irresponsible age were admitted to testify against their parents; perjurers, felons, and individuals of disrepute were invited to offer testimony; even defense lawyers could be forced to give evidence against their clients.[2] Ultimately, in cases of witchcraft, torture was considered *probatio probatissimi*, "the proof of all proofs." In this chapter I describe the judicial torture system in great detail so that the reader may obtain a precise understanding of the force of torture in bolstering demonology and fueling the persecutions.

Large-scale witch-burnings took place only where torture of the most brutal sort was employed to extract the names of accomplices. According to the historian Burr, "No confession was complete and no witch released from her agony until accomplices had been named. Nor were they satisfied with one or two only. I have read a list of no less than a hundred and fifty accomplices taken down from the lips of a single witch; and I know of several others who accused upwards of a hundred each. A record of confessions kept by one local court during the space of seven years—you may still read the document yourself—contains some six thousand accusations from about three hundred witches: that is to say, an average of twenty apiece."[3] In the words of a contemporary eyewitness: "A single innocent person, compelled by torture to confess guilt, is forced to denounce others of whom she knows nothing; it is the same with them, and thus there is scarce an end of accusers and accused, and, as none dare to revoke, all are marked for death."[4]

Every witch-hunt thus had the potential of increasing exponentially, as more and more victims were drawn into the snares. The dynamics of witch-hunting lie in the forced confessions and the pain and violence inflicted upon innocent victims, not in the scattered folklore of peasant superstitions, or in the "subjective realities" of the people accused of witchcraft, as mentalist writers would like us to believe.

By law, torture was not to last more than approximately thirty minutes, nor was it to imperil life or injure limb. In practice, however, each new question put to the accused justified an additional half- or one-hour torture session.[5] Del Rio reported one case in Westphalia in which a man suspected of lycanthropy was tortured no less than twenty times.[6] During the 1501–1505 witch-hunts in Tyrol, a woman accused of witchcraft was tortured eighteen times;[7] and in Rottenburg, Germany, in 1530, three women were subjected to a total of 186 applications of torture.[8] These were by no means exceptional or atypical incidents. Such use of torture in early modern Europe confirms the observation by modern researchers that people in authority, even if they initially set narrow limits on the use of torture, progressively expand the circle of victims and increase the level of violence.[9]

Johann Matthäus Meyfarth, doctor of Holy Writ and professor at the university of Erfurt, gave a horrifying first hand account of the ruthlessness of the torturers in a book entitled *Christliche Erinnerung* (1635) [Christian Remembrances]: "There are men who in this art [of torture] exceed the spirits of hell. I have seen the

Figure 5.1 The horrors of the torture chamber. From Samuel Chandler's *The History of Persecution* (1736). By permission of Special Collections and Archives, Milton S. Eishenhower Library, The Johns Hopkins University.

limbs forced asunder, the eyes driven out of the head, the feet torn from the legs, the sinews twisted from the joints, the shoulder blades wrung from their place, the deep veins swollen, the superficial veins driven in, the victim hoisted aloft and now dropped, now revolved around, head undermost and feet uppermost. I have seen the executioner flog with the scourge, and smite with rods, and crush with screws and load down with weights, and stick with needles, and bind around with cords, and burn with brimstone, and baste with oil and singe with torches. In short I bear witness, I can describe, I can deplore how the human body is violated."[10]

Frederick von Spee, a Jesuit priest who acted as confessor for many condemned witches during the savage witch-burnings in Würzburg in 1627, under Prince-Bishop Philipp Adolf, similarly wrote, "I know that many die under the enormous tortures, many are crippled for life, many are so torn that when they are to be beheaded the executioner does not dare to bare their shoulders and expose them to the people. Sometimes they have to be hurried to the place of execution, lest they die by the way."[11]

What material benefits did the authorities gain by the brutal torment and maiming of women, men, and children? The greed of local judges and witch-hunters, desiring to acquire the wealth and properties of convicted witches, certainly played a part. But this was a secondary factor;[12] economic motives cannot explain the widespread use and official endorsement of torture. The function of such institutionalized violence becomes evident only when we look past the abominable activities in the torture chambers.

Ultimately, torture is an act of oppression that goes beyond the actual tormenting of any single person: it is a form of violence intended to undermine and neutralize resistance by creating an emotional environment of extreme fear.[13] Studies of the use of torture during the twentieth century support this assertion. For those who govern without the consent of the people, torture is an effective method of maintaining power. Torture inspires terror— terror ensures submission.[14] Setting torture as the price of dissent guarantees that only a small minority will act. With the majority thus paralyzed by fear, the well-equipped forces of repression are able to focus exclusively on isolated deviants and troublemakers.[15]

Torture is likely to be used toward these ends when those in power are beset by persistent economic problems, political violence, and disruptive cultural changes.[16] These were precisely the kinds of conditions prevalent in territories where the most horrendous witch-hunts took place.[17]

Discovering Witches

Witchcraft was a secret crime and authorities seldom had direct evidence, such as the discovery of a *grimoire* (book of magic), a jar of ointment, a pot full of toads, human limbs, or other instruments of sorcery. Witch-hammerers and demonologists therefore had to rely on other diagnostic criteria to justify sending their prisoners to the torture chamber.

Old age or ugliness were always good indications that a suspect had commerce with evil spirits, for everyone knew that looking upon demons caused an "aspect savage and awry" (i.e., a grotesque physiognomy). Thus physical appearance could serve as *indicium ad torturam*, evidence warranting the use of torture.

Another criterion for torture included a prisoner's inability to look judges and prosecutors straight in the eye. If the suspect stammered, or exhibited signs of trepidation once hauled before the tribunal, he or she could be put to the torture on the basis of such "witch-like" behaviors. The inability to shed tears was also a sure sign of witchcraft.[18] "Tears," however, meant "tears of repentance," the witch-hammerers expounded, and not ordinary tears, which sorcerers and witches shed in abundance out of cowardice, grief, and the pains of torture.

A most persuasive evidence of witchcraft was the "Devil's mark," or the *stigma diabolicum*, an insensitive spot on the skin where Satan branded those who sealed pacts with him. The mark was said to be about the size of a pea and resemble a hare's or a toad's foot. A needle could be driven into the mark to the bone without producing any sensation.

The discovery of a mark was deemed infallible evidence of guilt. The following incident, which took place on October 30, 1590, at Porrentruy, illustrates: When authorities shaved a suspected woman's head looking for the mark, "A scar on the top of her forehead was thus plainly brought to light. Thereupon the Judge, suspecting the truth, namely that this was the mark of the Demon's talon, which had before been hidden by her hair, ordered a pin thrust deeply into it; and when this was done it was seen that she felt no pain, and that the wound did not bleed in the very least. Yet she persisted in denying the truth, saying that her numbness to pain was due to an old blow from a stone; but after she was brought to the torture she not only acknowledged that the mark had been made by the Demon, but recounted several other cruel injuries which she had received from him."[19]

However, even if the mark could not be detected, the accused could still be tortured, for it was commonly known that Satan only branded disciples of doubtful loyalties. The Devil's steadfast adherents, the witch-doctors pointed out, almost never bore the mark.

Matthew Hopkins, the ruthless Witch Finder General of England, was considered an expert in detecting the mark by probing a suspect's flesh with long, sharp needles.[20] During the course of one year, between 1645–1646, amidst the chaos of the English Civil War, Hopkins sent more people to the gallows for witchcraft than were executed in nearly a century of witch-hunting in that country.[21] Since England did not have a legalized system of torture, Hopkins adopted the technique of probing with needles as his primary means of witch-detection. This procedure was not considered a form of torture, although the witch-finding specialists continued piercing the suspect's flesh with their needles until either an insensitive spot was discovered, or the pain they inflicted led to a confession.

Sometimes the witch-detectors used retractable needles to convince onlookers that an insensitive mark had been found, thus confirming the guilt of their unwitting victims.[22] Needle-specialists, who had become paid professionals both in England and Scotland by the seventeenth century, were also aware of, and undoubtedly capitalized on, the knowledge that some areas of skin have more pain receptors than others. Fingertips, for instance, carry a large number of pain receptors, whereas in certain areas of the back, a site commonly used for probing with the needles, such receptors are more scattered.[23]

Hopkins' repertoire of witch-finding techniques—described and defended in his hideous pamphlet, Discovery of Witches (1647)—also included the "swimming ordeal." According to James VI's Daemonologie (1597), the authoritative source used by Hopkins, "God has appointed (for a super-natural sign of the

Figure 5.2 Matthew Hopkins, the ruthless Witch Finder General of Manningtree, Essex, and his victims. Frontispiece of Hopkins' *The Discovery of Witches* (1647). By permission of The Pepys Library, Magdalene College, Cambridge.

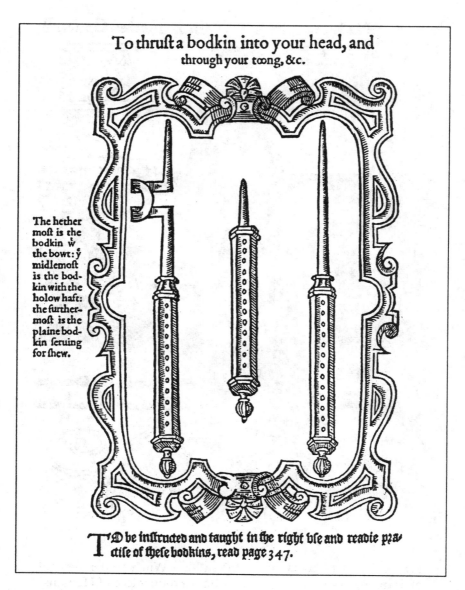

Figure 5.3 Retractable and trick needles used by witch-finders to search for the mark of Satan's talons. After a page from Reginald Scot's *The Discouerie of Witchcraft* (1584).

monstrous impiety of the Witches) that the water shall refuse to receive them in her boson, that have shaken off them the sacred Water of Baptism, and willfully refused the benefit thereof."[24]

Figure 5.4   The swimming ordeal. Title page of *Witches Apprehended, Examined and Executed ...* (1613). By permission of the Bodleian Library, Oxford.

The ordeal was designed to test a suspect's buoyancy by immersion in a pool or pond. Floating was a sign of guilt, whereas if the presumed miscreant sank, and sometimes drowned, this was an indication of his or her innocence.[25] First, the suspect's left thumb was tied to his right big toe, and his right thumb to his left big toe. Then two ropes were fastened around his waist, while a pair of witch-finders, taking the end of each rope, positioned themselves on opposite sides of the pool. When the prisoner was maneuvered over the deepest part of the water, the ropes were slackened to allow the suspected culprit to sink. By controlling the amount of tension, the ropes could be manipulated in such a way that the subject was prevented from sinking, and was thereby demonstrably guilty of witchcraft.[26]

Figure 5.5 The witch-finder collects his fees (right), while those he marked for death are executed by hanging. From Ralph Gardiner's *England's Grievance Discovered in Relation to the Coal Trade* (1796 [1655]). By permission of Special Collections and Archives, Milton S. Eishenhower Library, The Johns Hopkins University.

John Gaule, the Vicar of Huntingdonshire village of Great Staughton, the man who turned public opinion against the ruthless Witch Finder General, described some of Hopkins' other methods in a pamphlet Entitled *Select Cases of Conscience Touching Witches and Witchcraft* (1646): "The 'Witch-finder General' used to take the suspected witch and place her in the middle of a room, upon a stool or a table, cross-legged, or in some other uneasy posture. If she refused to sit in this manner, she was bound with strong cords. Hopkins then placed persons to watch her for four-and-twenty hours, during which time she was to be kept without meat or drink. It was supposed that one of her imps would come during that interval and suck her blood. As the imp might come in the shape of a wasp, a moth, a fly, or other insect, a hole was made in the door or window to let it enter. The watchers were ordered to keep a sharp look-out, and endeavour to kill any insect that appeared in the room. If any fly escaped, and they could not kill it, the woman was sentenced to be guilty; the fly was her imp, and she was sentenced to be burned, and twenty shillings went into the pockets of Master Hopkins. In this manner he made one old woman confess, because four flies had appeared in the room, that she was attended by four imps....."[27] There was no escape from the clutches of this vicious witch-catcher.

Hopkins, accompanied by assistants, traveled from village to village amassing a fortune from the fees he charged for disclosing the identity of witches. Although several hundred people were executed because of the evidence provided by Hopkins,[28] no one was legally tortured.

Methods and Technology of Torture

It is undeniable that without judicial torture the witch-hunting catastrophe would never have taken place. The enormous role played by torture in sustaining the witch-hunts becomes evident as soon as we scrutinize the pain-inflicting techniques and devices to which presumed witches were subjected.

European torture technicians were aware that the pain response can be affected by tissue damage and other variables, such as the social setting and psychological stimuli before and during the experience of pain,[29] and they used this knowledge to their full advantage. The torture room itself was designed to horrify the victims. According to Philip Limborch's *The History of the Inquisition* (1692): "The place of torture ... is generally an under-ground and very dark room, to which one enters through several doors. There is a tribunal erected in it, in which inquisitor, inspector, and secretary, sit. When the candles are lighted, and the person to be tortured brought in, the executioner, who is waiting for the other, makes an astonishing and dreadful appearance. He is covered all over with a black linen garment down to his feet, and tied close to his body. His head and face are all hid with a long black cowl, only two little holes being left for him to see through. All this is intended to strike the miserable wretch with greater terror in mind and body, when he sees himself going to be tortured by the hands of one who thus looks like the very devil."[30]

Before the actual torture began, the accused was stripped, shaved of all body hairs (female victims were often raped during the stripping), and probed in every orifice: mouth, nose, ears, and "secret parts" for hidden charms and talismans. This is an outrage, decried Meyfarth, to which all are subjected, maids, wives, and widows.[31] After being thus degraded and dehumanized, the wretched suspect was conveyed to the instruments of pain.

During torture, the prisoner was made to wear a dingy white robe, so that the torture technician could operate unhampered by the prisoner's clothing. The magistrate, accompanied by a notary, and sometimes a physician (whose job, like that of the modern "torture physicians," was to stop the torment just short of the prisoner's death), then came into the chamber and warned the suspect that should he be crippled or killed by the torture, he had only himself to blame for not having voluntarily confessed the truth.[32] The prospect of such a death was all the more appalling because victims were denied proper Christian burial, and were unceremoniously interred beneath the gallows.

There were several levels of torture, ranging from first to third degree. First-degree torture involved psychological techniques such as intimidation and verbal persuasion, or giving the prisoner a tour of the torture room and a demonstration of the sundry devices prominently displayed. These surprisingly effective procedures are detailed in the *Malleus Maleficarum*, a book one modern researcher[33] has appropriately referred to as the first widely-known handbook for torture technicians.

Leaving prisoners chained up in damp, dark, vermin-infested cells—based on the Inquisition's maxim of "chains and starvation in a stifling hole"—was itself often sufficient to elicit a confession. As one eyewitness tells us: "The cruelty ... [is] aggravated by the miseries of the prisons, where [the suspects] are confined in dark, narrow, underground holes, where there is no distinction between day and night, where they lie in their own filth, are devoured by vermin, are imperfectly fed, are exposed to such cold that their feet freeze and, if they are discharged, are crippled for life, and are ill-treated, ridiculed and abused by the jailers and their servants. In some of them are stocks confining arms and legs so that the prisoner cannot move; or large crosses of wood or iron to which he is fastened by the neck, back, arms and legs; or long iron rods, chained at the middle to the wall, with iron bands at the ends in which the hands are fastened, and sometimes to this are added heavy iron weights attached to the feet. Sometimes the cells are so small that a man can neither stand, sit, nor lie down. In some there are deep pits with cells in which prisoners are put and abandoned. In such places they are often kept so long that those who enter strong and intelligent become weakened in mind and body and half insane."[34]

In one case in Eichstätt, in 1381, a heretic imprisoned in this manner for only eight days confessed to dealing with evil spirits after having asserted upon his arrest that he would not admit guilt were heaven and earth to pour forth bloody tears, and his body burned and torn apart.[35] Modern studies confirm that solitary confinement is an effective technique for extorting confessions, a procedure used on prisoners-of-war by the North Koreans and also employed during the propaganda trials in Stalinist Russia.[36]

Sleep deprivation, or *tormentum insomniae*, used in Germany, Italy, England, and Scotland, was at times more effective in extracting confessions than the application of mechanical devices, such as thumbscrews or the rack.[37] Modern clinical research has shown that sleep loss of as little as thirty to sixty hours often leads to confusion, delusions, and finally, hallucinations, when the subject seems convinced of the reality of his false perceptions.[38] Cases reported in China and East Germany during the 1950s and 1960s, when prisoners were forced to undergo sleeplessness, indicate that this procedure (termed "torture without violence" by one writer), is extraordinarily effective in the "breaking of a prisoner's will" and rendering him susceptible to voluntarily confessing to any crime suggested by the interrogators.[39] The hallucinogenic effects of the sleep deprivation techniques were well-know to the authorities in early modern Europe.[40] Matthew Hopkins, who regularly employed this technique, was more successful in extorting confessions of pact and Devil-worship than any of his English counterparts.[41]

Isolation and sleep deprivation, along with techniques such as pulling out fingernails and toenails and scourging, were regarded as preliminary torture.[42] If these failed, the prisoner was subjected to the second degree of torture. This commonly involved the use of thumbscrews, the rack, and countless other devices and techniques designed to inflict great pain by the effects they produced on the human anatomy.

Among the miscellaneous devices used on Dr. Fian, one of the North Berwick witches, were the "boots." Torturers strapped the prisoner's feet into metal boots, and then pounded wooden wedges all around them, crushing the bones to a pulp. Afterward, to heighten the effects of the procedure, boiling water or hot oil was poured on the remaining bloody mass of the prisoner's feet.[43] The following excerpt describes Fian's torture, which included the application of this device: "His nails upon all his fingers were ruined and pulled off with an instrument called in Scottish a Turkas, which in England we call a pair of pincers, and under every nail there was thrust in two needles ... up to the heads. At all which torments notwithstanding the Doctor never shrunk any whit, neither would he then confess it the sooner for all the tortures inflicted upon him.... Then was he with all convenient speed, by commandment, conveyed again to the torment of the boots, wherein he continued a long time, and did abide so many blows in them, that his legs were crushed and beaten together as small as might be, and the bones and flesh so bruised, that the blood and marrow spouted forth in great abundance, whereby they were made unserviceable forever."[44]

On the rack the prisoner's arms and legs could be stretched in opposite directions, causing excruciating pain as sinew ripped, muscles tore, and joints dislocated. A variant of the rack involved stretching a prisoner on a ladder, while candles or feathers dipped in burning sulfur were applied to his underarms, ribs, or groin.

During the second degree of torture, interrogation specialists also used the thumbscrews, a simple vice-like contraption applied

Figure 5.6 Torture with the boots. By permission of the Hulton Getty Picture Library, London.

to the tips of the fingers and toes to crush the bones. Johannes Junius, the Burgomaster of Bamberg, tried and executed in 1628 as a witch, described his ordeal with the thumbscrews in a letter secretly sent from prison to his daughter: "And then came also— God in highest Heaven have mercy!—the executioner and put the thumbscrews on me, both hands bound together, so that the blood spurted from the nails everywhere, so that for four weeks I could not use my hands, as you can see from my writing."[45]

Another method of torment was the water-torture, described by Samuel Clarke in his *A General Martyrology* (1677): "[the prisoner is placed on his back,] his arms, thighs, and legs bound with strong small cords, and wrested with short truncheons, till the cords pierce almost to the very bones. Then they take a thick fine lawn cloth, laying it over the [prisoner's] mouth, as he lies ... on his back, so that it may stop his nostrils also, then taking a quantity of water, they pour it in a long stream like a thread, which falling from on high, drives the cloth down into his throat, which puts the poor wretch into as great an agony, as any endure in the pains of death: For in this torture he has not liberty to draw his breath, the water stopping his mouth, and the cloth his nostrils; so that when the cloth is drawn out of the bottom of his throat, it draws forth blood with it, and a man would think that it tore out his very bowels. This is iterated as oft as the Inquisitor please, and yet they threaten him with worse torments, if he confesses not. And so he is returned to his prison again."[46] The anxiety of suffocation, along with pain from visceral distention, and the physiological damage caused by the withdrawal of the cloth from the victim's esophagus, combined to produce this extremely agonizing and hideous torture.[47]

The next level of torture—the third degree—was divided into "ordinary torture" and "extraordinary torture." Ordinary torture involved the *strappado* (*estrapade*). The victim's hands were tied behind his back with a rope connected to a pulley. He was then hoisted to the ceiling, and thus inflicted with excruciating pain from the dislocation of the shoulders. Sometimes the *strappado* was used in conjunction with thumbscrews, scourging, and burning with candles.

Extraordinary torture, a variation of the *strappado*, was described by Limborch as follows: "The prisoner has his hands

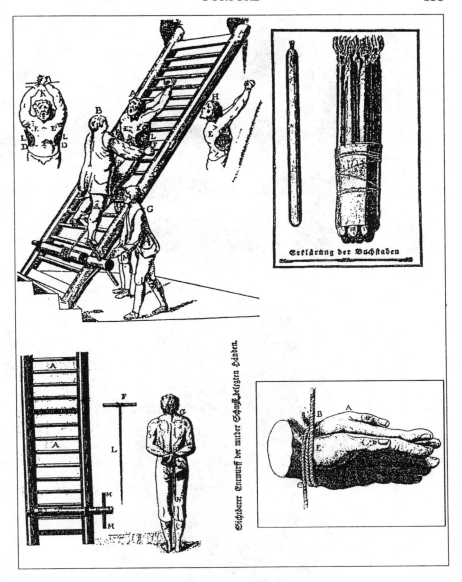

Figure 5.7 The rack was designed to stretch the prisoner's arms and legs in opposite directions, resulting in dislocated joints, torn muscles and ligaments, and excruciating pain. From *Constitutio Criminalis Theresiana* (1769). Courtesy of Department of Special Collections, Case Western Reserve University Library.

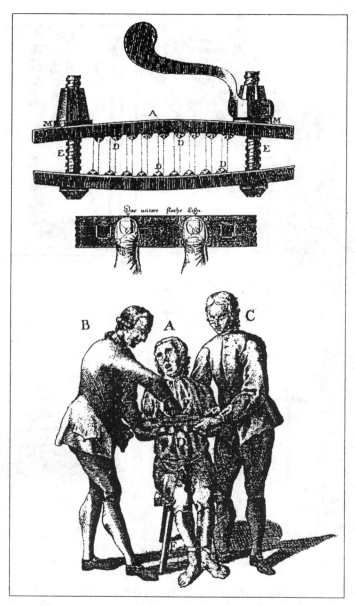

Figure 5.8 The thumbscrew and its application. From *Constitutio Criminalis Theresiana* (1769). Courtesy of Department of Special Collections, Case Western Reserve University Library.

Figure 5.9 The *Strappado*. From *Constitutio Criminalis Theresiana* (1769). Courtesy of Department of Special Collections, Case Western Reserve University Library.

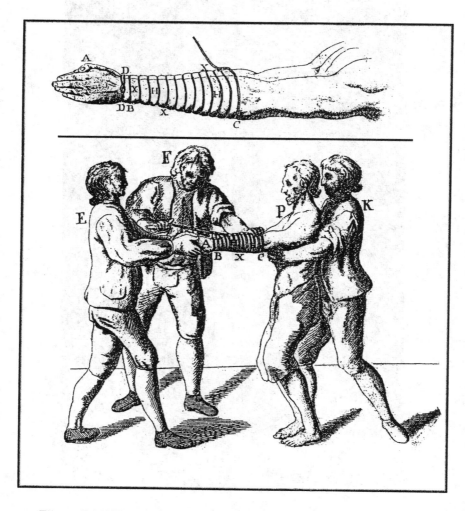

Figure 5.10 Torture with tourniquets. From *Constitutio Criminalis Theresiana* (1769). Courtesy of Department of Special Collections, Case Western Reserve University Library.

bound behind his back, and weights tied to his feet, and then he is drawn up on high, till his head reaches the pulley. He is kept hanging in this manner for some time, that by the greatness of the weights hanging at his feet, all his joints and limbs may be dreadfully stretched, and on a sudden he is let down with a jerk, by the slacking [of] the rope, but kept from coming quite to the ground, by which terrible shake his arms and legs are all disjointed, whereby he is put to the most exquisite pain—the shock which he receives by the sudden stop of his fall and the weights at his feet stretching his whole body more intensely and cruelly."[48]

Torture technicians took great pride in their craft, and deemed failure to obtain a confession a professional disgrace. Rather than face such an embarrassment in the eyes of their peers, they would often kill their victims, and claim that "Satan broke their back to prevent confession."[49] Critics, however, were aware of the deceptions perpetrated by the witch-hammerers. As an eyewitness wrote: "There is also the falsehood ... of concealing the foulest murders—this one was choked by a catarrh, that one killed himself, the other was poisoned, and the devil twisted the neck of another—excessive torture and prolonged squalor of the prison are never referred to—no inspection is made of the corpses and they are thrust into the grounds under the gallows."[50]

The physical assault on a prisoner's body was so severe that some victims remained silent during interrogation and displayed an inability to feel any pain, a phenomenon demonologists termed "taciturnity," or *maleficium taciturnitatis*. Francesco Maria Guazzo, the seventeenth-century friar and demon specialist from Milan, related one such case: "a woman of fifty ... endured boiling fat poured over her whole body and severe racking of all her limbs without feeling anything. For she was taken from the rack free from any sense of pain, whole and uninjured, except that her great toe, which had been torn off during her questioning, was not restored, but this did not hinder or hurt her at all."[51] Modern studies of torture have confirmed this phenomenon. During torture, a paradoxical situation may occur in which the victim develops a condition of complete denial, "switching off" all awareness, looks untroubled, and displays no response to pain.

He may lose his memory or voice and he may lie apparently paralysed.[52]

Figure 5.11 If a prisoner died at the hands of his torturers, it was said that "the Devil broke his back to prevent him from confessing." From Hermann Löher's *Hochnötige unterthänige wemütige Klage der frommen Unschultigen* (1676), Rare Bd Ms 37 (Witchcraft Collection, 4621). By permission of the Rare and Manuscript Collections Department, Cornell University Library.

Taciturnity could have resulted from several other causes as well. Studies on the physiology of pain have revealed that autosuggestion can raise the threshold of pain.[53] Some modern researchers have pointed out that narcotic potions may have been used by some "witches" to produce hyperaesthesia.[54] Boguet also remarked that witches have drugs which procure taciturnity.[55]

Perplexed demonologists argued, however, that taciturnity was caused by magical spells, or by Satan himself. The Devil did this, it was believed, either by interfering with the instruments of torture, rendering them ineffective, or more commonly, by entering the body of the witch and closing her mouth from the inside so as to prevent confession. Alternatively, the Devil sometimes obstructed the witch's ears, demonographers explained, so that she would not hear the judge's questions and thus remain silent.[56]

But many reported cases of taciturnity were false. Torturers made such claims because signs of taciturnity could be considered *novum indicium*, new evidence, and grounds for further torture. As Spee decried: "What are the signs ascribed to the *maleficium taciturnitatis*? They say that some do not feel pain, but laugh. This is a lie, and I speak knowingly. If to endure great torment one grinds her teeth, compresses her lips and holds her breath, they say she laughs. They say that some are silent and sleep. This is also a lie; some faint under torture and they call it sleep; some shut their eyes and, exhausted with pain, bow their heads and remain quiet, and this they call sleep."[57]

Torture technicians used other deceptions as well. Justus Oldekop, a seventeenth-century critic of the persecutions, tells us that torturers surreptitiously concealed tiny parchments on the bodies of their victims during the process of securing them to the rack. They later pretended to discover these articles and announced that they had detected a charm of taciturnity, thereby obtaining license to torture their prisoners more savagely.[58]

When dealing with suspects thought to be especially stubborn, judges summoned special torture experts, celebrated for their ability to extract confessions from even the most recalcitrant subjects. Before subjecting the prisoners to the instruments of pain, these torture specialists forced them to imbibe a "witch-broth," a foul drink allegedly made from the ashes of burnt witches.[59] The specialists maintained that the administration of the potion was necessary to protect them while they interrogated witches and wizards. The witch-broth in fact contained psychotomimetic drugs (substances producing psychosis-like conditions), and their use can conceivably account for the bizarre and detailed confessions on record. Critics, such as Spee, Weyer, and Oldekop were well aware that the authorities often employed such mind-altering potions in order to dupe their victims into confessing to outrageous crimes.[60]

As one contemporary observer complained, "Still more abominable it is that when you have those (whom you mockingly call your birds that must sing at your pleasure) who will not for any torture confess what you want [about] themselves and others, your turn to the devil and his arts to rob them of their senses; the executioner gives them a draught ... so that they become senseless and assent to all that you wish."[61] The use of mind-altering drugs was an extraordinarily effective means of procuring confessions. Thus, the so-called cases of spontaneous confessions with esoteric details that demonographers proclaimed to be voluntary, "*sans question ny torture*," and which mentalist writers attribute either to neurotic fixations,[62] or to recondite pagan magico-religious customs,[63] were often nothing more than deceptions perpetrated by the torture technicians.

Once a confession was obtained, the torture technicians warned their victims, saying: "If you intend to deny what you have confessed, tell me now and I will do better. If you deny before the court, you come back to my hands and you will find that I have only played with you thus far, for I will treat you so that it would draw tears from a stone."[64] Those who retracted their statements were made to suffer the entire procedure from the start, the shaving of the hair, the probing, sexual abuse, and countless insufferable torments. As Meyfarth tells us: "The executioner goes on, trying one torture after another, until he has extracted all that he can, or what satisfies the officials, and of course the accused inculpates enough to satisfy them. Whoever confesses, dies; whoever is silent, offers his body to the fifth, sixth and seventh torture and then follows to the place of execution."[65]

Many punishments prescribed for witchcraft, breaking on the wheel for instance, were also forms of torture. Such events were always held in the early morning, allowing a large number of people to view the spectacle, hear the ear-piercing cries and shrieks of the prisoner as he or she was methodically mutilated and slowly deprived of life, and thus learn its object-lesson. Stripped of clothing, except linen undergarments, the prisoner was taken to a public place where justice was to be meted. The prisoner was then laid out and tied by the waist to a large oak wheel. The executioner bound each arm at the elbow to the spokes of the wheel, and then, with a powerful blow from a heavy metal rod, he broke each limb to make them fit the rim of the wheel. The prisoner's legs were shattered and twisted in the same manner. A perfect fit required several well placed blows to each limb. Executioners took great pride in their ability to crack and splinter bones while leaving the skin unbroken.

Sometimes, before being dispatched on the wheel, the prisoner's flesh was torn with red-hot pincers. In Munich, in 1600, during a sensational and highly publicized case, eight men and three women convicted of witchcraft were treated in this fashion. On route to the place of execution, six of the men were torn with red-hot pincers six times, one female had her breasts cut off, five of the men were broken on the wheel, one man was impaled. Finally, they were all burned at the stake.[66]

Torture: The Validation of Demonology

Using a wide variety of brutal pain-inflicting techniques, witch-hunters carefully and conscientiously extracted new data on witches and their activities. In the deft hands of members of the educated upper class—learned and pious men such as Binsfeld, Boguet, Remy, Grillandi, Bodin, Del Rio, De Lancre, and others, whose sanguinary works stimulated horrendous persecutions— this mass of evidence coming out of the torture chambers was sifted, elaborated, analyzed, and then compiled into official instruction manuals for judges, prosecutors, and Inquisitors.[67] Systematized demonological ideas were then fed back to the general population through secular and ecclesiastical channels.

Thus, some suspects were found during interrogation to have intimate knowledge of what transpired at the witches' Sabbat, having heard the horrid details *ad nauseam*, as Spee put it, during repeated public readings of the catalogue of crimes and sentences, in sermons, and during the public remonstrations against witches.[68] The witch-hammerers, however, proclaimed that such cases proved conclusively that Europe was teeming with witches and sorcerers, stressing the urgency of their righteous duty to eradicate the poison of witchcraft that was spreading far and wide. As more victims were herded through the torture chambers and forced to confess, the myth of diabolical witchcraft fostered by the authorities appeared to be confirmed empirically: Europe was indeed infested with countless witches.

Figure 5.12 The torture and execution of the Pappenheimer family in Munich, in 1600, before a mass audiance. From Michael Kunze's *Highroad to the Stake: A Tale of Witchcraft*. Copyright © 1987. Courtesy of the University of Chicago Press.

The use of the same manuals, identical interrogatories (lists of leading questions acquired from Inquisitorial manuals, or from the records of previous witch-trials), along with similar expectations on the part of the prosecutors regarding appropriate responses, led to a remarkable uniformity in the data being generated about the minions of Satan and their nefarious activities.[69] The extent to which torture technicians shaped the content of the confessions through their exhortations was noted by Meyfarth, who described one case: "How suggestive were the questions put by the executioner is shown by the fact that nobody had heard of a second baptism by Satan and no one knew anything about the [diabolical] mass; but, after an executioner from elsewhere had been called in, the confessions became full of second baptisms and of sacrilegious masses celebrated in the Sabbats."[70] Clearly, the esoteric details recorded as emanating from the mouths of accused witches—details upon which mentalist writers such as Ginzburg have constructed elaborate theories—may well have originated for the most part in the imaginations of the friars, torture technicians, and Inquisitors.

When responding to their critics, the witch-doctors emphasized the countless confessions obtained "voluntarily" as proof that a witches' organization did indeed exist and that the witches' diabolical conspiracy to destroy the world was real. But in fact most "voluntary confessions" had been extracted by means of subterfuge, psychological duress, threats, intimidation, and deception. Indeed, critics were aware of the gross deceptions perpetrated by the witch-doctors and would not accept such cases without reservations. "Notaries are in error in recording that the accused confessed spontaneously," wrote one observer, "though he may have been led to it by terror or threats or promises of impunity, which is a great impediment to justice. No one can be so demented as to spontaneously confess a capital crime."[71] In numerous trials, including the infamous witch-trial in Arras, northern France, in 1459–1460, prisoners were promised clemency, freedom, and pardons, in exchange for noncompulsory confessions, only to be ruthlessly executed once they admitted guilt to a suggested offense.[72]

Confessions obtained through the use of sleep deprivation, extended solitary confinement, the administration of psychotomimetic drugs, or those extorted in prison cells under threat of repeated torture, were also recorded as voluntary, since they had either been made outside the actual torture chamber, or did not involve the use of mechanical devices. Moreover, in many instances, those persons recorded as having confessed voluntarily were subjected to the first degree of torture, considered too trivial for documentation. As Spee explained: "There is a frequent phrase used by judges, that the accused has confessed without torture and thus is undeniably guilty. I wondered at this and made inquiry and learned that in reality they were tortured, but only in an iron press with sharp-edged channels over the shins, in which they are pressed like a cake, bringing blood and causing intolerable pain, and this is technically called without torture, deceiving those who do not understand the phrases of the inquisitors."[73]

Spee was fully convinced that innocent people were being tortured into false confessions and sent to the stake. "Torture fills Germany with witches and unheard-of wickedness," he lamented, "and not only Germany but any nation that tries it. The agony is so intense that to escape it we do not fear to incur death ... many to avoid it will falsely confess whatever the examiner suggests or what they have excogitated in advance. The most robust who have thus suffered have affirmed to me that no crime can be imagined which they would not at once confess to if it would bring ever so little relief, and that they welcome ten deaths to escape a repetition."[74] "It is marvelous," Spee added, "that the learned writers who teach the world about witchcraft base their whole argument on this deceitful foundation."[75]

Of the two hundred convicted witches to whom Spee administered last rites, all asserted their innocence, but asked him not to mention this, preferring death to further visits to the torture chamber.[76] This humane priest, it was said, was so astounded by what he saw and heard that his hair prematurely turned white.[77] Spee remarked, "often I have thought that the only reason why we are not all wizards is due to the fact that we have not all been tortured. And there is truth in what an inquisitor dared to boast lately, that if he could reach the Pope, he would make him confess that he was a wizard."[78] Spee's own conclusion is poignant: "Hitherto it never came to my mind to doubt that there were many witches in the world; now, when I closely examine the public judgments, I find myself gradually led to doubt whether there are scarce any."

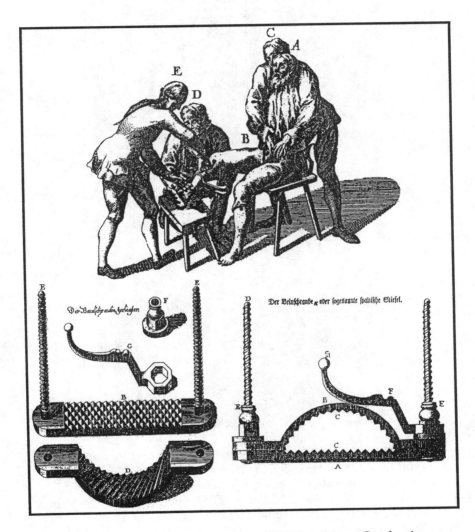

Figure 5.13 The shin-vice described by Spee. Confessions extorted by means of this torture were recorded as "voluntary." From *Constitutio Criminalis Theresiana* (1769). Courtesy of Department of Special Collections, Case Western Reserve University Library.

Figure 5.14 Application of the shin-vice (top); torture on heated metal seat (bottom). From Hermann Löher's *Hochnötige unterthänige wemütige Klage der frommen Unschultigen* (1676), Rare Bd Ms 37 (Witchcraft Collection, 4621). By permission of the Rare and Manuscript Collections Department, Cornell University Library.

Distinguished historians such as Henry Charles Lea, George Lincoln Burr, and Joseph Hansen, well aware of the force of torture and the deceptions perpetrated by the witch-slayers, argued that it was the authorities, law-makers, magistrates, churchmen, and Inquisitors who invented the idea of the witches' diabolical conspiracy, made it a part of criminal jurisprudence, and instigated the large-scale persecutions. In recent years, however, it has become fashionable to criticize such views. The mentalist historian Scarre argues, almost apologetically, that such a perspective "paints an excessively black picture of human nature not called for by the historical evidence, which does not support the view that people prosecuted others as witches without really believing in witchcraft." He adds: "While most of the accused would, no doubt, not have confessed had they not been tortured, several seem to have believed sincerely in their guilt, beseeching their judges to pray for their soul, and thanking them for the trouble they had taken in trying them." [79]

Such confessions, enumerated in accounts written by witch-hammerers, cannot and should not be accepted as trustworthy. As I have shown, the testimonies of allegedly self-confessed witches were seldom voluntary, but were extorted through psychological manipulation, intimidation, false promises, the threat of torture, administration of psychotomimetic drugs, or by the lesser of the three degrees of torture, considered too trivial to document. Such cases were often cited by demonologists in order to depict the witch-hunts and torture as religious services of the highest moral value rendered by the civil and ecclesiastical establishments.

Scarre goes on to assert that "a belief in the reality of witchcraft was shared by judges and defendants, and was critical to sustaining the trials." [80] Attributing the large-scale witch-hunts simply to a sincerity of beliefs, except in a small number of cases, is a naive and untenable position contradicted by even a cursory glance at the historical data. We may consider what Johannes Junius the Burgomaster of Bamberg wrote in the secret letter to his daughter: "When at last the executioner led me back into prison [after a brutal torture session], he said to me: 'Sir, I beg you, for God's sake confess something, whether it be true or not. Invent something, for you cannot endure the torture which you will be put to; and, even if you bear it all, yet you will not escape, not even if you were an earl, but one torture will follow after another until you say you are a witch. Not before that,' he said, 'will they let you go, as you may see by all their trials, for one is just like another.'"[81] At length the hapless Junius confessed and was accordingly burned at the stake on July 24, 1628.

Figure 5.15 Officials writing down a confession during torture. Hasty trials and brutal torture characterized the witch-persecutions. From *Bamberger Halsgerichtordnung* (1508). Courtesy of Historisches Museum, Bamberg.

The witch-hunts conducted by the Prince-Bishops of Bamberg and Würzburg, between the years 1624 and 1631, involved brutal torture and hasty trials, leading to the executions of close to one thousand people. These can hardly be said to have been motivated by sincere beliefs.[82] The promoters of the trials lined their pockets with money generated from confiscated possessions and, despite great public outcry and outrage over the injustice, and appeals by citizens to the Emperor, continued to send innocent people to the stake as long as the witch-hunts served their interests.[83] Cases in which actual written contracts with Satan were introduced as evidence, such as the trial of Urbain Grandier in Loudun, in 1634 (see Chapter Six, below), indicate flagrant fraud. There are countless other similar incidents.

Scarre's claim that witch-hunters honestly believed in what they were doing follows the same line of reasoning by another mentalist writer that, "What people believe to be true influences their actions more than what is objectively true, and the conviction that this picture [of satanic witchcraft] was accurate brought about the executions of hundreds of thousands of people."[84] One can approach the problem of the European witch-trials strictly in terms of the evolution of ideas regarding heresy and sorcery, as some historians have done,[85] but such an analysis is lopsided unless analytical priority is given to the more significant material forces—torture, false confessions, show trials, and official propaganda—which upheld and promoted these ideas.

Mentalist perspectives which stress the role of beliefs at the expense of concrete sociological variables misconstrue history by failing to distinguish between diffuse beliefs in witchcraft, which are near universal cross-culturally, and the systematic policy of oppression and terror—the catalyst for the large-scale witch-hunts in Europe—which was particular to a specific time and place.[86]

Torture: Economic Motives

Under some circumstances a large-scale witch-hunt meant profit for all involved, although this was not necessarily the primary motive behind the persecutions. If the suspect was wealthy, frequently his properties were seized, sold, and the money divided among the princes and bishops under the guise of "trial costs." Although in some places the confiscation of property was restricted by law, e.g., Charles V's *Constitutio Criminalis Carolina* (1532) in the Holy Roman Empire, such ordinances were not always adhered to strictly. Indeed, deviations from the letter of the law with respect to confiscation of property and torture were the main points of contention by critics of the witch-persecutions. Furthermore, the very fact that such legislation was thought necessary suggests that the confiscation of property had become a considerable problem.

As Meyfarth remarked, "the object of the officials is not to seek the truth, but to find pretext for the jailer to imprison and to chain, the *Hexenmeister* [= witch-finder] to condemn, the executioner to torture, burn, and behead, the judge to punish and seize the property."[87] Nor were other economic motives lacking. As Spee observed, "[the] inquisitor is not incorruptible who sends agents to places to inflame the minds of the peasants about witches and promises to come and destroy them, if a proper collection is made for him; when this is done he comes, celebrates one or two *auto de fé*,[88] excites the people still more with the confessions of the accused; pretends that he is going away and has another collection made; when he has exhausted the district, he moves off to another and repeats the game."[89]

Johan Linden, a canon of the Cathedral of Trier, provides us with an unnerving but revealing account of the horrendous witch-hunts in Trier (beginning in the principality in 1582, and in the city itself around 1586): "Inasmuch as it was popularly believed that the continued sterility of many years was caused by witches through the malice of the Devil, the whole country rose to exterminate witches. This movement was promoted by many in office, who looked for wealth in the ashes of the victims. And so, from court to court, throughout all the towns and villages in the diocese, scurried special accusers, inquisitors, notaries, jurors, judges, constables, dragging to trial human beings of both sexes and burning them in great numbers. Scarcely anyone who were accused escaped punishment. Nor were even the leading men spared in the city.... For the judge [Dietrich Flade[90]], two burgomasters, several councilors and associated judges were burned. Canons of sundry collegiate churches, parish priests, rural deans, were swept away in ruin. So far at length, did the madness of the furious populace and of the courts go in this thirst for blood and booty that there was scarcely anybody who was not smirched by some suspicion of this crime. Meanwhile, notaries, copyists, and innkeepers grew rich. The executioner rode on a blooded horse, like a nobel of the court, and went clad in gold and silver; his wife vied with the noble dames in the richness of her array. The children of those convicted and punished were sent into exile; their goods confiscated; plowman and vintner failed—hence came sterility. A direr pestilence or a more ruthless invader could hardly have ravaged the territory of Trier than this inquisition and persecution without bounds: many were the reasons for doubting that all were really guilty. This persecution lasted for several years; and some of those who presided over the administration of justice gloried in the multitude of stakes, at each of which a human being had been given to the flames."[91]

Cornelius Loos' assessment of the witch-persecutions in his ill-fated manuscript *De Vera et Falsa Magia* (1592)[92] is also relevant to our discussion: "Wretched creatures are compelled by the severity of the torture to confess to things they have never done; and so by cruel butchery innocent lives are taken; and, by a new alchemy, gold and silver are educed from human blood."[93] In a number of instances, however, when potential revenue seemed to be depleted, the hunts ceased.[94] In the case of Trier, Linden tells us: "At last, though the flames were still unsated, the people grew impoverished, rules were made and enforced restricting the fees and costs of examinations and examiners, and suddenly, as when in war funds fail, the zeal of the persecutors died out."[95] Similar episodes occurred elsewhere. Such somber and revealing accounts make it perfectly clear that, despite claims by mentalist writers to the contrary, profit and greed did indeed play a considerable part in numerous witchcraft trials.

Notes

1. Burr (1897:5–6).
2. Lea (1973 [1866]:128–9; 1887:129).

3. Burr (1943a:149). The data come from the records of the Benedictine Abbey of St. Maximin, in Trier, covering the years 1587 to 1594.
4. Spee (1631); Lea (1939:707).
5. Pratt (1915:111).
6. Lea (1973 [1866]:103).
7. Lea (1939:257).
8. Midelfort (1972:245, note 19)
9. Staub (1990:71).
10. Lea (1939:735).
11. Lea (1939:706).
12. Mora (1991:lii); Lea (1939:669, 702, 741, 863).
13. Suedfeld (1990:2); Staub (1990:50–51).
14. Walter (1969:26).
15. *Report on Torture* (1975:22).
16. Staub (1990:62–63).
17. Mora (1991:lii); Levack (1987:58); Kunze (1987).
18. Boguet (1929 [1602]:121–123).
19. Remy (1930 [1595]:9–10).
20. Lea (1939:1124). Hopkins' repertoire of witch-finding techniques are described and defended in his *Discovery of Witches* (1647).
21. Robbins (1981:249); Notestein (1911:164–205).
22. Oldekop (1698); Lea (1939:857).
23. Witters and Jones-Witters (1975:43–44).
24. *Daemonologie* (1597:81).
25. Verstegan (1605:66-67).
26. Holmes (1974:137).
27. Gaule (1646:77–79).
28. Davies (1947:153).
29. Christopherson (1971:33–37).
30. Limborch (1816 [1692]:413).
31. Meyfarth (1635); Lea (1939:738).
32. Lea (1973 [1866]:106).
33. Suedfeld (1990:5).
34. Anonymous, *Malleus Judicum* (circa 1630); Lea (1939:694).
35. Kieckhefer (1976:89).
36. Soloman, et al. (1957:357–363); Bexton, et al. (1954:70–76).
37. Lea (1878:483, 508). The fact that such devices were so frequently used, however, suggests that physical violence and the infliction of pain were vital and indispensable components of the witch-persecutions (see Chapter Nine, below).
38. Suedfeld (1990:10); Williams et al. (1962:158, 164).
39. J. A. C. Brown (1968:285–289). West (1985:72) describes sustained sleep deprivation as "the most potent of all the debilitating elements of softening up prisoners;" Ames (1985:86) calls it "the ultimate torment."
40. Larner (1983:107–108).
41. Thomas (1985:617).
42. Shumaker (1972:64).
43. Mannix (1986:122).
44. *Newes from Scotland* (1591:27–28).
45. Robbins (1981:497).

46.   Clarke (1677:106–107).
47.   Limborch (1816 [1692]:421).
48.   Limborch (1816 [1692]:416).
49.   Seligmann (1948:269).
50.   Oldekop (1698); Lea (1939:862–863).
51.   Guazzo (1929 [1608]:56). This wretched prisoner subsequently committed suicide in prison (see Chapter Four, above).
52.   *Report on Torture* (1975:42).
53.   Wolff and Wolf (1958:13).
54.   Conklin (1958:173).
55.   Boguet (1929 [1590]:125).
56.   Lea (1961:898).
57.   Spee (1631); Lea (1939:710).
58.   Lea (1939:857).
59.   Carus (1900:330).
60.   Lea (1939:857, 879, 903).
61.   Anonymous, *Malleus Judicum* (circa 1630); see Lea (1939:695).
62.   For example, Trevor-Roper (1988:51).
63.   For example, Ginzburg (1990, 1991).
64.   Meyfarth (1635:); Lea (1939:742).
65.   Meyfarth (1635); Lea (1939:738).
66.   Lea (1939:1126). See Kunze (1987) for a detailed account of the fate of the Pappenheimers, a family of vagrants, who fell into the clutches of the authorities and were publicly tortured and executed in Munich, in 1600, as part of a sensational show trial designed to deter resistance and lawlessness.
67.   Lea (1939:202, 204).
68.   Spee (1631); Lea (1939:711).
69.   Trevor-Roper (1988:40–41); Midelfort (1972:105–106); Kieckhefer (1976:90–91).
70.   Meyfarth (1635); Lea (1939:739).
71.   Oldekop (1654); Lea (1939:856).
72.   Limborch (1816 [1692]:143).
73.   Spee (1631); Lea (1939:706).
74.   Spee (1631); Lea (1939:704).
75.   Spee (1631); Lea (1939:711).
76.   Barthel (1984:132–133); Lea (1939:1042).
77.   Burr (1897:30).
78.   In Kors and Peters (1972:356).
79.   Scarre (1987:46–48).
80.   Scarre (1987:47).
81.   Burr (1897:27).
82.   Burr (1897:23–29).
83.   See Robbins (1981:35–37).
84.   J. B. Russell (1980:37). For more recent estimates of the total number of witches tried and executed, see Chapter One, above.
85.   J. B. Russell (1980:15, 42).
86.   Trevor-Roper (1988).
87.   Meyfarth (1635); Lea (1939:734).

88. *Auto de fé*, literally "an act of faith," was a ritualized public trial and execution.
89. Spee (1631); Lea (1939:702).
90. Dietrich Flade, a man of learning, head of the secular courts of the city of Trier, Vice-Governor of that city in 1580, Rector of the University in 1586, was the voice of moderation against the zeal of the prosecutors. As a result he was denounced as a patron and defender of witches, imprisoned, savagely tortured, and finally executed in 1589.
91. In Burr (1897:13–14).
92. Cornelius Loos, a Dutch cleric who opposed the persecutions in Germany, was jailed, publicly humiliated, forced to recant, and banished for questioning the veracity of demonological premises and criticizing the horrendous acts of torture and mass murder perpetrated by the witch-hammerers (Burr 1897:14–18). His manuscript *De Vera et Falsa Magia* (1592) [On True and False Witchcraft] was seized and destroyed by the authorities. A partial copy of the original manuscript, however, miraculously survived in the library of Trier, where it was recovered in the late 1800s by the historian George L. Burr (1943b:154–155).
93. In Robbins (1981:16).
94. Robbins (1981:221–222).
95. Burr (1897:13–14).

Chapter Six

Demonic Possession, Witchcraft, Deception, and Disease

The belief that spirits can enter a human body is found cross-culturally, and among many societies spirit possession is seen as a legitimate means of contacting the supernatural world.[1] In Europe during the medieval and early modern period, however, possession was believed to be caused by evil or unclean spirits.[2] According to one theologian: "The torment of possession is the greatest that man can suffer—the longest, for the demon never tires; the cause is invisible; the most-dangerous, for it leads to the irreparable ruin of the soul and body."[3] Hence, whenever cases of possession arose, experts were called in to oust or exorcise the intruding spirits.

In Christianity, the idea of possession by demons is based on The New Testament and the miracles performed by Jesus. Mark 5:2–13 relates the following:

> And when he [Jesus] was come out of the ship, immediately there met him out of the tombs a man with an unclean spirit ... [who] said, What have I to do with thee, Jesus, thou Son of the most high God? I adjure thee by God, that thou torment me not. For he said unto him, Come out of that man, thou unclean spirit. And he asked him, What is thy name? And he answered, saying, My name is Legion: For we are many. And he besought him much that he would not send them away out of the country. Now there was there neigh unto the mountains a great herd of swine feeding. And all the devils besought him, saying, Send us into the swine, that we may enter into them. And forthwith Jesus gave them leave. And the unclean spirits went out, and entered into the swine....

In Luke 10:1 Christ bestowed upon the Apostles the ability to cast out evil spirits: "Then he called his twelve disciples together and gave them power and authority over all devils." Likewise in Mark 14:17 Jesus says: "In my name shall they cast out devils." There is nothing in the Bible to suggest, however, that witches can cause possession by demons. This idea was forwarded in the *Malleus Maleficarum*[4] and in the *Rituale Romanum*, the official manual of exorcism of the Roman Catholic Church published in 1614, by the order of Pope Paul V.[5]

Once connected with witchcraft, demonic possession not only reached epidemic proportions, it also became a basis for witch-hunting. As Oesterreich pointed out in his now classic book on the subject, *Possession and Exorcism* (1930), "veritable epidemics [of demonic possession] were lacking [earlier] and epidemics only occurred after the belief in the devil reached its height in Europe—that is to say, in the time of the witchcraft trials."[6] Thus, as Boguet the witch-hammerer of Burgundy observed, "Everyday in our town we continually meet with large numbers of [possessed] persons who, for the most part impute their possession to certain *vaudois* [witches] or sorcerers."[7] In this chapter I shall examine the phenomenon of demonic possession and its role in the European witch-persecutions.

The characteristic symptoms of possession were fits and convulsions. Those demonically possessed also displayed autonomous excitement, disordered agitations of the limbs, changes in physiognomy, and invasion of the body by an alien personality.[8] Other symptoms included the ability to speak in a language not known to the patient (i.e., speaking in tongues), clairvoyance, uncanny strength, and revulsion of holy objects, Holy Water, and words from the Scriptures.[9] The inability to recite the Lord's Prayer correctly was both a sign of demonic possession and witchcraft.

Theologians, priests, and demonologists devised complex procedures for driving out possessing spirits. A demon, these experts said, could be expelled by making it reveal its name. Exorcists were directed that, should the spirit not reveal its name, one was to be imposed on it.[10] The names *Draco, Bestia, Mendax, Spiritus nequam, Asmodeus,* or the more popular *Beelzebub* were often used. But exorcists were warned not to interrogate a possessing demon out of sheer curiosity, not to become too familiar with it, or allow it to volunteer information, and never to ask its advice, because the Devil is "the father of lies" and will defame the innocent. In practice, however, it was often the words of possessing spirits which initiated a witch-hunt, leading to the execution of those named by the patient's supposed demons. The identity of witches who cause demonic possession, Boguet pointed out, "is confessed by the devils themselves, being wrung from them by the might and virtue of exorcisms."[11]

An effective cure for possession among Catholics was the use of the Host and holy relics. According to Sinistrari: "for, however, obstinate those evil spirits may be, however, resistant to the injunctions of the exorcist who bids them leave the body they possess, yet, at the mere utterance of the most holy names of Jesus or Mary, or the recitation of some verses of Scripture, at the imposition of relics, especially of the wood of the most holy cross, or at the sight of pictures and statues of the saints, they roar fearfully from the mouth of the possessed person, they gnash, shake, quiver, and display fright and terror."[12]

The formal ceremony of exorcism was designed to be dramatic and awesome, and involved a wide array of symbols and magical procedures. First, Holy Water was sprinkled on the patient, often eliciting frantic fits and convulsions from the possessing demons. Then lengthy prayers were recited, and extracts from the Scriptures were read aloud. Next, the exorcists chanted a litany of saints. Finally, the priests addressed the demon, shouting: "In the name of God ... depart with all thy noxious and accursed works and attempts from this servant of God, nor presume longer to injure him and his property."[13] Such exorcisms were also employed against insect infestations of homes (believed to be caused by supernatural means), as well as against disturbances due to witchcraft-induced *poltergeist* manifestations. The demand for this service was apparently very high, as there are numerous formulae for this type of spirit expulsion.[14]

The highly publicized cases of possession and successful exorcisms during the witch-hunt years functioned as powerful tools for religious propaganda.[15] Christ and the Apostles used exorcisms to validate the truth of their beliefs. By the time of the Reformation, exorcisms and cases of possession were being

Figure 6.1 Success in driving out possessing demons served to demonstrate the efficacy of the magical rituals of the exorcists. The devils infesting the body of the patient in this sixteenth-century illustration are shown departing from her mouth. From *Encyclopedia of Witches and Witchcraft*, by Rosemary Ellen Guiley. Copyright © 1989 Rosemary E. Guiley. Published by permission of Facts on File, Inc., New York.

employed by contending religious factions to establish the sanctity of their respective doctrines. Luther utilized exorcisms to demonstrate that it was the power of prayer and not "popish rituals" that was effective in expelling demons.[16] Catholics, on the other hand, held highly publicized exorcisms, conducted on stages before mass audiences, to vindicate beliefs in transubstantiation, holy relics, blest objects, the sign of the cross, and the power of names.[17]

A dramatic example was the case of Nicole Obry, a girl from Laon, France (1566), believed to be possessed by the demon *Beelzebub*. This spirit laughed and entered into lengthy discourses with the attending priests, who for nearly two months exorcised the girl daily before mass audiences. Acting as a spokesman for Catholicism, *Beelzebub* proclaimed that God had sent him to show that the heretical Reformation was the Devil's work. One writer estimates that 150,000 people witnessed the antics[18] of the possessed girl and the daily exorcisms, during which the clairvoyant spirit often accused onlookers of unconfessed sins, motivating them to go to confession.[19] The demon also declared that the Huguenots (French Calvinists) were in league with Satan. The final and dramatic expulsion of this articulate supernatural creature convinced many onlookers to convert to Catholicism.[20]

Aside from its utility for the purposes of religious propaganda, cases of demonic possession also served as an excuse to launch accusations of witchcraft against enemies, rivals, and political opponents. This is clearly illustrated by the infamous outbreak of demonic possession in Loudun, France, narrated by Aldous Huxley in his book *The Devils of Loudun* (1952).[21] On the second of June, 1630, Father Urbain Grandier, the parish priest of St.-Pierre-du-Marché in Loudun, was accused of witchcraft by a group of nuns from the local Ursuline convent. Grandier was a politically influential priest whose life-style, romantic adventures, and scandalous affairs with the daughters of prominent officials had made him many enemies. In 1618 he had written a sarcastic discourse about Cardinal Richelieu, who by 1630 had become one of the most powerful men in France and was to play a key role in the Loudun possession case.

During wild fits and convulsions, the nuns cried out that the priest had sent demons to possess them. Father Mignon, their confessor and Grandier's enemy, took up the role of exorcist. In an attempt to defame Grandier, Mignon intentionally encouraged the nuns in their demonic antics,[22] rather than attempting to cure them.[23]

The accusations of witchcraft against Grandier were temporarily put to rest when Archbishop Sourdis of Bordeaux prohibited Mignon from further exorcisms, but the machinations against Grandier were far from over. A short time later, Laubardemont, one of Richelieu's officials (and a relative of one of the possessed nuns), arrived in Loudun to supervise the tearing down of the town's fortifications, as part of the Cardinal's program of eradicating Huguenot strongholds by systematically demolishing local bastions. Both Catholic and Protestant inhabitants of Loudun opposed such an action, since without the defensive walls and battlements their town would be left unprotected against mercenary armies. Grandier prevented Laubardemont from dismantling the town's fortifications by citing a promise made by the King, that Loudun's defensive walls would not be demolished. Thus hindered by the troublesome priest, and having heard the allegations of the demonic nuns against Grandier, Laubardemont reported the situation to Richelieu. The Cardinal saw this as an excellent opportunity both to display his political might and to avenge himself on Grandier, whose insulting treatise he had not forgotten. Richelieu promptly appointed an investigative committee and allocated large sums of money for engaging exorcists and to provide care for the demonic nuns.

Both the investigators and the demonic nuns appear to have been familiar with the widely publicized case of Father Louis Gaufridi, executed in 1611 for sending "devils" into the nuns of the Ursuline convent at Aix-en-Provence.[24] Accused by *Beelzebub's* own words—from the mouth of a possessed nun—the priest was tortured with the *strappado*, forced to confess to all that was required, and was condemned "to be burned alive in the sight of the people." Gaufridi, however, was granted the mercy of strangulation before being set ablaze.

Among the expert demon-removers at Loudun were the Franciscan Lactance, the Capuchin Tranquille, and the Jesuit Surin. These zealous priests, employing dramatic rituals, threats, and commands, encouraged and directed the demonics in their accusations against Grandier, and transformed the situation into a bizarre circus by holding public exorcisms, in order that the devils' accusations against Grandier could be heard by the citizens of Loudun. At times as many as seven thousand spectators attended these obscene and horrifying spectacles.[25] Des Niau gave the following description in his *The History of the Devils of Loudun* (1634): "[The nuns] struck their chests and backs with their heads, as if they had their necks broken, and with inconceivable rapidity; They twisted their arms at the joints of the shoulder, the elbow, or the wrist, two or three times around. Lying on their stomachs, they joined the palms of their hands to the soles of their feet; their faces became so frightful one could not bear to look at them; their eyes remained open without winking. Their tongues issued suddenly from their mouths, horribly swollen, black, hard, and covered with pimples, and yet while in this state they spoke distinctly. They threw themselves back till their heads touched their feet, and walked in this position with wonderful rapidity, and for a long time. They uttered cries so horrible and so loud that nothing like it was ever heard before. They made use of expressions so indecent as to shame the most debauched of men, while their acts, both in exposing themselves and inviting lewd behavior from those present would have astonished the inmates of the lowest brothels in the country."[26]

With public opinion generated against Grandier, he was arrested on November 30, 1633, and jailed in the Castle of Angers. Investigators immediately examined his body for the "Devil's mark." Grandier's torments are detailed in Nicholas Aubin's treatise *The Cheats and Illusions of Romish Priests and Exorcists Discovered in the History of the Devils of Loudun* (1693):"They sent for Mannouri the surgeon, one of [Grandier's] enemies, and the most unmerciful of them all; when he [came] into the chamber, they stripped Grandier stark naked, blinded his eyes, shaved him every where, and Mannouri began to search him. When he would persuade them that the parts of his body which had been marked by the Devil were insensible, he turned that end of the probe which was round, and he guided it in such manner, that not being able to enter into the flesh, nor to make much impression, it was pushed back into the palm of his hand; the patient did not then

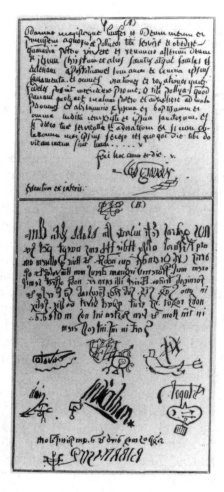

Figure 6.2   Part of the evidence presented against Urbain Grandier, the parish priest of St.-Pierre-du-Marche, in Loudun, were the actual contracts he signed with Satan. The documents are written from left to right with Latin words spelled backwards. They bear Grandier's signature and are countersigned by Satan, Lucifer, *Beelzebub,* and several other high-ranking infernal beings. These crucial bits of tangible evidence, the prosecution claimed, were handed to the tribunal by the demon *Asmodeus,* who had conveniently pilfered them from the Devil's own file cabinet. From Des Niau's *The History of the Devils of Loudun* (1887).

cry out, because he felt no pain; but when the barbarous surgeon would make them see that the other parts of his body were very sensible, he turned the probe at the other end, which was very sharp pointed, and thrust it to the very bone; and then the abundance of people [outside] heard complaints so bitter, and cries so piercing, that they [were] moved ... to the heart.... "[27]

Normal criminal procedure of trial by a secular court, with possibility of appeal to the Parliament of Paris, was denied the prisoner, and Richelieu's committee took charge of the legal proceedings. Part of the evidence presented by the prosecution was a document, allegedly written and signed in Grandier's own hand, and said to be his actual contract with Satan. The document was also signed by Lucifer, *Beelzebub, Leviathan, Astaroth*, as well as an array of other popular infernal beings.

As Grandier's situation looked grave, some nuns wanted to retract their allegations, but the officials prevented them from doing so, asserting that this was the Devil's ploy to save his disciple. Laubardemont made it clear, moreover, that any citizen of Loudun testifying in favor of Grandier would himself be subjected to arrest and his worldly possessions confiscated. Not surprisingly, Grandier was convicted on all counts. On August 18, 1634, the sentence was pronounced:

> We have ordered and do order the said Urbain Grandier duly tried and convicted of the crime of magic, *maleficia*, and of causing demoniacal possession of several Ursuline nuns of this town of Loudun, as well as of other secular women, together with other charges and crimes resulting therefrom. For atonement of which, we have condemned and do condemn the said Grandier to make *amende honorable*, his head bare, a rope round his neck, holding in his hand a burning taper weighing two pounds, before the principle door of the church of St. Pierre-du-Marché, and before that of St. Ursual of this town. There on his knees, to ask pardon of God, the King, and the law; this done, he is to be taken to the public square of St. Croix, and fastened to a stake on a scaffold, which shall be erected on the said place for this purpose, and there to be burned alive ... and his ashes scattered to the wind. We have ordered and so do order that each and every article of his moveable property be acquired and confiscated by the King; the sum of 500 livres first being taken for buying a bronze plaque on which will be engraved the abstract of this present trial, to be set up in a prominent spot in the said church of the Ursulines, to remain there for all eternity. And before proceeding to the execution of the present sentence, we order the said Grandier to be submitted to the first and last degrees of torture, concerning his accomplices.[28]

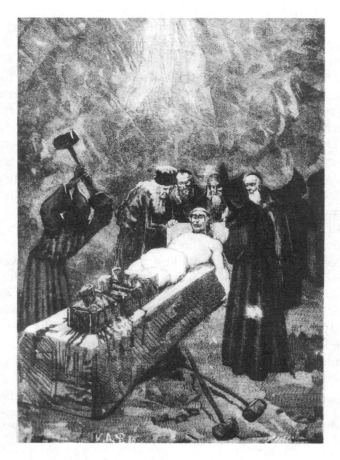

Figure 6.3 The torture of Urbain Grandier. By permission of the Mary Evans Picture Library, London.

The sentence was carried out to the last detail.

Grandier's torture was supervised by the vicious Tranquille, who subjected him to the leg-vices. Aubin described this harrowing torture as follows: "[they put] the legs of the patient between two planks of wood, which they bind with cords, between which they put wedges, and make them enter by blows of a hammer to squeeze the legs ... [and] the bones of the legs do crack and fall in pieces when they are unloosed; and those who have undergone this torture, die a little time after."[29] The torture was administered by the priests themselves: "The Recollect and [Capuchins] who were present to exorcise the wedges, the planks, and the hammers for the torture, fearing that the exorcism had not effect enough, and lest the Devils should have the power to resist the blows of a profane man, such as the hangman was, they themselves took the hammers and tortured the unhappy man...."[30]

Figure 6.4 The execution of Urbain Grandier. The demonic antics of the nuns are depicted in the background, to the right, while the exorcisms of the possessed sisters is shown in the background, to the left. Lactance, who is said to have personally lit the fire (according to some accounts), is shown standing before the condemned prisoner. By permission of Bibliothèque Nationale, Paris.

The torture was so severe that blood and marrow flowed out of Grandier's legs. Whenever the wretched man cried to God, his tormentors proclaimed that these were actually cries to Satan, Grandier's true god. Despite subjecting his prisoner to the most grievous pains, Tranquille was unable to extort either a confession or the names of accomplices. Crippled by the torture, Grandier was dragged to the place of execution, while, some sources say, the exorcists doused him with large quantities of Holy Water to prevent his last words from being heard.[31] Unlike Gaufridi at Aix-en-Provence, Grandier was shown no mercy and was burned alive. Cardinal Richelieu's power had been demonstrated in a very tangible and horrifying manner.

The Ursuline nuns continued their demonical antics until Richelieu cut off their funding, thus ending one of the most infamous cases of demonic possession in Europe. The Loudun affair was considered by many as concrete proof of both witchcraft and possession by demons. A few townspeople even converted to Catholicism as a result of this event, although in the long run the clearly fraudulent elements of the case contributed to skepticism regarding the reality of witchcraft.

Demonic Possession and Disease

As the incident in Loudun and numerous other such cases demonstrate, many instances of possession were hoaxes, perpetrated because of personal animosity, political motives, or simply through a desire for notoriety on the part of an accuser. There is evidence, however, that sometimes natural disease was confused with demonic intrusion. For this reason, Johann Weyer inveighed against priests and monks who, at the first indication of illness, cried witchcraft and demonic possession, their false accusations leading to the imprisonment and execution of innocent people.

The witch-hammerers, of course, saw matters differently. As a rejoinder to the argument that the physiological symptoms of possession could actually result from natural disorders, for example epilepsy, they maintained that the Devil, to hide himself from the Church which can expel him, conceals his possession by assuming the form of epilepsy, or the mask of lunacy.[32] This view was supported by *De Abditis Rerum Causis* (1548), the often quoted work of the famous French medical theorist, Jean Fernel, in which a case diagnosed as epilepsy was shown through astonishingly abstruse logic to be "an authentic" instance of possession by demons.[33]

The role of disease, however, cannot be overlooked. One possibility suggested from among an array of psychopathological conditions, such as schizophrenia, psychosis, etc., is the often unrecognized, bizarre neurological disorder known as Gilles de la Tourette's syndrome, named after the French physician who discovered it in 1885. The symptoms of this disease include involuntary nervous tics and paroxysms, and an uncontrollable urge to make obscene gestures and utter endless streams of profanities. The condition is thought to be caused by a deficiency in a particular neurotransmitter, and in some cases it is treatable with haloperidol, a tranquilizer prescribed for schizophrenia.

Those with severe cases of Tourette's disease could certainly have been mistakenly diagnosed as demonically possessed. The case of possession portrayed in the movie *The Exorcist*, according to one writer, was based on the symptoms of a Tourette's patient.[34] After viewing the motion picture, several individuals suffering from this affliction were convinced that their ailment was of a supernatural nature, and some even appealed to the Catholic Church for exorcism.[35]

However, Tourette's syndrome, which is relatively rare and afflicts particular individuals rather than whole communities, cannot account for the epidemics of demonic possession in Europe. A disease more likely to have been mistaken for demonic possession is ergot poisoning. A close examination of the historical periods in question reveals that the same geographical regions associated with rampant witch-hunting and epidemics of demonic possession were also areas subject to outbreaks of ergotism, a disease with significant psychotropic, convulsive, and hallucinatory dimensions that closely resemble the classic symptoms of demonic possession.

Ergot (*Claviceps pupurea*) is a species of the fungus *Claviceps* which infests various grasses, including wheat, barley, and oats. Rye, the staple grain on the European Continent, is especially susceptible to ergot infestation. In medieval and post-medieval

Figure 6.5 Ergot (*Claviceps pupurea*), a species of fungus with significant psychotropic and hallucinogenic properties. Photograph courtesy of Dr. Albert Hofmann, Burg I. L., Switzerland.

Europe, the ingestion of ergotized rye was responsible for incessant outbreaks of ergot poisoning, leading to countless deaths. Domestic animals fed ergotized grain died as well, often mysteriously, sparking accusations of witchcraft.[36]

The extraordinary psychotropic properties of ergot first came into public attention when Dr. Albert Hofmann produced an ergot derivative substance known as *d-lysergic acid diethylamide*, or LSD–25, one of the most powerful psychoactive substances ever found.[37] Compared to other psychotropic drugs, for example mescaline (a potent hallucinogen in its own right), the psychoactive properties of LSD–25 are of a "different order of magnitude," 5,000 to 10,000 times greater than mescaline.[38] The average psychoactive dose of LSD–25 is 100 micrograms, or one hundred millionth of a gram, and doses as low as 20 micrograms produce significant psychological changes in humans.[39] Ergot itself has ten percent the activity of LSD–25, making it an exceptionally potent psychotropic substance.[40] It can cause short-term or lasting psychosis, as well as other mental disturbances, such as panic attacks, illusions, hallucinations, and frightening dreams.[41]

In France epidemics of ergotism, called *ignis sacer*, or Saint Anthony's Fire (gangrenous ergotism), were generally characterized by hallucinations, delirium, intense sensations of burning, dry gangrene, and the loss of fingers, toes, or entire limbs.[42] It is perhaps no accident that Anthony, the Christian saint known specifically for his hallucinatory ordeals and visions of demons, was also selected as the patron saint of those afflicted by ergot poisoning. In Germany, ergotism, called *kriebelkrankheit*, was characterized primarily by epileptic fits (also known as "convulsive ergotism"). While France never experienced purely convulsive ergotism, there were cases of a mixed type, which displayed symptoms of both epileptic and gangrenous ergotism.[43]

In their milder forms, both gangrenous and convulsive ergotism share such symptoms as delirium, hallucinations, and other psychological aberrations.[44] Inhabitants of many areas also suffered "chronic unrecognized ergotism," which would have had similar physiological, psychological, and hallucinogenic effects.[45]

All of Continental Europe was affected by epidemics of ergotism, year after year, until improved agricultural techniques in the 1800s curtailed the outbreaks of this peculiar disease.[46] The social classes most prone to ergot toxins were the peasants and the

Figure 6.6 Saint Anthony being assailed by demons. Anthony, known specifically for his hallucinatory ordeals and visions of demons, was the patron saint of those afflicted by ergot poisoning—a disease characterized by intense and horrifying hallucinations. After a fifteenth-century engraving.

poor, whose staple grain was rye and who could not afford ergot-free grain.[47] It is significant to note that records of the witch-trials involving demonic possession indicate that both the accused and accusers were often from the poorest and weakest classes of society.[48]

Figure 6.7 Climate and geography were factors leading to ergot infestations which were localized at times to single fields. From Frank Bove's *The Story of Ergot*. Copyright © 1970. Courtesy of S. Karger AG, Basel, Switzerland.

Climate and local geography were important factors leading to a heavy infestation in one area, or even a single field, while adjoining plots would be ergot-free. According to Barger's classic monograph, *Ergot and Ergotism* (1931): "Apart from weather, local factors may have a considerable effect, particularly in hilly country. Often a particular valley or even a single low-lying field was much more heavily ergotized than its neighbors, and led to sporadic outbreaks of ergotism."[49] This produced a seemingly random pattern for the outbreaks of ergotism and, before widespread knowledge of its cause, would have ruled out diagnosis as a natural disease.[50]

Institutional settings such as nunneries and orphanages seem to have favored outbreaks of ergotism. Examples have been recorded in Heidelberg (1589), Turin (1789), Milan (1795), Braunsdorf in Saxony (1832), and Trier (1801).[51] The link between ergotism and institutional living arrangements may well shed light on the numerous outbreaks of demonic possession in convents and nunneries during the sixteenth and seventeenth centuries.

According to seventeenth-century accounts, victims of ergotism "often seemed to be bewitched, or possessed by demons; their cries could be heard four or five houses off."[52] As late as the 1700s, long after the cause of ergotism had been identified, and well past the height of the witch-persecutions, this disease was still being attributed to witchcraft. As Barger pointed out, "a belief in witchcraft was still prevalent and many believed the sufferers from convulsive ergotism to be possessed by demons."[53] Albrecht (1743), an eighteenth century chronicler, wrote: "through ignorance of natural causes the common people were apt to ascribe the symptoms of this peculiar disease to the action of spells."[54] One could not ask for stronger evidence suggesting a linkage between ergotism and witchcraft than these contemporary accounts.

Retrospective diagnoses, however, are always difficult and caution is advisable. Nevertheless, extant accounts do reveal that the specific symptoms of demonic possession, which included hysterical fits, convulsions, delirium, hallucinations, and analgesia, bear a striking resemblance to symptoms of ergot poisoning.[55] According to Lea: "Anesthesia and analgesia were frequently reported of the possessed. [A demonic], who was exorcised in 1599, *had no feelings when needles were thrust into her.* Needles could be thrust under the nails of ... one of the possessed nuns in a convent of Auxerre, in 1622, *without paining her.*"[56] Similarly, as an example of anesthesia of the fingers among those suffering from ergotism, Taube related the case of a woman who while sewing, *perforated her finger without knowing.*"[57] Another case of possession involved "[a] hysteric [who] ... in the excitement of

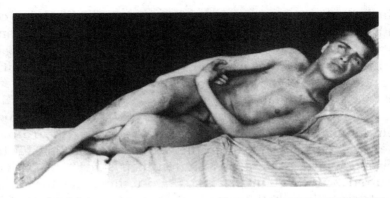

Figure 6.8 Convulsive ergotism (above), from George Barger's *Ergot and Ergotism* (1931). Demonic possession (below), from *The Encyclopedia of Witchcraft* by Rossell Hope Robins. Copyright © 1959 by Crown Publishers, Inc. Used by permission of Crown Publishers, Inc.

a hallucination opened an oven door and applied burning coals, with her hand to the pudenda. The hallucination stopped on the spot, but she felt no pain either at the time or during the long cure of the burns."[58] Victims of ergotism displayed similar insensitivity to hot coals, as in the case of one person who picked up a "red-hot" charcoal without pain.[59]

As another symptom of possession, European demonographers described the peculiar neurological phenomenon of formication, the abnormal sensation by those afflicted that ants were crawling on their skin: "The patient is tortured with certain *prickings*.... In some the throat is so constricted that they seem as if they are being strangled.... Sometimes the demon shows himself in some part of the body palpitating like a fish, or *like moving ants.*"[60] Likewise, symptoms of ergotism often included: "a tingling sensation *as if ants were running about under the skin*, hence formication.... In well-marked epidemics this sensation of *'pins and needles'* is said to have been experienced by all inhabitants of a village."[61]

Possession caused by witchcraft also involved "loss of reasoning power and idiocy, at intervals sometimes longer or shorter."[62] Ergotism was similarly known to produce "dullness of mind," "stupidity," "delusional insanity," and, in severe cases, dementia requiring confinement to an insane asylum.[63]

As to the onset of the affliction, demonic possession, according to contemporary accounts, "comes suddenly, and not gradually as a natural [disease] does ... the skin, especially of the face is yellow or ashen ... *there seems to be a lump at the orifice of the stomach or one passing up and down the throat; needle pricks are felt in the heart and other places*; sometimes the heart is corroded, or the kidneys are lacerated, or there are *convulsions and epileptic seizures*; they often are scarce able to look a priest in the face and the whites of the eyes are changed in various ways."[64] Similar symptoms of ergotism include "spasms of the face, the vocal cords, the aesophagus (simulating hydrophobia) and the diaphragm," as well as severe convulsions.[65] The onset of ergotism, likewise, was sudden, and there were cases in which convulsions came on so abruptly that "some at the table dropped knife or spoon and sank to the floor, and others fell down in the fields while plowing."[66]

Powerful muscular contractions were common in victims of both ergotism and demonic possession. "Often a strong man could not extend the limbs [of victims of ergotism]."[67] The possessed, similarly, underwent contortions and contractions of the limbs which required the strength of several people to extend.[68]

After convulsions, some ergotism patients experienced ravenous hunger, and several were reported to have eaten garments; a case of scatophagy was also reported.[69] Interestingly, the demonically possessed were known to vomit strange objects, such as stones, pieces of iron, and needles,[70] the consequence of having ingested them during periods of delusion.[71]

Objections to the possible involvement of ergotism in the European witch-hunts are based on the supposition that demonic possession afflicted only particular individuals in a given household or community, whereas ergot poisoning would have produced symptoms among a more inclusive category of victims.[72] For instance, in response to Parry's[73] suggestion that unusual weather conditions in Scotland conducive to ergot infestation during the years 1591–1598 and 1647–1649 may have had a bearing on the witch-hunts recorded there during these periods, Larner argues that in order to prove that ergot was involved, one must provide evidence of hysterical symptoms occurring exclusively among middle-aged women, the category of people usually accused of witchcraft.[74] Since cases of non-selective hysteria attributed to witchcraft are absent, Larner concludes, the involvement of ergotism in the Scottish witch-hunts can be ruled out. Thomas has also pointed to the selective nature of cases of demonic possession, and this selectivity, he argues, rules out ergotism as a cause of demonic possession.[75]

Another hypothesis, presented by Caporael (1976), and subsequently by Matossian (1982), posits that ergotism may have been a factor in the outbreak of demonic possession among several girls in Salem, Massachusetts, which sparked the infamous Salem witch-hunt of 1692. Spanos and Gottlieb (1976) have criticized Caporael's hypothesis on several points. Since their arguments have been applied inappropriately to European witchcraft,[76] they merit scrutiny.

Spanos and Gottlieb argue that if convulsive ergotism had been involved in the Salem witch-craze, all the individuals residing in the same households as the possessed girls should have displayed symptoms, because convulsive ergotism is not selective. Furthermore, they argue, children are more susceptible to ergotism than adults, and since only three out of the eleven possessed girls in Salem were under fifteen years of age, ergot could not have been involved. Moreover, Spanos and Gottlieb point out that convulsive ergotism occurs only among populations with a diet deficient in vitamin A; if vitamin A is plentiful (as would have been the case in Salem, an agricultural community, located near a seaport, giving it access to vitamin-rich seafoods), ergot poisoning leads to gangrene. The absence of gangrene in Salem, they conclude, rules out the presence of ergot.

For Spanos and Gottlieb, the demonic antics of the possessed girls in Salem more closely resemble Puritan notions of "demonic possession" than they do the symptomatology of ergotism. Moreover, because the possessed girls in Salem reported seeing apparitions with their eyes open, ergot could not have been present, they say, since experimental studies with LSD indicate that subjects rarely report seeing objects without closing their eyes. Finally, Spanos and Gottlieb argue that ergotism can be ruled out because none of the victims in Salem displayed permanent contractures, as would have been the case had convulsive ergotism been involved.

These objections, however, are ill-founded. A careful scrutiny of the literature indicates that, in cases of both convulsive and gangrenous ergotism, certain members of a family could be affected while others remained free of symptoms.[77] As to ergotism's selectivity by age, it is true that in some epidemics children were more susceptible; however, in many epidemics both children and teenagers were especially susceptible, suggesting that these categories would display symptoms of the disease.[78] Children and teenagers are more prone to ergot poisoning because they consume a greater amount of food in proportion to body weight than do adults.[79]

Similarly untenable is Larner's argument that a case for the role of ergotism depends on evidence that elderly females—the category of people often accused of witchcraft—were exclusively prone to ergot poisoning. Selectivity among the group accused of witchcraft is not crucial, contrary to Larner, because it was often the victims of possession who displayed symptoms and blamed others of causing their infirmity.

With regard to the role of vitamin A, the eminent medical historian Charles Creighton has pointed out that there are no clear lines between the two forms of the ergotism.[80] The crucial factor leading to gangrenous ergotism may either be the amount of ergot consumed,[81] or regional variations in the toxicity of the ergot fungus.[82]

As far as the perceptual effects of ergot alkaloids, Spanos and Gottlieb disregard the important fact that LSD hallucinations (as well as the psychotropic effects of other hallucinogens) are subject to a wide variety of extra-pharmacological variables.[83] This means that the cultural input into the subjective experience brought about by a hallucinogenic substance is as important as the drug itself.[84] It would be expected, then, that chemical psychosis express itself in accordance with the sociocultural and symbolic frame of reference of the person undergoing such an experience.

Spanos and Gottlieb also overlook the fact that ergot contains several different psychotropic alkaloids;[85] consequently, the psychological effects of ergotism would not be similar to those produced during experimental situations involving the use of LSD–25. Ergot often induced harrowing mental disturbances and permanent psychosis. Moreover, unlike subjects using LSD under clinical settings, the sixteenth- and seventeenth-century patients could not have known the cause of their unnerving hallucinations. This, in addition to the excruciating convulsions and other painful physiological symptoms associated with the disease, would have further reinforced the supposition that their affliction was of a supernatural nature.

Finally, that victims in Salem did not show permanent contractures does in fact accord with the symptomatology of ergotism. In less severe cases of ergotism an individual would suffer no permanent damage: "there would be an alarm in a village one day, and on the next the patient might be working in the fields."[86]

Thus, it is clear that ergotism can indeed be selective by socioeconomic class, age, and sex. Spanos and Gottlieb are totally wrong on the facts. The important question, therefore, is not whether ergotism can or cannot account for the physical symptoms attributed to demonic possession, but whether or not there was indeed an outbreak of ergotism in Salem in 1692. Evidence documenting an actual outbreak of ergot poisoning during the Salem witch-panic has not been produced. Caporael (1976) and Matossian (1982) make their case solely on the basis of climatic conditions conducive to ergot infestation. In fact, very few outbreaks of ergotism have been documented in the United States. As the eminent medical geographer August Hirsch has pointed out, "excepting a small epidemic of the convulsive form limited to a few persons in one of the New York city prisons [1825], I have not found any accounts of ergotism, although I have searched carefully in the very copious medico-topographical and epidemiographical literature of the United States."[87]

In Europe, on the other hand, there are no such difficulties, as we find the ubiquitous presence of ergotism throughout the years of witch-hunting and in the same geographical regions.[88] Indeed, when one compares existing records, fragmentary as they are, the geographical distribution of cases of demonic possession attributed to witchcraft seem to coincide with outbreaks of ergotism recorded in the same areas (Map 6.1). Epidemics of demonic possession characterized by "malignant spasms" were recorded in the years 1596 and 1597 in the areas of Cologne, Westphalia, and Hesse; these correspond to outbreaks of ergotism recorded there during the same years.[89] Additional epidemics of spasms attributed to witchcraft were recorded in 1648, 1649, and 1675 in the region of Plauen and Vogtland,[90] where outbreaks of ergotism have been recorded at the same time.[91]

Another outbreak of demonic possession corresponding to a period of ergotism occurred in 1717 in Annaberg.[92] Originating among some boys, this epidemic rapidly spread to the men and women of the community: "These all asserted that they saw spirits, when their eyes were open or closed, who told them of the future course of the disease, and molested them terribly. They had sharp pains and wonderful convulsions and contortions; some would be lifted from their beds; some would throw themselves on their heads and then on their feet, more than four hundred times a day, with incredible swiftness."[93]

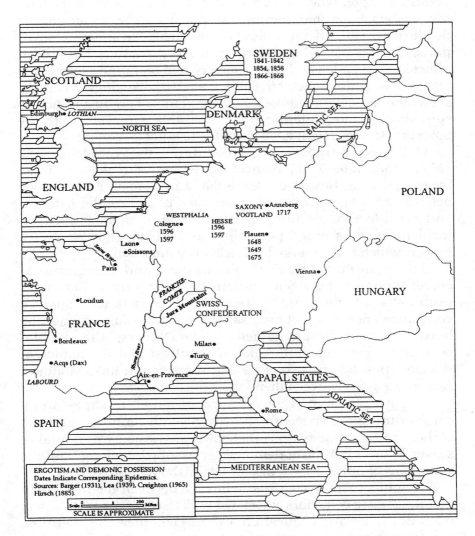

Map 6.1 Geographical distribution of ergotism, and correspondence between epidemics of demonic possession and ergot poisoning.

Outbreaks of ergotism and demonic possession also coincide in the Jura region between France and Switzerland. This area had more witches and demonics than any other place in Europe.[94] Episodes of widespread demonic possession were also reported in France, a region where ergotism was endemic. Pierre de Lancre, the vicious witch-hammering lawyer from the *parlement* of Bordeaux, recorded the following incident: "In a single small parish near Acqs [Dax] more than forty persons have been afflicted with epilepsy through sorcery and an infinite number of others have a disease which makes them bark like dogs"[95] Barking sometimes accompanied the other symptoms of ergotism, such as convulsions and epileptic fits,[96] and this suggests that the epidemic at Acqs might have been due to ergot poisoning.

Outbreaks of ergotism in Sweden during the years 1841–1842, 1854, 1858, 1866–1868, coinciding with outbreaks of "mass hysteria,"[97] offer further evidence that a mycotoxin can produce behavior akin to the "demonic possession panics" of the sixteenth and seventeenth centuries. Similar hysteria characterized an incident of mass bread poisoning, in 1951, in Pont St.-Esprit, France, which had a marked hallucinatory dimension.[98]

The symptomatological similarities and geographical correspondence between epidemics of ergotism and mass outbreaks of demonic possession are striking. Such a correspondence does not necessarily indicate a causal connection between the two phenomena. Nevertheless, the general correlation between outbreaks of ergotism and epidemics of demonic possession is so close that some causal linkage almost certainly existed between them.

The symptoms of ergotism were attributed to supernatural causes during the sixteenth and seventeenth centuries, and not earlier, for the same reasons that spirit possession was not taken seriously until European demonology ascribed it, along with the symptoms of other strange diseases, to diabolical forces.[99]

Creighton, who recognized a linkage between the mycotoxin and the bizarre behaviors associated with it, observed that: "There is, indeed, a larger question raised, whether the so-called psychopathies of the medieval and more recent periods may not have had a beginning, at least, in some toxic property of the staple food. The imagination readily fixes upon such symptoms as foaming at the mouth and barking noises, exalts these phenomena over deeper symptoms that a physician might have detected, and finds a simple explanation of the whole complex seizure as demoniac possession or, in modern phrase, as a psychopathy."[100]

Another of Creighton's observations is well worth considering, especially in light of the countless tautological mentalist explanations that have obfuscated the matter by ascribing demonic possession entirely to beliefs or hysteria: "Without questioning the subjective or imitative nature of many outbreaks which have been set down to hysteria, it may be well to use some discrimination before we exclude altogether an element of material poisoning such as ergot in the staple food."[101]

The historian Mary Matossian devotes a chapter of her *Poisons of the Past* (1989) to the role of ergotism in the European witch-hunts. Matossian draws attention, as I have, to the geographical and chronological correspondence between outbreaks of ergotism and epidemics of witchcraft. However, she does not cite specific instances where epidemics of demonic possession and ergotism have occurred simultaneously. Moreover, her conclusions are fundamentally different from mine. Matossian argues that anyone who has examined the records of the witch-persecutions will realize that actual harm ("bewitchment") was done.[102] The harm attributed to witches often manifested itself as outbreaks of "bizarre behavior" characterized by central nervous system symptoms: tremors, spasms, convulsive seizures, hallucinations, etc.[103] The target of the witch-persecutions, Matossian observes, were persons blamed for causing these horrible conditions, namely the witches. As Matossian sees it, "It simply will not suffice to discuss widespread beliefs about witches, tensions between factions in a witch-persecuting community, ruling-class repression, or legal and judicial arrangements for dealing with witchcraft. These were continuous cultural and social realities that did not vary in space and time as the distribution of 'bewitchment' varied. One cannot explain a variable with a constant."[104]

Matossian goes too far, however, by implying that the entire judicial and ideological basis of witch-hunting evolved as "a social response" to the effects of a mycotoxin, i.e., ergot poisoning, interpreted as bewitchment. "To blame witch accusers and the courts for witchcraft," she affirms, "is to mistake an effect for a cause. Witches were persecuted because harm had befallen a community, not just because there were people vulnerable to indictment and other people prone to indict them."[105] Simply because fraudulent accusations were possible does not mean that all episodes of bewitchment can be ascribed to invention, Matossian adds. Thus, she attributes the tragic fate of Urbain Grandier, not to gross subterfuge on the part of Richelieu's functionaries and the good sisters of Loudun's Ursuline convent, but to the misdiagnosis of the symptoms of a genuine central nervous disorder afflicting the nuns.[106]

Matossian's reductionist perspective is untenable. The witch-hunts, which were specific to a particular time and place, could not have been a response to a disease that was present for centuries prior to the witch-craze. (This criticism may also be directed at the speculations of Piero Camporesi, author of a rather garbled work entitled *Bread of Dreams* [1989], who attributes the witch-persecutions to "a hallucinating scenario" induced by tainted bread[107]). Furthermore, Matossian overlooks the fact that witches were hunted not just for precipitating nervous disorder symptoms, but for other calamities as well, such as lightning, storms, frosts, insect infestations, fires, plagues, economic slumps, etc. Satan's minions were also blamed for causing a host of illnesses that did not exhibit nervous disorder symptoms. Finally, and perhaps more importantly, innumerable witches were put to death, not for causing "actual harm," but for flying through the air, copulating with demons, conversing with spirits, making pacts with the Devil, possessing instruments of sorcery, and attending Sabbats. Records of the witchcraft trials do not reveal that actual harm was always done, as Matossian seems to think they do.[108] Explanations of the witch-persecutions, therefore, do not hinge on an explanation for their epidemiology, as she suggests, because there really was no "epidemiology of witchcraft" in the first place.

Finally, Matossian has not been able to establish a direct link between specific outbreaks of ergotism and outbreaks of witchcraft persecution, as noted above. Instead, she infers the presence of mycotoxins indirectly, from climatic factors conducive to ergot infestation in rye producing regions, and from the court cases of witchcraft accusations themselves.[109] In other words, incidence of microfungal epidemics are inferred from the recorded outbreaks of witch-hunting, the very phenomenon Matossian tries to explain as being the effect of these epidemics.

Although Matossian has exaggerated the role of mycotoxins in the European witch-persecutions, others[110] have altogether missed the significance of this potent environmental toxin and its influence on human behavior. Ergot poisoning, as I have argued, should not be ruled out as one plausible epidemiological explanation for the recurrent epidemics of demonic possession during the witch-hunt years.

Notes

1. See Bourguignon (1973, 1974, 1976) and Crapanzano (1977); see also the collection of essays on demonic possession in Noll (1992:139-230).
2. Oesterreich (1930:176); Bourguignon (1976:51–52).
3. Lea (1939:1060).
4. Kramer and Sprenger (1971 [1486]:124–27, 179–188).
5. Walker (1981:9); Oesterreich (1930:102); *Rituale Romanum* (1614).
6. Oesterreich (1930:188).
7. Boguet (1929 [1602]:10).
8. Oesterreich (1930:17–25).
9. Walker (1981:12).
10. Thorndike (1941:556–557).
11. Boguet (1929 [1602]:10).
12. Sinistrari (1927 [c.1690]:14).
13. Lea (1939:1066).
14. Lea (1939:1068).
15. See Walker (1981).
16. Oesterreich (1930:186–187).
17. Walker (1981:5–6, 47); Davies (1947:21).
18. See note 22, below, for the reason why I use the term "antics" to characterize the "demonic" behavior of the patients.
19. Walker (1981:25–28); Oesterreich (1930:103).
20. Walker (1981:25–28); Oesterreich (1930:103).
21. Ken Russell's controversial 1971 film, *The Devils,* is based on the Loudun case. See De Certeau (1970) and Carmona (1988) for other accounts of this case.
22. I use the term "antics" because there are sufficient grounds for us to conclude that the entire affair was staged. Indeed, a clearer case of fraud could not be found in the entire annals of European witchcraft. That the

demonic displays of the good sisters came to a halt as soon as Cardinal Richelieu (who subsidized the whole affair) withdrew his stipend, further reinforces my suspicions as to their complicity in the deception. A similar argument may be offered for countless other cases of demonic possession tied to political and economic interests and personal enmities of the individuals involved.

23. Aubin (1703 [1693]:20, 64).
24. See Michaelis (1613).
25. Oesterreich (1930:103).
26. Des Niau (1887: 206).
27. Aubin (1703 [1693]:93–94).
28. In Aubin (1703 [1693]:142–143).
29. Aubin (1703 [1693]:149–150).
30. Aubin (1703 [1693]:150).
31. Aubin (1703 [1693]:156).
32. Lea (1939:1060).
33. Walker (1981:11).
34. Garelik (1986:74–82). The movie, based on W. P. Blatty's novel, *The Exorcist* (1971), is said to have been modeled after an actual case (Bourguignon 1976:4–5).
35. Garelik (1986:74–82).
36. See Robbins (1981:209); Hoffer and Osmond (1967:84).
37. Furst (1982:59).
38. Hofmann (1980:45).
39. Claridge (1970:104).
40. Hoffer (1965:183).
41. See Matossian (1989:9–10).
42. Haggard (1929:216–219).
43. Bove (1970:156).
44. Barger (1931:21).
45. See Birt (1910:1580).
46. Bove (1970:153).
47. Barger (1931:25).
48. See Monter (1976:139).
49. Barger (1931:98–99).
50. See Bove (1970:27).
51. Barger (1931:24).
52. Barger (1931:69).
53. Barger (1931:71).
54. In Barger (1931:71).
55. Mentalist writers would claim that notions of health and disease must be interpreted in their cultural contexts and that it is very hazardous simply to impose Western medical categories upon other societies. Thus, they would say, one should be wary of categorical statements about epidemics of ergotism. So far as mentalist writers are concerned, accounts of possession and witchcraft in demonological texts were often written within a theological or eschatological framework and so are poor sources by which to determine the "reality" of the victims' suffering.

Perspectives which focus on and restrict themselves to concepts and distinctions that are "real," "culturally meaningful," and "appropriate" from the point of view of the actors necessarily eschew the legitimacy of scientific accounts of human behavior, as I have already argued. Commitment to such sterile and often misleading research perspectives entails the assumption that all knowledge is equally uncertain, hence scientific concepts and knowledge are inapplicable cross-culturally. Such research strategies diminish and reduce the intellectual enterprise undertaken to understand sociocultural phenomena to the status of mere aesthetic judgments. Herein lies the greatest defect in the mentalist approach. Brain tumors, viral infections, cancers cells, alkaloids, and mycotoxins exist apart from ideas, beliefs, theologies, and eschatological frameworks. One does not need to find out about thoughts, beliefs, or religious orientations in order to account for brain tumors, cancers cells, alkaloids, and mycotoxins using the data language of science and scientific medicine. I would argue, therefore, that it is not the documents in question that are poor sources of information, but rather it is the mentalist perspective that is inadequate as a way of knowing.

56. Lea (1939:1048), emphasis mine.
57. Taube (1783).
58. Lea (1939:1048).
59. Barger (1931:36).
60. Guazzo (1929 [1608]:167–168), emphasis mine.
61. Barger (1931:32), emphasis mine.
62. Lea (1939:1057).
63. Barger (1931:36).
64. Lea (1939:1064), emphasis mine.
65. Barger (1931:34).
66. Barger (1931:34).
67. Barger (1931:34).
68. Oesterreich (1930:23).
69. Barger (1931:35).
70. See Robbins (1981:395).
71. Lea (1939:1047). This phenomenon is known as allotriophagy.
72. For example, Klaits (1985:11–12); Larner (1983:220); Spanos and Gottlieb (1976:1390–1394); Thomas (1985:573).
73. Parry (1978:142).
74. Larner (1983:220).
75. Thomas (1985:573).
76. For example, Klaits (1985:11–12); Quaife (1987:203–204).
77. See Bove (1970:135).
78. Barger (1931:39).
79. Matossian (1989:29, 65, 77).
80. Creighton (1965 [1894]:56).
81. Barger (1931:26).
82. Hirsch (1885:216).
83. See Furst (1982).
84. See Blum, et al. (1964:xiv).
85. The alkaloids with hallucinogenic properties are *ergine, ergonovine,* and *lysergic acid hydroxyethylamide* (Matossian 1989:7–11). Sometimes *lysergic acid diethylamide* (LSD) may also appear in the natural ergot due to the action of other fungi.

86. Barger (1931:35).
87. Hirsch (1885:211–212).
88. Hirsch (1885:204–10).
89. Lea (1939:14); Hirsch (1885:206); Barger (1931:67).
90. Lea (1939:1472).
91. Hirsch (1885:206).
92. See Lea (1939:1474–1478); Barger (1931:67, 70–71); Hirsch (1885:207).
93. Lea (1939:1475).
94. Monter (1976:7).
95. Lea (1939:1475).
96. Creighton (1965 [1894]:61).
97. Creighton (1965 [1894]:62).
98. Fuller (1968) has attributed this epidemic to ergotism, while Bove (1970:160) has argued that the poisoning was due to an organic phosphorous chemical sprayed on the grain.
99. See Estes (1983).
100. Creighton (1965 [1894]:62).
101. Creighton (1965 [1894]:62).
102. Matossian (1989:70).
103. Matossian (1989:70).
104. Matossian (1989:71).
105. Matossian (1989:71).
106. Matossian (1989:151).
107. Camporesi (1989:124–125).
108. Matossian (1989:70).
109. Matossian (1989:14, 19, 57, 72, 80).
110. Writers who are themselves committed to the analysis of implausible and absurd details with respect to ideas and beliefs, and who are unfamiliar with the literature on ergotism and lack even a rudimentary understanding of the basic and pertinent variables, have disdainfully dismissed explanations attributing the witch panics to ergot poisoning, as "dubious," "biological determinism," or "banal."

For example, Ginzburg (1991:303–304, 312) writes a few hasty, indeterminate words about ergot and its symptomatology, but astonishingly misses the point of his own discussion. He even cites a couple of cases involving victims who experienced convulsive fits, visions, and who were thought by the people around them "to be possessed," only to conclude that, "All this leads us to think of evil spells rather than witches." Ginzburg (1984:46) also alludes to the ritual use of ergot in Europe during the witch-hunt years, for which there is absolutely no evidence. This further confirms my suspicions that this writer is unfamiliar with the literature on ergot and ergotism.

Another writer, who seems to be altogether oblivious to a possible connection between ergotism and the witchcraft phenomenon, even has the symptomatology of the disease wrong, including among the manifestation of ergotism "blindness" and "fornication" [sic] (Duerr 1985:146). Thomas' (1985:573) familiarity with ergotism—which he dismisses as a variable in the witchcraft trials—is based on just one source, Fuller's The Day of St. Anthony's Fire (1968), detailing an incident of bread poisoning that may well have been caused by something other than ergot (see note 98, above). Such a biased and prejudicial attitude among eminent men of letters, which is a detriment to knowledge, is most unfortunate indeed.

Chapter Seven

Hallucinogenic Drugs and Witches

European demonologists maintained that witches had the ability to fly through the air and that they often traveled in this manner to attend their hideous nocturnal assemblies. The idea of the witches' flight, or *transvection*, was rooted in myths from Classical times and elements of local folklore. Popular beliefs regarding the night-flying adherents of the pagan goddess Diana, or Herodius, are mentioned in the *Canon Episcopi*, a document incorporated into Canon Law during the twelfth century and considered the highest authority in matters of orthodoxy: [1]

> It is not to be omitted that some wicked women, perverted by the Devil, seduced by illusions and phantasms of demons, believe and profess themselves, in the hours of the night, to ride upon certain beasts with Diana, the goddess of pagans, and an innumerable multitude of women, and in the silence of the dead of night to traverse great spaces of earth, and to obey her commands as their mistress, and to be summoned to her service on certain nights. [2]

The possibility of the atmospheric transportation of witches was based on Matthew 4:5–8, which relates how the Devil transported Jesus through the air, setting him down on the Temple and then on the pinnacle of a mountain outside Jericho. [3] Citing this passage, as well as Thomas Aquinas' commentary on it, Bodin observed that "Satan, with God's permission, has no less power over men to transport them, since it is completely certain that Jesus Christ was a real man and not ghostlike." [4] Similarly, Boguet argued, "a fact which ... strongly inclines me to believe in the transvection of witches is that Jesus Christ himself was carried to the pinnacle of a mountain; for if this could happen to our Lord, why should it not happen to witches?"[5]

Thus, many demonographers were convinced that witches, when so empowered by the Devil, could soar through the air by rubbing themselves with certain magical ointments. Others maintained, however, that the witches' atmospheric transportations were diabolically-induced dreams and illusions. As one contemporary scholar noted: "[Satan] rarely carries witches from one place to another, but deludes them through illusions and dreams. If you ask why her ointment and fork are always found and are burnt with her, the answer is that she prepares the ointment as [the Devil] instructs her, mostly out of somniferous herbs, and smears herself and her broom or fork, falls into deep sleep and dreams that she flies hither and thither with others, some of whom she knows, eats, drinks, talks, jests, dances, has sexual intercourse—and admits it when tortured."[6]

Demonologists often related experiments in which women, after anointing themselves with a salve, fell into a stupor during which they fancied themselves to be transported through the air and enjoyed various pleasures, which they described upon awakening.[7] Johannes Nider, a Dominican professor of theology at the University of Vienna and pioneering demonologist, reported one such case in his *Formicarius* (1435):[8] "a Dominican ... in a village found a woman so demented that she believed herself to be carried through the air with Diana and other women. He could not convince her of this infidelity and asked to be present when next she flew away. She agreed and that witnesses should be present. When the time came, she placed a large bowl used for kneading dough on a bench, seated herself in it, rubbed herself with ointment and uttered certain magic words, whereupon she went to sleep at once and *opere daemonis* dreamed of Domina Venus and other superstitions so strongly that she exclaimed and moved her hands so that the bowl on which she was seated was shaken from the bench and severely injured her head in the fall. As she lay there, awakened, the friar told her that she had not moved; and thus with salutary exhortations he cured her of her error."[9] Nider, like many other demonographers, attributed the efficacy of the magical unguents to demonic forces (see below).

Figure 7.1 Witches transformed into animals depart for the Sabbat. European demonologists claimed that witches could fly through the air and assume the shape of beasts by anointing themselves with unguents made with the fat of slain children. After a page from Ulrich Molitor's *De Lamiis et Phitonicis Mulierbus* (1489).

Figure 7.2 Flying witches circle overhead in preparation for landing at their diabolic assembly, while other witches pay homage to the Devil in the shape of a goat. From Johannes Tinctoris' *Tractatus Contra Sectum Valdensium* (c. 1400). Cabinet des manuscripts, fonds français 961. By permission of Bibliothèque Nationale, Paris.

Adversaries of the witch-hunters, men such as Scot, Weyer, Nynauld, Porta, and Laguna, attempted to refute demonological allegations regarding the witches' night-flights and sexual encounters with demons, by attributing such escapades to a natural cause: the action of drugs. The celebrated physician Andrés de Laguna described the contents and effects of a witches' ointment in his commentary on Dioscorides' *De Medica Materia* (1529):[10] "Among the materials found in the hermitage of ... [a] wizard and witch (executed by the authorities) was a pot full of [a] certain green ointment ... composed of soporific herbs such as hemlock, nightshade, henbane, and mandrake. Through the constable, who was a friend of mine, I obtained a good supply of the ointment and later in the city of Metz I had the wife of the public executioner anointed with it from head to foot. She through jealousy of her husband had completely lost power of sleep and had become half insane in consequence. This seemed to me to be an excellent opportunity to undertake a test of the witch's ointment. And so it turned out, for no sooner did I anoint her than she opened her eyes wide like a rabbit, and soon they looked like those of a cooked hare when she fell into such a profound sleep that I thought I should never be able to awake her. However ... after the lapse of thirty-six hours, I restored her to her senses and sanity. Her first words were, 'Why did you awaken me, badness to you, at such an inauspicious moment? Why I was surrounded by all the delights in the world.' Then turning her eyes toward her husband (he was beside her, she stinking like a corpse) and smiling at him she said: 'skinflint! I want you to know that I have put the horns on you, and with a younger and lustier lover than you.' Many other strange things she said, and she swore herself out beseeching us to allow her to return to her pleasant dreams. Little by little we distracted her from her illusions, but forever after she stuck to many of her crazy notions. From all this we may infer that all that those wretched witches do and say is caused by potions and ointments which so corrupt their memory and imagination that they create their own woes, for they firmly believe when awake all that they had dreamed when asleep."[11]

Giovanni Della Porta, a physician who opposed witch-hunting, provided detailed information about the witches' flying ointments in his *Magiae Naturalis* (1561): "They take the fat of an infant and boil it in a brazen vessel, then strain it; they then knead the residue. With it they mix eleoselinum, aconite, poplar leaves, and soot. Or in some cases [they use] sium, common acorum, cinquefoil, and the blood of a bat, sleep-inducing nightshade, and oil. After the unguent has been prepared, they rub all parts of their bodies exceedingly, till they look red, and are very hot, so that the pores may be opened, and their flesh soluble and loose. They add either fat or oil so that the force of the ointment may pierce inwardly, and so be more effectual. Thus on a moonlit night they seem to be carried in the air, to feasting, singing, dancing, kissing, culling, and other acts of venery, with such youths as they love and desire most: for the force of their imagination is so vehement, that almost all that part of the brain, wherein the memory consists, is full of such concepts. And whereas they are naturally prone to believe any thing: so do they receive such impressions and steadfast imaginations into their minds, as even their spirits are altered thereby; not thinking upon any thing else, either by day or by night.... "[12]

As evidence of the ointment's hallucinatory effects, Porta described an actual instance in which he (like Laguna) had observed a witch who was under the influence of an unguent: "I considered thoroughly hereof, remaining doubtful of the matter, when there fell into my hands a witch, who of her own accord did promise to fetch me an errand out of hand from far countries, and willed all them, whom I had brought to witness the matter, to depart out of the chamber. And when she had undressed herself, and smeared her body with certain ointments (which action we beheld though a chink or little hole in the door) she fell down through the force of those soporiferous or sleepy ointments into a most sound and heavy sleep: so as we did break open the door, and did beat her exceedingly; but the force of her sleep was such, as it took away from her the sense of feeling: and we departed for a time. Now when her strength and powers were weary and decayed, she awoke of her own accord, and began to speak many vain and doting words, affirming that she had passed over both seas and mountains; delivering to us many untrue and false reports: we earnestly denied them, she impudently affirmed them."[13]

Figure 7.3 A sixteenth-century woodcut showing a man peeking through a crack in a door, witnessing witches anointing themselves with their magic grease and flying through the chimney. From *Encyclopedia of Witches and Witchcraft*, by Rosemary Ellen Guiley. Copyright © 1989 Rosemary E. Guiley. Published by permission of Facts on File, Inc., New York.

The Witch Ointments: Pharmacological Composition

Surviving lists of ingredients indicate that the witches' flying-ointments contained powerful hallucinogenic substances.[14] The principal psychotropic ingredients of the ointments belong to the nightshade or Solanaceae family. Gustav Schenk, the noted

German toxicologist, observed that, from ancient times Solanaceae have been the true magic plants, capable of putting the human mind into states of consciousness impossible to enter and experience without them.[15]

The Solanaceae family has over 3,000 species world-wide, including potato, tomato, eggplant, and tobacco, as well as a variety of medicinal species. Belladonna (*Atropa belladonna*), henbane (*Hyoscyamus niger*), datura (*Datura stramonium*), and mandrake (*Mandragora officinarum*)[16] all belong to this family. These plants contain the psychoactive alkaloids *atropine, d,l-hyoscyamine*, and *scopolamine*,[17] which are anticholinergic substances—they block the action of acetylcholine on the peripheral cholinergic receptors in the brain, producing intense visual, gustatory, and olfactory hallucinations.[18]

These drugs differ from other natural hallucinogens, however, in their extreme toxicity.[19] Dr. Karl Kiesewetter, author of *Geschichte des Neueren Occultismus* (1891) and *Die Geheim-wissenschaften* (1895), died after an experiment with a flying-ointment containing extracts of some of these plants, clearly demonstrating the potential dangers of such compounds.[20] (This case should stand as a warning to those foolish enough to contemplate experiments with such dangerous and potentially deadly compounds.)

In large doses anticholinergic drugs are in some respects similar to LSD, and experienced users, as well as clinical diagnosticians, can sometimes confuse anticholinergic intoxication for LSD psychosis.[21] What distinguishes the two drugs, however, is that anticholinergic substances tend to induce hallucinations which appear to exist externally, with the subject losing all sense of reality.[22] LSD psychosis, on the other hand, is more ideational in nature, with the subject often able to distinguish the drug-induced state from his objective surroundings.[23]

This may explain why people under the influence of *atropine, hyoscyamine*, and *scopolamine* sometimes emerged from their psychosis convinced that what they experienced had really taken place. Thus, according to Lewin, one of the pioneers in the field of pharmacology, "Magic ointments or witches' philtres procured for some reason and applied with or without intention produced effects which the subjects themselves believed in, even stating that

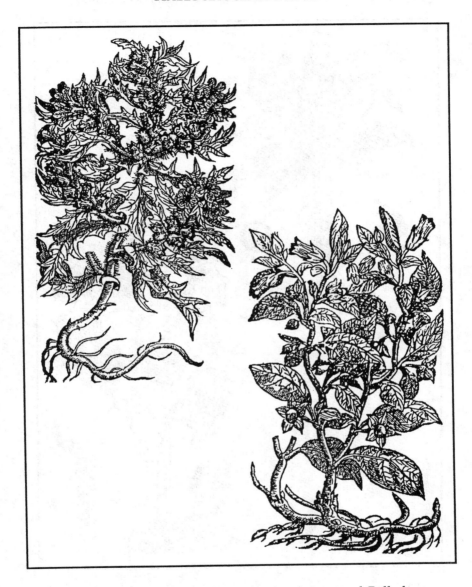

Figure 7.4 Henbane (*Hyoscyamus niger*), top, and Belladonna (*Atropa belladonna*), bottom, hallucinogenic plants used in the preparation of the witches' ointments. From John Gerard's *The Herbal, or, General Historie of Plantes* (1636). Courtesy of the Walter Havighurst Special Collections, King Library, Miami University.

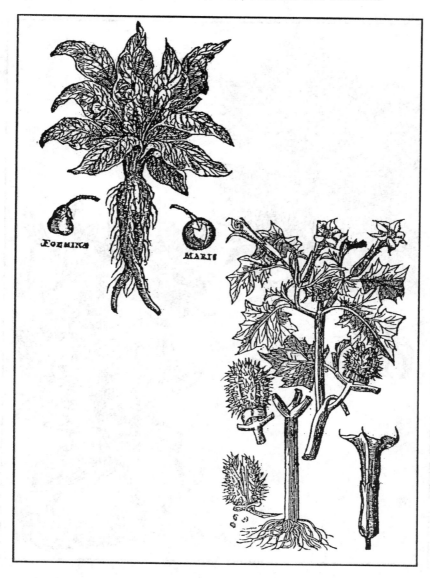

Figure 7.5 Mandrake (*Mandragora officinarum*), top, and Datura (*Datura stramonium*), bottom, hallucinogenic plants used in the preparation of the witches' ointments. From John Gerard's *The Herbal, or, General Historie of Plantes* (1636). Courtesy of the Walter Havighurst Special Collections, King Library, Miami University.

they had intercourse with evil spirits, had been on the Brocken [a peak in the Harz mountains in Germany] and danced at the Sabbat with their lovers, or caused damage to others by witchcraft....."[24]

Hallucinogens and the Witches' Sabbat

Some of the first modern researchers who assessed the flying-ointment recipes, acknowledged that these preparations contained potent hallucinogens which, when mixed with fat and applied to the skin (as several of the recipes indicate), could be absorbed into the bloodstream.[25] *Atropine* is fat-soluble, and therefore topical applications are easily absorbed; likewise, medicinal belladonna plasters to the skin have resulted in serious poisoning.[26] *Scopolamine*, the active alkaloid in datura, can also readily enter into the bloodstream through the skin.[27]

Experiments with these drugs suggest that they sometimes produce the sensation of flight and other subjective impressions not unlike those reported by people thought to be witches.[28] Schenk described his own experience after inhaling henbane smoke: "I was permeated by a peculiar sense of well-being connected with the crazy sensation that my feet were growing lighter, expanding and breaking loose from my body. This sensation of gradual bodily dissolution is typical of henbane poisoning. Each part of my body seemed to be going off on its own. My head was growing independently larger, and I was seized with the fear that I was falling apart. At the same time I experienced an intoxicating sensation of flying.... The frightening certainty that my end was near through the dissolution of my body was counterbalanced by an animal joy in flight. I soared where my hallucinations—the clouds, the lowering sky, herds of beasts, falling leaves which were quite unlike any ordinary leaves, billowing streamers of steam and rivers of molten metal—were swirling along. All this time I was not peacefully sleeping with limbs relaxed, but in motion. The urge to move, although greatly curtailed, is the essential characteristic of *Hyoscyamus* intoxication."[29] The sensations of floating in the air and of flight have also been reported during LSD intoxication,[30] indicating that experiences of this nature are not improbable during drug-induced altered states of consciousness.

Such evidence has prompted a number of modern writers—especially those influenced by the "drug culture" of the 1960s—to argue that the witches' night-flights, encounters with demons, communion with the Devil, and metamorphosis, were actually hallucinatory phenomena, stemming from the ritual use of psychotropic drugs during the Sabbats.[31] Charles Hoyt has suggested, for example, that hallucinogenic drugs were used by leaders of witch-covens in order to produce a state of awe among their followers.[32] Schultes and Hofmann have forwarded a comparable idea, maintaining that henbane was employed in the induction ceremonies of the witch-sects to produce highly impressionable states of mind among young recruits.[33]

Not everyone, however, shares the conviction that hallucinogenic drugs played some role in European witchcraft; some writers have altogether dismissed the involvement of drugs, asserting that the idea of magical ointments was a fabrication of European demonologists, intended to make the sinister picture they had painted of the "witch" more believable.[34] The historian Klaits has argued that although witches were usually arraigned for using diabolical salves, more often such charges were false.[35] To illustrate his point, he cites an experiment conducted in 1611 by Alonso Salazar y Frias, who, having acquired some ointments from Basque witches, administered them to animals, but with negative results.[36] Klaits, however, has ignored the fact that most hallucinogenic substances tend to affect higher-order mental functions, and consequently animal experiments are useless in demonstrating the effects these drugs have on human subjects. As Dr. Hofmann has pointed out concerning LSD—a drug with properties resembling hallucinogens found in the witches' ointments[37]—experiments with animals provide little information on the psychotropic effects of LSD, because these animals cannot express the subtle but important psychic changes.[38]

Demonologists themselves considered the ingredients of the witches' lotions to be inert materials, incapable of producing any effects without the aid of demons. Del Rio observed, for instance, that "the ointment used is made of various foolish things, but chiefly of the fat of slain infants; sometimes only the staff is

Figure 7.6 A witch preparing the flying grease with the aid of a demon. European demonologists attributed the efficacy of the witches' ointments to the action of demons, not the natural qualities of their ingredients. Title page of Henning Grosse's *Magica de Spectris et Apparitionibus Spiritu* (1656). Illustration courtesy of the Franklin D. Schurz Library, Indiana University South Bend.

anointed, sometimes the thighs or other parts of the body. The transport could be effected without, but the demon insists on it to stimulate infanticide."[39] The Inquisitor Valle de Moura affirmed that, "The poisons from which the *Veneficae* [poisoners-witches] derive their name have their potency, not from the natural qualities of the ingredients, but from the charms and incantations used in their preparation, the demon thus contributing their effectiveness."[40] Remy (1595) likewise remarked that, "the drugs owe their potency to the Demon, not to any inherent properties of their own."[41] And Johann Geiler von Kaysersberg (1517), the famous Strasbourg theological teacher, observed: "If a witch sits on a pitchfork which she rubbed with salve and speaks the prescribed words, she can ride about wherever she will. It is not any virtue in the fork or in the salve that does it, therefore, it is the devil who does it, who carries her away on the fork, when he sees his signs used by the witch."[42]

One could argue that, if the erudite witch-doctors were trying simply to paint a sinister picture of witches and their activities, the list of obnoxious and loathsome ingredients for the ointments should have varied considerably among the sources, rather than remaining, as they did, confined almost exclusively to psychotropic substances. Indeed, the medical historian Fletcher, who surveyed the extensive literature of folk-beliefs associated with the witches' pharmacopoeia, observed that "it will be found that the same ingredients have been made use of through many ages to produce the like results."[43]

Thus, the objection that the witches' salves were entirely the fabrication of European demonologists may not be well founded. On the other hand, explanations which posit the presence of "drug-using sects," whose members were persecuted because of their dreams and hallucinations,[44] are equally tenuous, inasmuch as concrete evidence for the existence of such organizations does not exist. In the remainder of this chapter I shall suggest alternate explanations for the role of hallucinogens in European witchcraft.

Drugs, Poisons, and Chemical Ecstasy

Reginald Scot equated one type of witchcraft, which he called *veneficium*, with dealers in poisons: "As touching this kind of witchcraft, the principal part thereof consists in certain confections prepared by lewd people to procure love; which indeed are mere poisons, bereaving some of the benefits of the brain, and so of the sense and understanding of the mind. And for some it takes away life, and that is more common than the other."[45] Such practitioners not only existed, they apparently possessed considerable knowledge of poisons and the utilization of various alkaloids.

Figure 7.7 Witches adding toads to their magical brew. From Pierre de Lancre's *Tableau de l'inconstance des mauvais anges et démons* (1612). By permission of Special Collections and Archives, Milton S. Eishenhower Library, The Johns Hopkins University.

Take for example, toads, dreaded during the Middle Ages because of their association with witchcraft.[46] According to Fletcher: "The toad figures constantly in necromantic charms and its venom, if it have any, is supposed to reside in the glands of the skin."[47] Toads also appear in flying[48] and killing ointment recipes. Although the role of the toad in the witches' recipes has long been dismissed as folklore, the skin secretions of the toad family *Bufonidae* (which includes the common European toad) are now known to contain the alkaloid *bufotenine*, which has significant hallucinogenic properties.[49] This alkaloid was employed by the Pokoman Maya of Guatemala, who added it to their fermented drinks, and is still part of the pharmacopoeias of local curers in Veracruz.[50] We can infer from this and similar evidence that individuals versed in *veneficium* had a sound empirical knowledge of alkaloids.

Those skilled in the art of poisons were greatly feared and were believed to possess supernatural powers, with which they could both heal and kill.[51] There is no reason to assume, however, that these specialists acted collectively, worshipped the Devil, or made pacts with evil spirits. Indeed, *veneficium* was originally altogether distinct from the ecclesiastical notion of diabolical witchcraft. For example, the Benedictine abbot Johann Trithemius, author of *Antipalus Maleficorum* (1555), distinguished between those practitioners who caused injury by using deadly drinks, herbs, and roots, and witches who were in league with the Devil.[52] According to Weyer's *De Praestigiis* (1568), "Witches [are] poor ignorant creatures, old and powerless, who without instruction imagine themselves, in their desperation and degradation, to be the cause of the evils which God sends to man and beast. Unlike magicians, they have no books, nor exorcisms, nor signs, nor other monstrous things, nor teachers except a corrupt imagination or a mind diseased by the devil. They are also to be distinguished from *Veneficae*, who injure men and beasts by poisons swallowed or rubbed in, or by their breath."[53] Pierre de Lancre also recognized two types of witches: those who dealt in poisons and botanical drugs, and those who performed their occult feats miraculously with the aid of Satan.[54]

Conceivably, the witches' ointments were invented and dispensed by *veneficae*, specialists in botanical drugs. As *veneficium* was gradually assimilated into the stereotype of diabolical witchcraft, its practitioners came under persecution as witches, and the ecstatic states induced by the unguents they dispensed acquired sinister attributes in the minds of churchmen, magistrates, and Inquisitors. Demonological propaganda may have also convinced some of those who used such ointments that their drug-induced dreams and hallucinations were indeed diabolical in nature.

Figure 7.8 *Veneficae* about to poison a sleeping woman. From Francesco Maria Guazzo's *Compendium Maleficarum* (1626 edition). Courtesy of the Special Collections Library, Duke University.

But why were hallucinogenic salves used in the first place? The pharmacological properties of these compounds suggest a possible answer. Dr. Ludwig Mejer, author of *Die Periode der*

Hexenprocesse (1882), argued that the idea of sexual intercourse with demons, which figured so prominently in European demonology—and the timing of witch-trials themselves—coincided with the introduction and use of thorn apple (*Datura stramonium*) during the late Middle Ages. Datura, he argued, produces intense hallucinations with sexual characteristics so vivid in nature that they are often mistaken for actual events.[55]

The drug, introduced into Europe by gypsies, according to Mejer, soon became popular among members of the indigent classes, who began to depend upon it more and more as a means of relieving the tedium of their miserable existence. However, some users were so terrified by what they experienced (i.e., hallucinations of intercourse with what were thought to be demonic creatures) that they revealed in the confessionals what they believed to have really taken place. Perplexed churchmen immediately issued warnings about, and took steps to counteract, the new crime of sexual intercourse with the minions of hell.[56] "And it is perfectly obvious" wrote Mejer, "that the thorn apple and witch-trials followed the same path, and it was the thorn apple that invariably made its appearance shortly before the commencement of witch-trials in a given area—at least, as far as we can establish this, given the secrecy that at first surrounded the planting of the thorn apple."[57]

It may be argued that the fantastic elements in the Sabbat imagery of the demonologists (i.e., magic flight, metamorphosis into animals, encounters with supernatural beings), may well have been rooted in drug-induced hallucinations. Such a contention would certainly entail fewer leaps of logic, than attempts "to decipher" or seek the presence of ancient pagan beliefs or archaic shamanistic survivals in the rhetoric of the witch-doctors and witch-burning judges, as writers such as Thomas or Ginzburg have done.[58]

Mejer's argument has some merit. In small doses, *atropine*, *scopolamine*, and *hyoscyamine* do act as sedatives, producing pleasing hallucinations and vivid erotic dreams.[59] According to Hesse: "[Solanaceae] hallucinations are frequently dominated by the erotic moment.... In those days, in order to experience these [erotic] sensations, young and old women would rub their bodies with the 'witches' salve,' of which the active ingredient was belladonna or an extract of some other solanaceae."[60] Solanaceae are still used in this manner by the peasantry in parts of western and central Europe.[61] Thus, it is quite possible that the witches' ointments may have been employed simply for recreational purposes.

Figure 7.9 *Datura stramonium*. Some researchers have posited that the idea of sexual relations with demons and the timing of the witch-trials coincided with an epidemic of drug abuse stemming from the recreational use of datura. From James W. Hardin and Jay M. Arena, *Human Poisoning from Native and Cultivated Plants*, fig. 63 p. 138. Copyright © 1974, Duke University Press, Durham, NC. Reprinted with permission.

From their prominence in documents we can surmise that hallucinogenic drugs were used extensively.[62] Indeed, medieval and post-medieval European society may have been experiencing epidemics of drug abuse,[63] as Dr. Mejer maintained. The prolonged use of Solanaceae alkaloids can lead to acute psychotic reactions, conditions conducive to charges of witchcraft. The indiscriminate use of datura, one of the ingredients frequently found in the witches' salves, for instance, can lead to permanent insanity,[64] a fact which may account for at least some of the cases involving individuals who voluntarily came forward and confessed to outlandish witchcraft-related crimes. As Lewin wrote, "The mental disorder caused by ... datura has ... instigated some persons to accuse themselves before a tribunal. The peculiar hallucinations evoked by the drug had been so powerfully transmitted from the subconscious mind to consciousness that mentally uncultivated persons, nourished in their absurd superstitions by the Church, believed them to be reality."[65]

Such observations do not warrant the conclusion, however, that the demonological theory of witchcraft and its sequela, witch-hunting, had their origins in the drug-induced psychosis of particular individuals. The theory of witchcraft, as we have seen, comprised sets of logically coherent axioms founded on Christian theology and formulated in the context of particular sociopolitical circumstances. Hence, European witchcraft is better understood in sociological rather than psychological or pharmacological terms.

Psychochemical Torture

Drugs administered by torturers and exorcists to produce desired states of mind among their victims and patients, respectively, may prove to be more significant than any opiate or narcotic used by alleged witches. In his *Cautio Criminalis* (1632), Spee wrote that torture technicians who were unable to extract a confession from their victims forced them to drink a potion which produced disorders of the brain, thus leading to bizarre confessions.[66] Similarly, Weyer, in his treatise *De Lamiis* (1577), pointed out that confessions to impossible crimes were "elicited by administering potions causing drunkenness or mental disturbance."[67] In Rottenburg, Germany, in 1530, authorities obtained confessions from three women suspected of witchcraft, who had resisted 186 applications of the *strappado*, through the administration of a special potion.[68] A similar concoction was employed for the same purpose in the German town of Esslingen in 1562.[69] Likewise, an accused werewolf from Westphalia, who resisted twenty applications of torture, finally confessed after being forced to imbibe an intoxicating draught.[70] A comparable incident occurred in Denham, England (1585-1586), when an intoxicating potion was used by exorcists to induce their patient into believing that she really was possessed.[71]

Figure 7.10   Confession to impossible crimes were elicited through psychochemical persuasion. Hallucinogenic potions administered by torture-technicians to produce desired states of mind among their victims may prove to have played a more significant role in European witchcraft than any opiate or narcotic used by alleged witches. From Samuel Chandler's *The History of Persecution* (1736). By permission of Special Collections and Archives, Milton S. Eishenhower Library, The Johns Hopkins University.

European torture technicians, we have already seen, had a wide assortment of tools and techniques at their disposal for extracting confessions, ranging from mechanical devices designed to inflict gross tissue damage, to psychological and physiological techniques, such as solitary confinement and sleep deprivation. Hallucinogenic or psychotomimetic drugs appear to have been part of this arsenal of weapons at the disposal of the interrogators. Although drugs have not proven to be effective tools for "brainwashing," i.e., radically and permanently altering the personality,[72] drug-induced psychosis can be an extremely unnerving experience, and chemical torture can thus be a formidable tool.

Atropine and *scopolamine*, for instance, often produce frightening and disagreeable symptoms, and subjects who have experienced such effects rarely use these drugs a second time.[73] This may explain why the witches' ointments were applied topically: inunction (introducing a drug into the body through the skin) is often used when it is necessary to maintain low levels of a drug in the blood stream.[74]

A person under the influence of *Atropine*, according to Schenk, "may easily be subordinated to another's will, for he is completely open to influence and will do whatever he is told. If he has swallowed a great deal of the poison, this state of confusion and sensory derangement leads to a temporary, but acute, mental disorder exactly resembling a symptomatic psychosis. Sudden outbursts of delirium and increasingly intense periods of mania create a terrifying and uncanny clinical picture, which finally ends in convulsions similar to those of epilepsy."[75] Similarly, *hyoscyamine*, when given even in moderate doses causes, among other symptoms, delirium, near blindness, and unbearable pain.[76] Mixtures containing both these drugs, as well as those containing extracts of mandrake and datura, which would have had similar effects, were administered to suspected witches prior to torture.[77]

Such drugs, used to induce debility, would, by disrupting the perceptual and conceptual processes, confuse and weaken the victim.[78] The result of such psychochemical torture would be a mixture of fantasy, delusional and hallucinatory memories, interspersed with random real ones,[79] precisely the kinds of confessions magistrates and torture technicians sought and obtained. Again, according to Lewin: "We find these plants [the Solanaceae species discussed] associated with incomprehensible acts on the part of fanatics, raging with the flames of frenzy and fury and persecuting not only witches and sorcerers but also mankind as a whole. Garbed in the cowl, the judge's robe, and the physician's gown, superstitious folly instituted diabolical proceedings in a trial of the devil and hurled its victims into the flames or drowned them in blood."[80] Given the propaganda value of confessions and cases of demonic possession, it is very likely that hallucinogenic drugs, administered to produce dramatic effects, may have been used more extensively for this objective than hitherto suspected.

Notes

1. The *Canon Episcopi*, incorporated into the *Corpus Juris Canonici* in 1140 A.D., was held as the highest authority on matters of orthodoxy. It dismissed witchcraft, night-flights, and metamorphosis as pagan superstitions and illusions.
2. In Kors and Peters (1972:29–31).
3. Burr (1943b:173–176).
4. Monter (1969:53–54).
5. Boguet (1929 [1602]:42).
6. Anonymous, *Malleus Judicum* (circa 1630); Lea (1939:691–692).
7. See Lea (1939:560, 911, 914).
8. Johannes Nider (1380–1438) wrote the book circa 1435. The first edition was published in Augsburg in 1475.
9. Lea (1939:260–261).
10. See Dioscorides' *De Medica Materia* (1529).
11. In Rothman (1972).
12. Scot's (1584:184–185) translation; Porta (1561:85).
13. In Scot (1584:185). Reginald Scot included Porta's account in his *The Discoverie of Witchcraft*. But, he pointed out that, "It shall not be amiss here in this place to repeat an ointment greatly to this purpose, rehearsed by [Porta] ... wherein although he may be overtaken and cozened by an old witch, and made not only to believe, but also to report a false tale; yet because it greatly overthrows the opinion of [the *Malleus Maleficarum*] Bodin, and such other, as write so absolutely in maintenance of witches transportations, I will set down his words in this behalf." Porta's tale, it may be noted, is remarkably similar to Nider's account. Scot's caveat

concerning the reliability of such information, ancient and modern, is therefore worth keeping in mind.

14. See Duerr (1985:140–141) for various formulae found in the demonological tomes.

15. Schenk (1955:33).

16. Taken internally, mandrake causes stupor and deep sleep which can last for days. During the time of the Roman occupation of Israel, in order to produce the appearance of death, Sanhedrin women sometimes administered *morian* (an infusion of wine laced with mandrake) to crucified prisoners by means of a sponge attached to the end of a pole. The apparently deceased prisoners were then taken down from the cross and afterward secretly revived (Blum et al. 1969:124). Some scholars have speculated that the death and resurrection of Jesus might have been achieved in this manner (Schonfield 1971:159; C. J. S. Thompson 1934:225–226). Thus, mandrake may have had a more significant role in the history of Christianity than simply its involvement in European witchcraft.

17. *Atropine* ($C_{17} H_{23} N_{03}$), *d,l-hyoscyamine* ($C_{17} H_{23} N_{03}$), and *scopolamine* ($C_{17} H_{21} N_{04}$).

18. Shader and Greenblatt (1972:104); Schultes and Hofmann (1979:86–87).

19. Shader and Greenblatt (1972:113); Schultes and Hofmann (1979:86–87); Siegel (1984:14).

20. See Hansen (1978:95).

21. Shader and Greenblatt (1972:124).

22. Schultes and Hofmann (1979:82).

23. Barber (1967:171).

24. Lewin (1931:130).

25. A. J. Clark (1971 [1921]:279–280); Führner (1930:37); Norman (1933:291–292).

26. Conklin (1958:173, note 7); Sollmann (1936:370); Levine (1973:89).

27. Thienes and Haley (1955:20).

28. For example, see Ferckel (1979:15–16).

29. Schenk (1955:48).

30. Kaye (1954:372).

31. For example, Hansen (1978:101–102); Barnett (1965a; 1965b); Harner (1973); Haarstad (1964); Emboden (1979:129); Harris (1975:217); Witters and Jones-Witters (1972:105); Duerr (1985).

32. Hoyt (1981:113).

33. Schultes and Hofmann (1979:87).

34. For example, Levack (1987:45).

35. Klaits (1985:11).

36. See Henningsen (1980:297–298).

37. Rothman (1972:562).

38. Hofmann (1980:24).

39. Lea (1939:970–971).

40. Valle de Moura (1620); Lea (1939:480).

41. Remy (1930 [1595]:2).

42. In Pratt (1915:60).

43. Fletcher (1896:148).

44. For example, see Hansen (1978:101–102); Barnett (1965a; 1965b); Harner (1973); Emboden (1979:129); Harris (1975:217); Quaife (1987:202); Witters and Jones-Witters (1972:105); Duerr (1985).
45. Scot (1584:121).
46. Schenk (1955:945).
47. Fletcher (1896:147).
48. See Allen (1979). One writer, who attributes an unwarranted degree of sophistication to the witches' lotions, believes that *bufotenine* was used specifically to produce the hallucination of flight (Quaife 1987:201).
49. Hollyhock (1965:226); Schultes (1976:28); Duerr (1985:138–140); Allen (1979:265–268).
50. Furst (1982:161).
51. Trachtenberg (1987 [1939]:5); Hansen (1978:79). One of the poisons closely associated with *veneficium* and sorcery was Aqua Tofana, a toxin invented in the mid-seventeenth century by an Italian sorceress named Teofania di Adamo. Four to six drops of this odorless, colorless, tasteless, and deadly toxin was allegedly sufficient to cause death. By regulating the dose and frequency of administration, it was said, death could come within anywhere from one day to several months (The Society For the Diffusion of Useful Knowledge 1846:204, 443–444). During the eighteenth century, Mozart thought himself poisoned at the hands of his enemies by means of this lethal liquid (Carr 1983:370).
52. Pratt (1915:63).
53. Lea (1939:491).
54. Langdon-Brown (1942:29).
55. Lea (1939:1076); Duerr (1985:76, 291–292).
56. Credit for the so-called "pharmacological theory of witchcraft" unquestionably belongs to the imaginative Dr. Mejer.
57. In Kunze (1987:271).
58. See Ginzburg (1991:303).
59. Conklin (1958:172); Hansen (1978:55); Sollmann (1936:374); Taylor (1963:148–149).
60. Hesse (1946:103).
61. Baroja (1964:256–257); Hesse (1946:103); Risso and Böker (1968:966–967).
62. Pratt (1915:112).
63. See Surawicz and Banta (1975:537–540) and Camporesi (1985:123–130, 134).
64. Furst (1982:140).
65. Lewin (1931:130).
66. Lea (1939:903).
67. Lea (1939:542).
68. Midelfort (1972:91, 245 note 19).
69. Midelfort (1972:245 note 19).
70. Mackay (1932 [1841]:538).
71. Walker (1981:46–47).
72. Schlaadt and Shannon (1982:169).
73. Hollister (1968:13).
74. Schlaadt and Shannon (1982:45, 57).
75. Schenk (1955:36–37).
76. Le Strange (1977:141).

77.   Hansen (1978:36); Lewin (1931:134–135).
78.   Barber (1967:162).
79.   *Report on Torture* (1975:56).
80.   Lewin (1931:129–131).

Chapter Eight

Werewolves and Witches

Toward the end of the sixteenth century, while the witch-hunts gained terrible momentum across Europe, numerous people were tried and executed as werewolves. In France werewolves, or lycanthropes (from the Greek *lukos*, "wolf," and *anthropos*, "man"), were known as *loup-garou*, in Germany, *währ-wölffe*, and in Italy, *lupo manaro*.[1] The increasing preoccupation with, and apprehension concerning, lycanthropy is reflected both in the numbers of people brought to trial and in the fact that between 1591 and 1686 no less than fourteen major treatises were written on the subject.[2]

Demonologists maintained that werewolves were actually witches who, through magical procedures and diabolical pacts, changed themselves into wolves and, while in the form of these ravenous and ferocious beasts—possessing supernatural cunning, strength, and speed—committed unspeakable atrocities, killing men, women, children, and livestock. Witches transformed themselves, or shifted shape, into wolves, demonographers argued, because of their innate greed, cruelty, lust for human flesh, thirst for human blood, and a desire to execute their heinous works without being identified.[3]

One skilled in this witchcraft, according to Bishop Olaus Magnus' *A Compendious History of the Goths, Swedes, & Vandals, and Other Northern Nations* (1658): "when he pleases ... may change his human form, into the form of a wolf entirely, going into some

Figure 8.1 A werewolf devouring a woman. Werewolves were witches who changed their shape by magical procedures and diabolical pacts. From a 19th century engraving. By permission of the Mansell Collection, London.

private cellar or secret wood. Again, he can after some time put off the shape he took upon himself, and resume the form he had before at his pleasure."[4] Such a metamorphosis was achieved by the witch donning a wolf's skin, uttering incantations, and anointing his or her body with magical unguents. As the historian Richard Verstegan observed in his *Restitution of Decayed Intelligence* (1605): "werewolves are certain sorcerers, who having anointed their bodies, with an ointment which they make by the instinct of the devil; and putting on a certain enchanted girdle, do not only unto the view of others seem as wolves, but to their own thinking have both the shape and nature of wolves, so long as they wear the said girdle. And they do dispose themselves as very wolves, in worrying and killing, the most human creatures."[5]

Werewolves appear to have been particularly troublesome in northern Europe. According to Olaus Magnus: "In Prussia, Kurland [Latvia], and Lithuania, although the inhabitants suffer considerably from the rapacity of wolves throughout the year, in that these animals rend their cattle, which are scattered in great numbers through the woods, whenever they stray in the very least, yet this is not regarded by them as such a serious matter as what they endure from men turned into wolves.... On the feast of the Nativity of Christ, at night, such a multitude of wolves transformed from men gather together in a certain spot, arranged among themselves, and then spread to rage with wondrous ferocity against human beings, and those animals which are not wild, that the natives of these regions suffer more detriment from these, than they do from true wolves; for when a human habitation has been detected by them isolated in the woods, they besiege it with atrocity, striving to break in the doors, and in the event of their doing so, they devour all the human beings, and every animal which is found within. They burst into the beer cellars, and there they empty the tuns of beer or mead, and pile up the casks one above another in the middle of the cellar, thus showing their difference from natural and genuine wolves...."[6] France, Switzerland, Germany, and Italy also suffered the predations of these human-wolves.[7]

The idea of werewolves and were-animals (zooanthropes) dates back to antiquity and, like the concept of *maleficium*, is found cross-culturally.[8] During the sixteenth and seventeenth centuries in Europe, however, beliefs concerning werewolves and the metamorphosis of people into animals were assimilated into the demonological theory of witchcraft. It is this particular conception of lycanthropy which is the focus of the present chapter.

Experts on witchcraft agreed that shape-shifting was achieved through demonic agencies and pacts with the Devil, but they disagreed among themselves over the precise mechanisms by which such a metamorphosis was accomplished. A major difficulty was posed by the *Canon Episcopi*, which stated that,

> Whoever ... believes that anything can be made, or that any creature can be changed to better or to worse or to be transformed into another species or similitude, except by the Creator himself who made everything and through whom all things were made, is beyond doubt an infidel.[9]

In an attempt to reconcile the demonological position with the edicts of the *Canon Episcopi*, the *Malleus Maleficarum* forwarded the idea of prestidigitory transmutations and glamour, "by which things seem to be transmuted into other likenesses."[10] After a tortuous and convoluted argument, the *Malleus* asserted that the Canon referred to "real" transformations, whereas the transubstantiation of witches was simply an exterior illusion. According to Guazzo, one advocate of this theory: "the demon surrounds a witch with an aerial effigy of a beast, each part of which fits on to the correspondent part of the witch's body, head to head, mouth to mouth, belly to belly, foot to foot, and arm to arm.... In this ... case it is no matter for wonder if they are afterwards found with an actual wound in those parts of their human body where they were wounded when in the appearance of a beast; for the enveloping air easily yields, and the true body receives the wound."[11]

Boguet forwarded a somewhat different explanation, thereby avoiding the dilemma posed by Canon Law: "My own opinion is that Satan sometimes leaves the witch asleep behind a bush, and himself goes and performs that which the witch has in mind to do, giving himself the appearance of a wolf, but that he so confuses the witch's imagination that [the witch] believes he has really been a wolf and has run about and killed men and beasts.... And when it happens that they find themselves wounded, it is Satan who immediately transfers to them the blow ... which he has received in his assumed body."[12]

Alternatively, the theologian Geiler von Kaysersberg maintained that the Devil compelled natural wolves to kill humans and livestock, and then impressed upon the witch the idea that it was he or she who had committed the savage acts. Diabolically energized the Devil, or wolves possessed by the Devil, were especially feared, because such creatures were thought to be impossible to capture, injure, or kill.[13]

Figure 8.2   In the view of some demonologists, the metamorphosis of men into beasts was achieved by the Devil, who surrounded the witch with an aerial effigy, giving him the appearance of a wolf. From Francesco Maria Guazzo's *Compendium Maleficarum* (1626 edition). Courtesy of the Special Collections Library, Duke University.

Other demonologists argued that the belief in the physical transformation of humans into animals was so widely and obstinately held that it could not be entirely without foundations. As Remy observed: "It is not only the external physical shape that appears to be changed; the witch is also endowed with all the natural qualities and power of the animal into which she is seemingly changed. For she acquires fleetness of foot; bodily strength; ravenous ferocity; the lust of howling; the faculty of breaking into places, and of silent movement; and other such animal characteristics, which are far beyond human strength or ability. For it is a matter of daily experience that Satan does actually so empower them. Thus they easily kill even the biggest cattle in the fields, and even devour their raw flesh.... Now this cannot be explained away as mere glamour or prestige by which our senses are deceived ... for they leave behind them concrete traces of their activities."[14] Bodin also believed that shape-shifting involved an actual physical transformation.[15] Proponents of this perspective attempted to accommodate the interdictions of the *Canon Episcopi* by arguing that although the human form was altered during metamorphosis, the soul—God's perfect creation—remained unchanged.

Wolves and Werewolves

The common European wolf (*Canis lupus*) became particularly troublesome after the massive casualties of the Black Death led to the abandonment of formerly cultivated lands and inhabited villages (a phenomenon known as *Wüstungen*), reversing the deforestation of the previous centuries and facilitating the resurgence of dwindling wolf populations.[16] Indeed, fifteenth- and sixteenth-century European chroniclers frequently reported the presence of roaming wolves in both urban and rural areas.[17] Wolves preyed heavily on livestock and other domestic animals (due to the extermination of many of their natural prey by hunters), and on occasion they also attacked humans. Sometimes such depredations were imputed to werewolves, i.e., cruel, treacherous, and ferocious wolves possessing the reasoning power and intelligence of a human.[18] The heightened fear of werewolves

Figure 8.3 A witch traveling to the Sabbat astride a wolf. Demonological propaganda caste the already dreaded wolf as a diabolical creature associated with evil. After a page from Ulrich Molitor's *De Lamiis et Phitonicis Mulierbus* (1489).

appears to have been partially connected to the increasing fear and terror inculcated by demonological propaganda.[19]

In France, a country which historically experienced severe onslaughts by wolves,[20] a large number of people were executed for shape-shifting. Similarly, in the wolf-infested Franche-Comté, numerous men and women were burned as werewolves.[21] In the wolf-ridden Pyrenees, at least two hundred individuals were put to death for lycanthropy.[22] In countries such as England, on the other hand, where a combination of large-scale, organized hunting and massive deforestation resulted in the extermination of wolves by the sixteenth century,[23] werewolves, and even tales about werewolves, were nearly absent.[24]

Figure 8.4 A contemporary engraving depicting the pursuit and capture of the monstrous Werewolf of Anspach. By permission of the Mansell Collection, London.

The ascription of anthropomorphic attributes to wolves suggests the horror and trepidation generated by these animals— reactions evident on numerous occasions. In 1685, for example, the inhabitants of Anspach [now Ansbach], Germany were terrorized by a wolf reported to have killed a number of women, children, and domestic animals. This creature was thought to be a werewolf, the reincarnation of the town's detested Burgomaster who had recently died. After a long and difficult search by local hunters, the presumed werewolf was found, chased into a well, and killed. The townsmen then retrieved the wolf's carcass, dressed it in a flesh-colored suit, and adorned its head with a mask, wig, and beard, giving the dead beast the appearance of the Burgomaster. They hung the creature from a gibbet, where it could be viewed publicly, and later put it on permanent display at a museum to prove that werewolves did indeed exist.[25]

A more dramatic incident took place in Gévaudan, south-central France, between the July, 1764 and June, 1767, when a pair of extremely large and peculiarly colored man-eating wolves, responsible for the death of sixty to one hundred people, caused great terror in the community.[26] Many who believed the killings to be the work of a single creature—an infernal werewolf—named it the "Beast of Gévaudan."[27] Professional wolf-hunters and teams of dogs were brought in, along with several detachments of dragoons, to stalk the fiendish animal, while the authorities posted huge bounties. At one point nearly 20,000 men from seventy-three parishes joined the hunt; and as a consequence more than a thousand wolves were slaughtered, although the "Beast" was not among them.[28] The elusive creatures remained at large and continued their destructive habits, until the male of the pair was finally killed on September 21, 1766, and the female some nine months later.

In both of these instances, actual wolves were killed. But far more often than not, during the sixteenth and seventeenth centuries, it was presumed shape-shifters who, on the basis of highly circumstantial evidence, were blamed for general misfortunes, or damage caused by wolves, and were sought out and executed as werewolves.

Indeed, in some of the most sensational cases of werewolfism,[29] the coincidence of two separate and often totally unrelated events—the sighting of a wolf, on the one hand, and the subsequent presence of a human in the vicinity, on the other—was sufficient ground for legal action. Sometimes the concrete evidence in these cases was the discovery of "sympathetic wounds" (i.e., injuries found on the body of a suspect corresponding to wounds inflicted on a wolf). A typical trial of this nature occurred in 1521, when Jean Boin, the Inquisitor of Besançon, tried Pierre Bourgot, Michel Verdun, and Philibert Montot, "the werewolves of Poligny," for lycanthropy and for having made a compact with the Demon.

These men came under suspicion when a traveler passing through the area was attacked by a wolf. While defending himself, he was able to wound the animal, forcing it to retreat. Following the trail of the injured creature, the man came upon a hut were he found a local resident, Michel Verdun, under the care of his wife, who was washing a wound on his body. Believing Verdun's injury to be a sympathetic wound, the man notified the authorities. Arrested and tortured, Verdun admitted that he was a shape-shifter; he also revealed the names of his two werewolf accomplices, as well as confessing to hideous crimes: diabolism, murder, and eating human flesh.[30] The three men were promptly executed.

The widely publicized and often cited trial of Gilles Garnier, the Hermit of Dôle (St. Bonnot), is another instance when wolf depredations comprised part of the tangible evidence against an alleged human shape-shifter. Details of the incident are to be found in Baring-Gould's *The Book of Werewolves* (1865): "[On the 8th of November, 1573] some peasants of Chastenoy were returning home from their work, through the forest, [when] the screams of a child and the deep baying of a wolf, attracted their notice, and on running in the direction whence the cries sounded, they found a little girl defending herself against a monstrous creature, which was attacking her tooth and nail, and had already wounded her severely in five places. As the peasants came up, the creature fled on all fours into the gloom of the thicket; it was so dark that it could not be identified with certainty, and whilst some affirmed that it was a wolf, others thought they had recognized the features of the hermit."[31]

This incident was followed by the disappearance of a boy, on November 15, and shortly after, by the murder of two girls and the slaying of a young boy. The children were presumed to have fallen victim to the *loup-garou*.

In the following weeks, the frequency of werewolf's attacks seems to have increased, and the creature began seeking adult victims. Meanwhile, suspicions about the hermit were heightened. The authorities, alarmed at the number of werewolf attacks, gave permission for the residents of Franche-Comté to hunt the monster that scourged the countryside. The decree issued on December 3, 1573, reads as follows:

> According to the advertisement made to the sovereign Court of the Parliament at Dôle, that, in the territories of Espagny, Salvange, Courchapon, and the neighbouring villages, has often been seen and met, for some time past, a were-wolf, who, it is said, has already seized and carried off several little children, so that they have not been seen since, and since he has attacked and done injury in the country to some horsemen, who kept him off only with great difficulty and danger to their persons: the said Court, desiring to prevent any greater danger, has permitted, and does permit, those who are abiding or dwelling in the said places and others, notwithstanding all edicts concerning the chase [i.e., a ban on hunting] to assemble with pikes, halberts, arquebuses, and sticks, to chase and to pursue the said were-wolf in every place where they may find or seize him; to tie and to kill, without incurring any pains or penalties....[32]

The ensuing werewolf-hunt ended with the apprehension of Garnier, who was discovered dragging the body of a young boy into the forest. The suspect was described as follows: "The man, Gilles Garnier, was a somber, ill-looking fellow, who walked in a stooping attitude, and whose pale face, livid complexion, and deep-set eyes under a pair of coarse and bushy eyebrows, which met across the forehead [one of the signs of werewolfism], were sufficient to repel any one from seeking his acquaintance. Gilles seldom spoke, and when he did it was in the broadest patois [vernacular] of his country. His long gray beard and retiring habits procured him the name the Hermit of St. Bonnot, though no one for a moment attributed to him any extraordinary amount of sanctity."[33]

Because of his marginal position, reclusive life style, and atypical behavior (common characteristics of the majority of accused werewolves), Garnier was an ideal candidate for accusations of witchcraft, or in this case, werewolfism. In the lurid accounts made public following his capture, he was said to have savagely slain several children while in the shape of a wolf, eating part of their flesh immediately and taking the rest home to share

Figure 8.5 A werewolf who has slain several people, carries off an infant in his mouth. On occasion, werewolves killed and ate their victims without shifting shape. From a sixteenth-century engraving by Lucas Cranach. By permission of Bibliothèque Nationale, Paris.

with his wife. On one occasion, according to Boguet, the monstrous Garnier had even attempted to kill and eat a young boy without shifting shape.[34]

The motives behind Garnier's offenses were as shocking as his crimes. According to a contemporary account written by one Daniel d'Ange to the Dean of the Church of Sens, "Gilles Garnier, lycophile, as I may call him, lived the life of a hermit, but has since taken a wife, and having no means of support for his family fell into the way, as is natural to defiant and desperate people of rude habits, of wandering into the woods and wild places. In this state he was met by a phantom in the shape of a man, who told him that he could perform miracles, among other things declaring that he would teach him how to change at will into a wolf, lion, or leopard, and because the wolf is more familiar in this country than the other kinds of wild beasts he chose to disguise himself in that shape, which he did, using a salve with which he rubbed himself for this purpose, as he has since confessed before dying, after recognising the evil of his ways."[35] Garnier's confession was extorted on the rack; he was burned at the stake on January 18, 1574.[36] What possessions he had were sold to cover the costs of his trial and execution.[37]

Garnier was probably guilty of murder, or perhaps, as Barry Lopez suggests in his splendid book, *Of Wolves and Men* (1978), guilty of scavenging a dead body in the forest and of being a recluse and a beggar.[38] In any case, it is possible that at least some of the damage attributed to Garnier, the presumed human-wolf, was simply the work of ordinary wolves.

The trial of Jacques Roulet, the werewolf of Angers, another widely sensationalized case, followed the same pattern. Details of the incident, which took place in 1598, are provided by Baring-Gould: "In a wild and unfrequented spot near Caude [in the vicinity of Angers, France], some countrymen came one day upon the corpse of a boy of fifteen, horribly mutilated and bespattered with blood. As the men approached, two wolves, which had been rending the body, bounded away into the thicket. The men gave chase immediately, following their bloody tracks till they lost them; when suddenly crouching among the bushes, his teeth chattering with fear, they found a man half naked, with long hair and beard, and with his hands dyed in blood. His nails were long as claws, and were clotted with fresh gore, and shreds of human flesh."[39] Although the miscreant was immediately arrested on the basis of the physical evidence, exactly how the authorities determined that the "gore" under Roulet's fingernails was human flesh (an impossible task without a modern forensic laboratory) is never mentioned.

The suspect, a beggar and vagabond, admitted under severe duress that he was able to transform himself into a wolf by means of a salve given to him by his parents. He also revealed that in the company of his brother Jean and cousin Julien—shape-shifters as well—he had killed numerous women and children and devoured their flesh. The *lieutenant criminel* of Angers condemned Roulet to death for werewolfism, murder, and cannibalism; however, on appeal to the Parliament of Paris, Roulet was committed to an insane asylum for two years because the authorities in Paris deemed his confession to be unreliable on account of his feeblemindedness.

In the case of the Gandillon family, another infamous werewolf trial, the activity of a wolf once again constituted the solid evidence. The incident took place in 1598, in the Jura Mountains, when a young boy and girl were attacked by a huge wolf: the girl was instantly killed, while the boy, who defended himself with a knife and injured the creature, was mortally wounded and died later. A party of men pursued the beast, but a short time later encountered Perrentte Gandillon, a simpleminded woman from St.-Claude. Suspected of being the wolf in question based on the evidence of a sympathetic wound,[40] she was seized and killed by an enraged peasant mob. The authorities went on to apprehend her sister, Antoinette, who was accused of witchcraft, her brother, Pierre, and his son, Georges Gandillon.

While in captivity, the Gandillon men behaved like animals, howling, barking like dogs, and crawling on all fours, presenting a frightening spectacle to all who saw them. Pierre Gandillon, Boguet wrote, "was so much disfigured ... that he bore hardly any resemblance to a man, and struck with horror those who looked at him."[41] Pierre and his son both confessed to having attended Sabbats and worshipping the Devil while they assumed the shape of wolves; and Antoinette admitted to being a witch. The community of St.-Claude was much relieved when these three remaining members of the disdained and cantankerous Gandillon family, long suspected of wrongdoings, were burned alive at the stake.

Finally, in 1603, in the St.-Sever district of Gascony, France, a community which had experienced a series of wolf attacks and disappearances of children, found a human malefactor, a thirteen-year-old boy named Jean Grenier, a beggar and part-time cowherd who had boasted to some girls that he could transform himself into a wolf.[42] On the basis of this evidence, the Parliament of Bordeaux convicted Grenier to life imprisonment in a monastery.

Werewolf-Hunts and Lycanthropy Trials

Trials and executions for lycanthropy occurred in France, Franche-Comté, Switzerland, Italy, and Germany. One of the earlier legal proceedings against a suspected werewolf took place in Basel, Switzerland, in 1407 (Map 8.1); and a woman in Andermatt, Switzerland, was beheaded, in 1459, for turning herself into a wolf and causing an avalanche while in the company of the Devil.[43] Another werewolf was executed in 1448, in Switzerland's Pays de Vaude. The majority of werewolf-hunts and persecutions in Switzerland, however, occurred during the sixteenth and seventeenth centuries. In Neuchâtel's Val de Travers, two lycanthropes were apprehended around 1580.[44] In Pays de Vaud werewolves were caught in 1602, 1624, and 1670.[45] In his *De la lycanthropie, transformation, et extase des sorciers* (1615), the physician Jean de Nynauld discussed the five werewolves of Cressi (Lausanne) who were put to death in 1604 for the crimes of lycanthropy, murder, cannibalism, and attending the Sabbat.[46]

A number of sensational werewolf trials were held in Franche-Comté. The first of these was the prosecution of the werewolves of Poligny in 1521, followed by the conviction of Gilles Garnier in Dôle, mentioned earlier. Another werewolf case was reported in Dôle in 1605. In St.-Claude the Gandillons were tried and executed in 1598. Also apprehended and burned alive for lycanthropy at about the same time were Clauda Jamprost, Thievenne Paget, Clauda Jamguillaume, Jacques Bocquet, Clauda Gaillard, la

Micholette, and Françoise Secretain. Finally, one *loup-garou* was apprehended in Baume in 1599 and one in Orgelet in 1610.

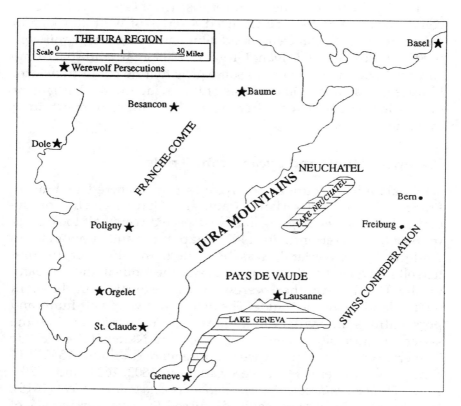

Map 8.1 Werewolf Trials in Switzerland and Franche-Comté

Lorraine (Map 8.2) had a total of five werewolf trials.[47] In 1530, a woman in Poitiers, France, was put to death for werewolfism on the basis of a sympathetic wound.[48] Another woman was executed in Auvergne, in 1558, because of similar circumstances. Boguet related the case: "One evening a gentleman, standing at the window of his chateau, saw a huntsman whom he knew passing by, and asked him to bring him some of his bag on his return. As the huntsman went his way along a valley, he was attacked by a large wolf and discharged his arquebus at it without

Map 8.2 Werewolf Trials in France, Northern Europe, and Germany.

hurting it. He was therefore compelled to grapple with the wolf, and caught it by the ears; but at length, growing weary, he let go of the wolf, drew back and took his big hunting knife, and with it cut off one of the wolf's paws, which he put in his pouch after the wolf had run away. He then returned to the gentleman's chateau, in sight of which he had fought the wolf. The gentleman asked him to give him part of his bag; and the huntsman, wishing to do so and intending to take the paw from his pouch, drew from it a hand wearing a gold ring on one of the fingers, which the gentleman recognized as belonging to his wife. This caused him to entertain an evil suspicion of her; and going into the kitchen, he found his wife nursing her arm in her apron, which he took away, and found that her hand had been cut off. Thereupon the gentleman seized hold of her; but immediately, and as soon as she had been confronted with her hand, she confessed that it was no other than she who, in the form of a wolf, had attacked the hunter.... This was told me by one who may be believed, who went that way fifteen days after this thing had happened."[49] The woman was handed over to the authorities who had her burned alive at the stake in Ryon, before a crowd of several thousand spectators.[50] Of course, the man's real motives for having his wife put to death, rendered inconsequential in light of demonological speculations and the general level of attendant hysteria over werewolves, were never investigated.

In 1598 three werewolves were apprehended in Anjou, including Jacques Roulet (convicted in Angers). In the same year the Parliament of Paris sentenced a man from Châlons to death for werewolfism. Reverend Summers described this particularly horrifying case: "On the 14th of December ... at Paris, a tailor of Châlons was sentenced to be burned quick for his horrible crimes. This wretch was wont to decoy children of both sexes into his shop, and having abused them he would slice their throats and then powder and dress their bodies, jointing them as a butcher cuts up meat. In the twilight, under the shape of a wolf, he roamed the woods to leap out on stray passers-by and tear their throats to shreds. Barrels of bleached bones were found concealed in his cellars as well as other foul and hideous things. He died (it was said) unrepentant and blaspheming. So scabrous were the details of the case that the Court ordered the documents to be burned."[51]

In Germany, the infamous Peeter Stubbe was captured in the Bishopric of Cologne in 1589 (see below). One case of lycanthropy was reported in the Bishopric of Münster in 1615, and another in the city of Hamburg in 1631. Werewolves were also apprehended in the electorate of Trier in 1615 and 1652, a werewolf was reported in Palatinate in 1663, and in Hesse werewolves were caught in 1656 and again in 1683.[52]

Many of the charges of lycanthropy were undoubtedly false: such indictments were used to incriminate irksome neighbors or enemies for misfortunes, such as the loss of livestock or the disappearance of children. These accusations resemble charges of *maleficium*; werewolves, after all, were witches in animal form. A case related by Boguet illustrates the close parallel between witchcraft and lycanthropy: "three wolves ... were seen ... in the district of Douvres and Jeurre about half an hour after a hailstorm had very strangely ruined the fruit of that country. These wolves had no tails; and, moreover, as they ran through herds of cows and goats they touched none of them except one little kid, which one of them carried a little distance away without doing it any harm at all. It is apparent from this that these were not natural wolves, but were rather witches who had helped to cause the hailstorm, and had come to witness the damage they had caused."[53]

Werewolf-hunts instigated by the authorities seem to have had the same sociological functions as witch-hunts: both were public demonstrations against diabolism and deviance, and both served to explain certain kinds of misfortunes. Werewolf alarms were also another means of reifying the threat of the Devil, who was now said to be prowling amidst hamlets, villages, and towns, fiendishly slaying "the Christian flock" while assuming the form of the already sinister and dreaded wolf.[54]

As with witchcraft accusations, it was often beggars, non-conformists, and the socially marginal and expendable who were accused of lycanthropy. Occasionally, suspected mass-killers, such as the tailor from Châlons, were tried as werewolves. Baring-Gould was keenly aware of this fact and devoted several chapters of his *The Book of Werewolves* to the affiliation between mass-murder and lycanthropy.[55]

The most sensational werewolf trial involving multiple murders was that of Peeter Stubbe. Reports of this case, which, like the printed accounts describing cases of witchcraft and demonic possession, were widely circulated both on the Continent and in England, may well have served as both model and catalyst for the subsequent series of werewolf trials which occurred in France, Franche-Comté, Switzerland, and Germany toward the end of the sixteenth century.

The tale of Peeter Stubbe encompasses all the horrors associated with werewolfism: sorcery, diabolism, the use of magical means of transmutation, murder, cannibalism, and more. The English narrative of the proceedings is to be found in the pamphlet *A True Discourse Declaring the Damnable Life and Death of one Stubbe Peeter* (1590): "In the towns ... near Cologne in high Germany, there was continually brought up and nourished one Stubbe Peeter, who from his youth was greatly inclined to evil and practicing of wicked arts ... forgetting the God that made him, and that Savior that shed his blood for man's redemption: In the end, careless of salvation gave both soul and body to the Devil forever, for small carnal pleasure in this life, that he might be famous and spoken of on earth, though he lost heaven thereby. The Devil, who has a ready ear to listen to the lewd motions of cursed men, promised to give him whatsoever his heart desired during his mortal life: whereupon this wild wretch, neither desired riches nor promotions, nor was his fancy satisfied with any external or outward pleasure, but having a tyrannous heart, and a most cruel bloody mind, requested that at his pleasure he might work his malice on men, women, and children, in the shape of some beast, whereby he might live without dread or danger of life, and unknown to be the executor of any bloody enterprise, which he meant to commit: The Devil who saw him a fit instrument to perform mischief as a wicked fiend pleased with the desire of wrong and destruction, gave him a girdle which being put about him, he was straight transformed into the likeness of a greedy devouring wolf, strong and mighty, with eyes great and large, which in the night sparkled like brands of fire, a mouth great and wide, with most sharp and cruel teeth, a huge body, and mighty paws: And no sooner should he put off the same girdle, but presently he should appear in his former shape, according to the proportion of a man, as if he had never been changed...."

Stubbe was accused of numerous rapes and murders. He was also said to have lured his own son into the forest, where he savagely attacked and killed him, broke open his skull and devoured his brain. Stubbe's other crimes included incestuous sexual relations with his own daughter and sister, as well as consorting with a demon who, it was said, appeared to him in the guise of a woman.

The whole region was terrorized by the atrocities of this monster, according to contemporary accounts, and the inhabitants of the area continually found human limbs and other body parts strewn about the countryside. These, it became clear after the werewolf's capture, were the remains of Stubbe's wolfish feasts: "so much he had practiced this wickedness, that the whole province was terrified by the cruelty of this bloody and devouring wolf. Thus continuing his devilish and damnable deeds, within the compass of a few years, he had murdered thirteen young children, and two goodly young women big with child, tearing the children out of their wombs, in most bloody and savage sort, and after eat their hearts panting hot and raw, which he accounted dainty morsels and best agreeing to his appetite...."[56]

Like an ordinary lupus, however, this ravenous *währ-wölffe* also slaughtered livestock: "for when he could not through the wariness of people draw men, women, or children in his danger, then, like a cruel and tyrannous beast he would work his cruelty on ... beasts in most savage sort, and did act more mischief and cruelty than would be credible, although high Germany hath been forced to taste the truth thereof."[57]

Stubbe's capture and the evidence presented for his being a shape-shifter reveal the general pattern of the previously discussed cases, and the search for this monster was not unlike the hunt for the Beast of Gévaudan. The hunters who apprehended Stubbe were, in fact, pursuing an actual wolf at the time: "And although they had practiced all the means that men could devise to take this ravenous beast ... they could not in any wise prevail; notwithstanding they daily continued their purpose, and daily sought to entrap him, and for that intent continually maintained great dogs of much strength to hunt and chase the beast whoresoever they could find him. In the end it pleased God ... that they should spy him in his wolfish likeness, at what time they beset him round about, and most circumspectly set their dogs upon him, in such sort that there was no means to escape ... being hardly pursued at the heels presently he slipped his girdle from about him, whereby the shape of a wolf clean avoided, and he appeared presently in his true shape and likeness, having in his hand a staff as one walking toward the city, but the hunters whose eyes was steadfastly bent upon the beast, [saw] him in the same place metamorphosed contrary to their expectation.... Thus being apprehended, he was shortly after put to the rack in the town of Bedbur, but fearing the torture, he voluntarily confessed [sic] his whole life, and made known the villainies which he had committed for the space of 25 years...."[58]

Stubbe revealed how he had acquired his magic girdle from the Devil and said that he had cast this instrument of metamorphosis in a particular valley shortly before he was captured.[59] But, as is so often the case with such episodes, the crucial bit of tangible evidence somehow vanished. Thus, when men were sent to the spot where the magic girdle lay, "they found nothing at all, for it may be supposed that it was gone to the devil from whence it came, so that it could not be found."[60]

Stubbe was very likely guilty of multiple murders and also of being a sex offender, although his crimes were probably compounded by wolf attacks on livestock and children. The penalties for Stubbe's atrocities included his being torn with red-hot pincers, his limbs broken on the wheel, and finally, after experiencing sufficient anguish, being beheaded. The authorities also condemned Stubbe's daughter and mistress, as accomplices and for their obscene and amoral lifestyles, to be burned alongside Stubbe's decapitated cadaver, a sentence which was duly carried out on October 31, 1589, before a large crowd of spectators.

The sociological parallels between this episode and cases involving witchcraft are obvious: Stubbe's shocking crimes and misdeeds served as a convenient explanation for a series of misfortunes (wolf attacks on children and livestock, and actual murders); it enabled the community to purge from its midst a man

Figure 8.6 The execution of Peeter Stubbe. From a contemporary poster printed in Augsburg, Germany (1589). Courtesy of Staats- und Stadtbibliothek, Augsburg.

and two women who were perceived to be moral deviants; and it amplified the fear of the Devil and his emissaries.

Wolf Madness: Lycanthropy and Disease

The French physician Jean Nynauld, author of *De la lycanthropie, transformation, et extase des sorciers* (1615), maintained that shape-shifting was neither metamorphosis nor enchantment, but merely a delusion or hallucination brought on by drugs or sickness. Similarly, the Oxford cleric Robert Burton said in his *The Anatomy of Melancholy* (1621) that "lycanthropia," or *Lupina insania* (wolf madness), was a kind of mental illness.[61] Weyer and Scot had forwarded such an opinion earlier, asserting that lycanthropy—the fixation during which a patient believed himself to be a wolf—was a psychiatric pathology.

Although some demonographers also deemed lycanthropy to be altogether different from werewolfism, i.e., the ability of sorcerers and witches to transform themselves into wolves,[62] sixteenth- and seventeenth-century magistrates seldom recognized such a disparity while meting out justice, and often people believing themselves to be wolves were as readily executed as those who were denounced as werewolves by others. (The two exceptions among the cases discussed here were the trials of Roulet and Grenier.)

The following incident, which took place in Pavia, Italy, in 1541, illustrates: "a farmer ... as a wolf, fell upon many men in the open country and tore them to pieces. After much trouble the maniac was caught, and he then assured his captors that the only difference which existed between himself and a natural wolf, was that in a true wolf the hair grew outward, whilst in him it struck inward. In order to put this assertion to the proof, the magistrates, themselves most certainly cruel and bloodthirsty wolves, cut off his arms and legs; the poor wretch died of the mutilation."[63]

Approaching the problem from the perspective of those accused, one could assume that, in some cases, mentally disturbed individuals, exhibiting bizarre behavior, may have been suspected of lycanthropy and sent to the stake (although the same reservations concerning psychiatric explanations for witchcraft discussed in Chapter Four apply here as well). Rosenstock and

Vincent, medical researchers who have examined both the modern literature and medieval accounts of lycanthropy list the following possibilities: schizophrenia, organic brain syndrome and psychosis, psychotic depressive reaction, hysterical neurosis of the dissociative type, and manic-depressive psychosis.[64]

The eminent clinical neurologist Dr. Lee Illis suggests porphyria as another disease which may have conceivably led to accusations of lycanthropy.[65] A rare congenital disorder, porphyria is characterized by extreme sensitivity to light (exposure to sunlight causes vesicular erythema), reddish-brown urine, reddish-brown teeth, and ulcers which destroy cartilage and bone, causing the deformation of the nose, ears, and fingers. Mental aberrations, such as hysteria, manic-depressive psychosis, and delirium, characterize this condition as well. Illis argues that the physical deformities, in conjunction with psychopathology and nocturnal wandering due to photosensitivity, could have been mistaken as evidence of werewolfism.

Baxter, referring to the work of Bruno Bettelheim, has remarked that some cases of lycanthropy may have involved abandoned autistic children.[66] Bettelheim, a researcher at the Sonia Shankman Orthogenic School, a laboratory school of the University of Chicago, made a case that the so-called "feral children," human infants allegedly raised by wolves,[67] exhibit the same characteristics as autistic children who come not from the wild, but ordinary, middle-class American homes.

Yet the actions of those suffering from this heartrending condition so closely resemble those of animals that many observers could only explain their behavior by inferring a life in the wild. Such speculations, Bettelheim observes, perhaps originate in the narcissistic unwillingness of humans to admit that these animal-like creatures could have had pasts at all similar to their own.

Severely autistic children are extremely shy and withdrawn from their surroundings; some react with panic to the slightest visible external motion.[68] They prefer to crawl on all fours for some time, urinating and defecating as they walk or run about, and many do not tolerate clothing and run around naked. Often ferocious, these patients may howl and scream, eat only raw food, bare their canines when annoyed or angered, and attack with their

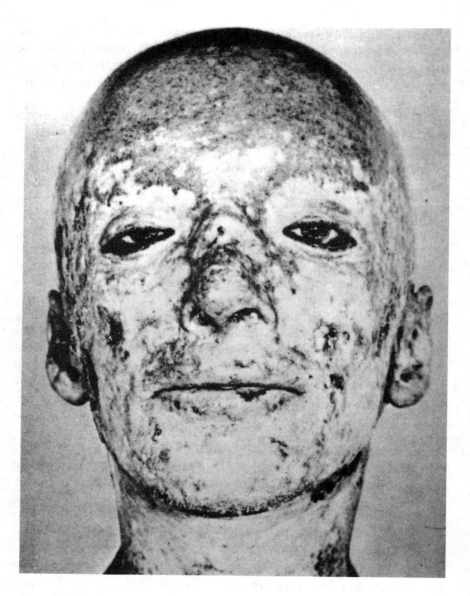

Figure 8.7 A porphyria patient. Victims of this disease might have been accused of werewolfism. From A. Goldberg and C. Riminton, *Diseases of Porphyrin Metabolism* (1962). Courtesy of Charles C. Thomas Publisher, Springfield, Illinois.

claws and teeth. Bettelheim adds, "There are ... more specific reasons to suggest comparing these children with animals. During one year a single staff member had to have medical help more than a dozen times for bites she suffered from [one of the children].... Different, and again reminiscent of animals, is their prowling around at night, in marked contrast to their quiet withdrawal into a corner during the day.... Some will go to almost any length to get raw onions and lettuce and similar food, and go into violent temper tantrums if they do not get them immediately. Others lick salt for hours, but only from their own hands. Others, again, build themselves dens in the dark corners or closets, sleep nowhere else, and prefer spending all day and all night there. Some build caves out of blankets, mattresses, or other suitable objects. They do not permit us to touch either them or their abodes, and at least two of them would eat only if they could carry their food into their self-created caves or dens, where they would then eat without utensils."[69]

Bettelheim argues that one need not suppose that such children were raised by wolves or other creatures in order to account for their pathological behavior. Yet such presumptions are often made, and during the sixteenth and seventeenth centuries this condition could easily have been misconstrued as lycanthropy. While embellishments by demonologists preclude diagnosis in most recorded incidents, the case of Jean Grenier, the young boy sentenced to life imprisonment in a monastery, is an example that comes to mind.[70]

According to Baring-Gould's account, "No sooner was [Grenier] admitted into the precincts of the religious house, than he ran frantically about the cloister and gardens upon all fours, and finding a heap of bloody raw offal, fell upon it and devoured it in an incredibly short space of time.... Delancre visited him some seven years after, and found him diminutive in stature, very shy, and unwilling to look anyone in the face. His eyes were deep set and restless; his teeth long and protruding; his nails black, and in places worn away; his mind was completely barren; he seemed unable to comprehend the smallest things."[71]

Mad Wolves and Wolf Madness

Another possible, and perhaps more probable, explanation for werewolfism is suggested when one examines the circumstances surrounding wolf attacks on people. The stereotype of wolves as human-eaters is not well-founded, as numerous ethologists have argued. An overwhelming number of reports about anthropophagic wolves[72] contain details, such as wolves howling while hunting humans (wolves hunt silently), or running in packs of hundreds (packs rarely exceed more than twenty-five animals), which cannot be reconciled with data generated by modern field studies of wolf behavior.[73]

Vilhjalmer Stefansson, a naturalist who investigated every case involving a human purportedly killed by wolves during the period between 1923 to 1936, covering the Caucasus region, the Near East, Canada, and Alaska, found them all to be spurious or exaggerated. Indeed, many incidents involving "man-eating" wolves have turned out to be sensationalized hoaxes, motivated by the economic interests of agricultural communities whose domestic animals were being preyed upon. Such prevarications have often been used to justify the ruthless and indiscriminate slaughter of entire wolf populations. There are also indications that in a number of cases, attacks by dogs, or feral dogs, have been blamed on wolves.[74]

Zimen, a modern authority on wolves, explains the origins of the stereotype of wolves as man-eater: "In wars and epidemics men died outside inhabited areas, and the wolves no doubt exploited this source of food.... Many assumed killings of human beings by wolves can probably be attributed to their eating corpses."[75] This does not mean, however, that wolves have never attacked people. As Zimen adds, "it would not be surprising if some wolves, having grown accustomed to men, both living and dead, and having learned to distinguish between dangerous and nondangerous ones, should have learned to kill them. Children above all must have been easy prey."[76]

Nevertheless, authenticated wolf attacks on humans are very rare. The naturalist C. H. D. Clarke maintains that ordinary wolves do not bite humans; but, he adds, rabid wolves do. In the majority of cases involving wolves which have killed and eaten human beings, Clarke observes, the animals were rabid.[77]

The notable exceptions were the beasts of Gévaudan. These, however, were not ordinary wolves, as contemporary accounts indicate. They had color markings which were abnormal, and they were exceptionally large for European wolves. Clarke argues convincingly that the beasts of Gévaudan were a dog-wolf cross, exhibiting hybrid vigor (and thus larger than their parents).[78] Such breeds are often more destructive than their wild parents and display less fear of people,[79] traits that would certainly account for the predatory behavior of the creatures of Gévaudan toward humans.

Figure 8.8 A werewolf attacking two men. Rabid wolves behave more like the stereotype of wolves—especially werewolves— than do their healthy counterparts. From Geiler von Kaysersberg's *Die Emeis* (1517). Courtesy of Special Collections and Rare Books, University of Minnesota.

This leaves for consideration rabid wolves, their attacks on *Homo sapiens*, and the consequences of such attacks. A rabid canine, according to clinical observations, becomes "increasingly irritable, restless, and nervous.... It shows exaggerated response to sudden stimuli of sight and sound. Excitability, photophobia, and hyperesthesia may become apparent ... the animal may begin to move and roam, and wander aimlessly, all the time becoming more irritable and vicious; at this stage the animal is now very dangerous because of its tendency to bite anything that it encounters, be it man, animal, or inanimate objects. If the animal is confined it will bite at chains or bars of the cage or kennel, breaking its teeth, and inflicting severe trauma on its oral tissues."[80]

There are numerous reliable reports of rabid wolves traveling long distances, invading villages, and attacking all humans they encountered. These animals show no fear and charge relentlessly, often inflicting massive injuries and deaths. The horror of a crazed beast, frantically assailing people, is often amplified by the hair-raising sounds which rabid animals emit due to the paralysis of their laryngeal musculature.

One such incident took place in 1851, near Hue-Au-Gal, France, where a rabid wolf bit forty-six people and killed eighty-two head of livestock in one day. A similar episode occurred in the Turkish town of Adalia, where another rabid wolf wounded 128 people and killed eighty-five sheep during a single rampage.[81] Many of the victims died of rabies.[82]

This raises an intriguing possibility: could rabid wolves have contributed to the belief in diabolically possessed werewolves who fiendishly and relentless attacked, killed, and sometimes devoured humans? Rabid wolves certainly behave more like the folk-stereotype of wolves—and especially werewolves—than do their healthy and normal counterparts.

But an attack by a rabid wolf had a repercussion which extended far beyond the immediate deaths or the lacerations received by those who survived the mauling: rabies-infected humans. Also known as "hydrophobia"—after the spasmodic laryngopharyngeal contractions experienced by patients upon seeing liquids, and their inability to drink water—rabies is a zoonotic malaise transmitted to humans through the bite of an animal carrying the virus in its saliva. The epidemiology of human rabies, therefore, closely parallels the epizootiology of animal rabies.

The incubation period of the rabies virus in humans averages from two to eight weeks, but may vary from ten days to ten months, or more, depending on the location of the bite, the severity of the wound, and its proximity to the central nervous system.[83] The symptoms of the disease in humans are relevant to our discussion. These, according to modern clinical observations, include: hyperactivity, disorientation, hallucinations, seizures, bizarre behavior, stiffness or paralysis of the neck. In most cases a period of marked hyperactivity (furious rabies) develops lasting hours to days. The hyperactivity consists of periods of agitation, thrashing, running, biting, or other bizarre behavior. These episodes may occur spontaneously or may be precipitated by tactile, auditory, visual, or olfactory stimuli.[84]

Many victims of rabies are reported to rage in delirium, howl like wolves in their agony, go into violent frenzies, and attack and bite those around them, producing horror among both medical personnel and casual onlookers.[85] Again, the absence of detailed and unbiased observations precludes a retrospective diagnosis with any degree of certainty in most of the recorded incidents of lycanthropy; however, these symptoms do bring to mind behavior such as that of the Gandillon men while in captivity. One wonders whether the often misunderstood but truly horrifying symptoms of rabies might not, under certain circumstances (e.g., long incubation periods disassociating the animal bite from the disease in the human), have been interpreted as evidence of werewolfism.

Finally, there is the close historical correlation between the werewolf trials in Europe and rabies epizootics (outbreaks of rabies among humans, as already mentioned, coincide with epidemics among animals). According to one authority on the subject, "until the middle ages epizootics were rare. Most cases were singular bites of rabid dogs, and occasionally wolves.... In 1500, Spain was said to be ravaged by canine rabies. By 1586 there were epizootics of rabies among dogs in Flanders, Austria, Hungary and Turkey. In 1604, canine rabies was widespread in Paris and caused great alarm."[86]

Russell and Russell have pointed to the possible connection between rabies and the belief in werewolves: "The occurrence of a terrible disease transmitted from wolf to man, providing a sinister linkage between the two species, may well have contributed to the werewolf belief. It is even possible that some of the convicted werewolves may have been suffering from rabies."[87]

Although rabies was known to the ancient Greeks, the Romans, early Christian writers, and medieval Arab physicians, and a sound naturalistic treatise on the subject was written in 1593 by Salius of Bologna,[88] such specialist knowledge rarely filtered down to local communities. Moreover, demonological speculation, interjecting demonic forces into nearly every kind of pathology, could very well have obfuscated the epidemiological basis of rabies in humans in favor of supernatural causes.

Hallucinogenic Drugs and Lycanthropy

Another explanation for lycanthropy, advanced both by sixteenth- and seventeenth-century demonographers and some modern writers, implicates hallucinogenic drugs. In an overwhelming number of lycanthropy cases, suspects were thought to effect their metamorphosis by means of magical salves. The objective of individuals who thus transformed themselves into animals, as I noted earlier, was to be able to inflict injuries on others without being identified.[89] Nathanial Crouch, the vehement English demonographer, related a typical account involving the use of such magical ointments in his *The Kingdom of Darkness* (1688): "That a certain woman being in prison on suspicion of witchcraft, pretending to be able to turn herself into a wolf, the magistrate before whom she was brought promised her that she should not be put to death in case she would then in his presence thus transform herself, which she readily consented to, accordingly she anointed her head, neck, and arm-pits, immediately upon which she fell into a most profound sleep for three hours, after which she suddenly rose up, declaring that she had been turned into a wolf, and had been at a place some miles distant, and there killed first a sheep and then a cow...."[90]

Pierre Bourgot and Michel Verdun, the werewolves of Poligny, testified that they used a magical ointment to effect their

Figure 8.9 Witches shifting their shapes by anointing with the werewolf ointment. Francisco Goya's "*La Cocina de las Brujas*" [The Witches' Kitchen] (1794-5). By permission of Ampliaciones Reproducciones MAS, Barcelona.

metamorphosis. Weyer, who cited this case in order to dismiss lycanthropy as a hallucination, described the ointment's effects: "On rubbing themselves with a salve they would be changed into wolves, and on rubbing with certain herbs would resume [their] human shape. As wolves they had marvelous swiftness.... They told various stories of killing and devouring children and animals. Michel would be transformed in his clothes, but Pierre took his off, and resumed them when retransformed."[91]

Testimony about magical ointments was likewise recorded during the trials of Gilles Garnier, Jacques Roulet, and Jean Grenier. Boguet also stressed the role of magical unguents in lycanthropy: "The confessions of Jacques Bocquet, Françoise Secretain, Clauda Jamguillaume, Clauda Jamprost, Thievenne Paget, Pierre Gandillon and George Gandillon are very relevant to our argument; for they said that, in order to turn themselves into wolves, they first rubbed themselves with an ointment, and then Satan clothed them in a wolf's skin which completely covered them, and then they went on all-fours and ran about the country chasing now a person now an animal according to the guidance of their appetite...."[92]

The drugs employed in shape-shifting were similar to those used in the witches' flying-ointments, discussed in the previous chapter.[93] The most complete list of ingredients for the werewolf ointment was provided by Nynauld in his *De la lycanthropie, transformation, et extase des sorciers* (1615): "Belladonna root, nightshade, the blood of bats and hoopoes, aconite, celery, soporific nightshade, soot, cinquefoil, calamus, parsley, poplar leaves, opium, henbane, hemlock, varieties of poppy, and crustaceans...."[94] Giovanni Della Porta described the relevant effects of some of these drugs in his *Natural Magic* (1658): "by drinking a certain potion, the man would seem sometimes to be changed into a fish; and flinging out his arms, would swim on the ground: sometimes he would seem to skip up, and then dive down again. Another would believe himself turned into a goose, and would eat grass, and beat the ground with his teeth, like a goose: now and then sing, and endeavour to clap his wings. And this he did with [mandrake, deadly nightshade, and henbane]."[95]

The question raised by such claims is this: can lycanthropy be explained in terms of the actions of psychotropic drugs? Some modern researchers, again those belonging to the 1960s "drug culture" generation, have noted that henbane and datura can produce the subjective impression of transformation into animals, and hence drugs can account for the phenomenon of lycanthropy in Europe.[96]

One authority cited in support of this argument is the noted German toxicologist, Erich Hesse, who has stated that, "A characteristic feature of the solanaceae psychosis is ... that the intoxicated person imagines himself to have been changed into some animal, and the hallucinosis is completed by a sensation of the growing of feathers and of hair, due probably to the main paraesthesia. In all these states the intoxicated person is loud, loquacious, restive; he laughs, and carries on animated discussions with people who are not there."[97]

The sensation of changing into a wolf and the urge to chase and eat animals have also occurred during LSD psychosis,[98] suggesting that such feelings are possible during drug-induced hallucinatory episodes. But whether lycanthropy (which, like witchcraft, was a socially defined crime) can be explained in terms of the subjective, mental states of the accused is a question to which we will turn next.

Sociological Considerations

The range of possible physiological and psychological variables discussed are obviously not mutually exclusive, although most of these conditions, with perhaps the exception of rabies, were generally rare. Drug-induced psychosis, possibly the aberrant side-effect of the recreational use of hallucinogens (see Chapter Seven, above), may account for manifestations of lycanthropism, although there is no objective evidence that such drugs were used by secret societies of shape-shifting sorcerers. Thus, apart from isolated instances, one needs to seek other determinants or variables with which to account for the many accusations of lycanthropy during the years of the witch-hunts.

In any legitimate explanation, the sociological correlates of accusations of witchcraft and lycanthropy cannot be outweighed by the suspects' states of mind. Indeed, we have seen that, in some of the most famous werewolf trials, the defendants fit the sociological criteria making them ideal for accusations of *maleficium*, or, in those particular instances, of werewolfism. False accusations and confessions originating on the rack unquestionably account for most, if not all, cases of lycanthropy.

Trumped up charges, psychosis, or the delirium of rabies notwithstanding, demonographers were convinced that lycanthropes were in league with the Devil and hence deserved death. Thus, Boguet aptly concluded his chapter "Of the Metamorphosis of Men into Beasts, and Especially of Lycanthropes or Loup-garoux," stating: "So much have I thought good to set down concerning Lycanthropes or were-wolves. Yet I should be sorry to leave this subject without reprimanding those who would excuse them and cast the blame for all that they do upon Satan, as if they were entirely innocent. For it is apparent from what I have said that it is the witches themselves who run about and kill people.... And even if they were guilty in nothing but their damnable intention, they should still be thought worthy of death, seeing that the law takes cognisance of the intention even in matters which are not very serious, although nothing has actually resulted from such intentions. I may add that such people should never have this intention, except those who have first renounced God and Heaven."[99]

Notes

1. Eisler (1951:148–149); MacCulloch (1915:200).
2. Summers (1933:x–xi); Eisler (1951:146–147).
3. Hamel (1915:2, 7); Lea (1939:940).
4. Magnus (1658 [1555]:193).
5. Verstegan (1605:237).
6. Magnus (1658 [1555]:193).
7. Peuckert (1951:118–121).
8. Shape-shifting is mentioned by Greek and Roman writers, such as Plato, Pliny, Virgil, Petronius, and Apuleius, and demonologists made free use of these authorities. As Scriptural evidence, demonographers usually made reference to the story of Nebuchadnezzer (Daniel 4:33), King of Babylon, who, it is said, God transformed into an ox for seven years. Also frequently cited were Homer's tale of Circe, the sorceress who transmuted Ulysses' companions into swine, and Ovid's recounting of the myth of Lycaon, King of Arcadia, who, having incurred the wrath of Jupiter

(Zeus), was metamorphosed into a wolf. See Stewart's (1909) and Noll's (1992:83-99) survey of the literature.

9. In Kors and Peters (1972:29–31).
10. Kramer and Sprenger (1971 [1486]:61–65, 122–124).
11. Guazzo (1929 [1608]:51).
12. Boguet (1929 [1602]:146).
13. Kramer and Sprenger (1971 [1486]:65); Baring-Gould (1865:61).
14. Remy (1930 [1595]:112).
15. MacCulloch (1915:212); Summers (1933:73).
16. Gottfried (1983:135–136).
17. Gottfried (1983:135–136); Pollard (1964:23–26); Russell and Russell (1978:158–159).
18. Zimen (1981:298).
19. MacCulloch (1915:217).
20. Pollard (1964:23–32).
21. Monter (1976:147).
22. Russell and Russell (1978:161).
23. Verstegan (1605:111); Zimen (1981:45, 310).
24. Baring-Gould (1865:100); Monter (1976:149). For a discussion of metamorphosis in the English context see Kittredge (1956:174–184).
25. Hamel (1915:65).
26. Pollard (1964:48–55); Summers (1933:235–236).
27. C. H. D. Clarke (1971:67–68).
28. C. H. D. Clarke (1971:50).
29. In other words, cases involving witches and sorcerers who were presumed to have the ability to transform themselves into wolves.
30. Summers (1933:223–225).
31. Baring-Gould (1865:75–76).
32. Baring-Gould (1865:74).
33. Baring-Gould (1865:74–75).
34. Boguet (1929 [1602]:140–141).
35. Hamel (1915:57–58).
36. Robbins (1981:212).
37. Mackay (1932 [1841]:485).
38. Lopez (1978:241).
39. Baring-Gould (1865:81–82).
40. Summers (1933:122).
41. Boguet (1929 [1602]:154).
42. Baring-Gould (1865:85–99).
43. Kieckhefer (1976:24).
44. Monter (1976:111).
45. Monter (1976:144–151).
46. Summers (1933:234–235).
47. Monter (1976:148).
48. Summers (1933:225).
49. Boguet (1929 [1602]:139).
50. Garinet (1818:150).
51. Summers (1933:230).
52. Cases of werewolfism continued to be reported in Germany and the Austrian Alps until the eighteenth and nineteenth centuries (Monter

1976:144–150; Baring-Gould 1865:1–5; O'Donnell 1912), while such incidents persisted in France well into the twentieth century (Pollard 1964:145–146; Summers 1933:236–238). See also Woodward (1979:23-29).

53. Boguet (1929 [1602]:139).
54. Otten (1986:5–8).
55. See also Eisler (1951).
56. *A True Discourse Declaring the Damnable Life and Death of one Stubbe Peeter* (1590).
57. *A True Discourse.*
58. *A True Discourse.*
59. Elich (1607:155).
60. *A True Discourse.*
61. Burton (1621:13–14).
62. Crouch (1688:69); Summers (1933:2–3).
63. Baring-Gould (1865:64–65).
64. Rosenstock and Vincent (1977:1142–1149).
65. Illis (1986:195–199).
66. Baxter (1977b:69).
67. The most celebrated feral child in modern times was Victor, discussed in J. M. Itard's *The Wild Boy of Aveyron* (1932); Amala and Kamala, the feral girls from India, subject of Singh and Zingg's *Wolf Children and Feral Man* (1940)—which Bettelheim refutes—represent the only documented modern cases of children allegedly raised by wolves.
68. Bettelheim (1959:456, 459, 460).
69. Bettelheim (1959:458).
70. Lopez (1978:244).
71. Baring-Gould's (1865:97).
72. For example Pollard (1964:17–22, 108–121).
73. Zimen (1981:328–329); Caras (1975:32–41).
74. Zimen (1981:328).
75. Zimen (1981:298, 300).
76. Zimen (1981:298).
77. C. H. D. Clarke (1971:69).
78. C. H. D. Clarke (1971:71–72).
79. Lopez (1978:71).
80. Tierkel (1975:125).
81. Steele (1975:13); See also Caras (1975:40–41).
82. See Pollard (1964:56–68) for additional incidents from the eighteenth and nineteenth centuries.
83. Acha and Szyfres (1980:295–296).
84. Hattwick and Gregg (1975:290).
85. Steele (1975:2, 5); Pollard (1964:57); Eisler (1951:34, 160, 166).
86. Steele (1975:6).
87. Russell and Russell (1978:164).
88. Steele (1975:1–6); Russell and Russell (1978:164).
89. Lea (1939:940).
90. Crouch (1688:69–70).
91. Lea (1939:938).
92. Boguet (1929 [1602]:154).
93. Baring-Gould (1865:149–150).

94. Nynauld (1615, Chapter Two); Duerr (1985:141).
95 Porta (1658:219–220).
96. For example, Barnett (1965a; 1965b); Harner (1973); Emboden (1979:129).
97. Hesse (1946:103–104).
98. Surawicz and Banta (1975:537–542).
99. Boguet (1929 [1602]:155).

Chapter Nine

Witch-Hunting, Terror, and Social Control

In the preceding chapters I have examined three aspects of the witch-persecutions: the acts of violence, coercion, and terrorism perpetrated by the engineers of the witch-hunts; the material conditions that inspired such acts; and the ideological means through which the witch-hammerers justified their actions. Here I wish to address several specific questions: why witches were persecuted; what effects these persecutions had on local communities; and why the witch-hunts lasted for so long.

Between 1550 and 1630 the witch-persecutions reached an unprecedented crescendo. This intense period of witch-hunting coincided with a time of prodigious calamities, as western Europe was jolted by profound economic crises, the trauma of the Reformation, incessant warfare, and recurrent outbreaks of the plague. To many, these events portended the capitulation and destruction of Christendom, the citadel of light besieged by the legions of darkness. The increase in witchcraft and sorcery marked this melancholy age of disasters and misfortunes.

Witches and sorcerers were multiplying daily, exasperated demonologists clamored, and this was an affront to God. Thus, the Almighty, moved to righteous wrath, was assailing mankind with famines, wars, pestilence, and manifold tribulations. Del Rio explained the reasons for the innumerable adversities besetting Europe by citing Isaiah's condemnation of Babylon: "All things are come upon thee because of the multitude of thy sorceries and for the great hardiness of thy enchanters."[1] To appease God, witches and sorcerers, the perfidious sowers of evil and disorder, had to be eradicated at all costs. The situation was grievous, demonologists explained, for the crime long lay hid, and its malignancy spread far and wide, so that it could be extirpated only with diligent effort and great difficulty. Magistrates were to act swiftly, decisively, and without mercy. Even if innocent people were sometimes condemned, the remorseless witch-hammerers declared, it was better to suffer this than to jeopardize the welfare of society by leniency or hesitation.

The war against witches was therefore a movement to restore moral order in a time of profound crises. The process of detecting, exhibiting, and ceremoniously destroying Satan's baleful agents conveyed the message that society was not out of control after all, that the majesty of the law reigned supreme, and that the Almighty was indeed in heaven.[2]

Through witchcraft accusations, problems arising from complex sociocultural forces, which people could neither explain nor control, were attributed to the magical spells of pretended miscreants. Such accusations personified society's troubles by laying blame on particular individuals and groups. Scapegoats offered easy answers and thus spared people from having to come to terms with the real reasons for their social, economic, and political woes. Those in power were all too eager to encourage accusations and even took the initiative in ferreting out the pernicious enemies of humankind, the devils in the midst of society, because this conveniently relieved them of having to bear responsibility for intolerable sociopolitical and economic conditions.

In reality, few executed as witches were ever actual threats to society. Indeed, as we have seen, the majority of those tried and put to death were drawn from among society's weakest and poorest elements. Moreover, unless one is willing to accept demonological propaganda as literal descriptions of actual occurrences, there is no solid evidence for the existence of a seditious organization of witches, sorcerers, shape-shifters, night-flying females, shamans, or Devil-worshippers, during or after the Middle Ages, whose personnel may have been targeted for elimination as witches.

Many of those prosecuted by the authorities as agents of the Prince of Darkness were initially accused of simple *maleficium*.

Vestitus relapsi vel impœnitentis comburendi qui vocatur Samarra.

Figure 9.1 Witches and heretics were depicted as the pernicious enemies of humankind, the devils in the midst of society. Problems arising from complex sociocultural forces, which people could neither explain nor control, were attributed to the magical spells and malice of these pretended miscreants. From Philip Limborch's *Historia Inquisitionis* (1692). Courtesy of the Rare Books and Manuscripts Department, The Ohio State University Library.

Some were guilty of ordinary antisocial crimes, such as murder or theft, but were prosecuted as witches or werewolves. But countless others were undoubtedly incinerated through deception, fraud, greed, and the animosities of their neighbors and local authorities. Witches, after all, were punished for crimes of which they manifestly could not have been guilty. As Spee lamented, envy, calumny, gossip, malicious rumors, and venomous tongues daily create suspicions of witchcraft for which the innocent are put to death.[3]

If the world really was inundated by Satan's fifth-column, as the witch-doctors wanted everyone to believe, why not simply execute these lethal magicians in prisons, instead of making public spectacles out of them? This would certainly have been a more efficient way of dispatching the plethora of witches being seized and detained. The answer is that the publicity generated by the exemplary punishment of pretended witches was frequently more important than the actual death of any single individual or group of individuals.

The spectacle of publicly executing witches before mass audiences, aside from being a display of power, afforded the authorities the opportunity to invite their citizens to vent their collective frustrations and heap their combined hatreds upon the presumed miscreants and public enemies on display—an effective strategy for distracting the pauperized masses from their existential woes.[4] The execution of every witch also demonstrated in a graphic and tangible form the might of the authorities and the price paid by the nonconformists.[5] More significantly, however, the witch-persecutions were a constant reminder of the threat posed by the Devil and his legions of darkness.

Regardless of their other consequences,[6] the witch-hunts invariably frightened and terrified a great many people. "There is fear and hatred and suspicion everywhere," decried Meyfarth, "in courts and castles, in churches and schools and between neighbors. Everyone suspects everyone and openly accuses him of witchcraft."[7] This has led one historian to conclude that the persecutions were sociologically dysfunctional because they heightened rather than dissipated fears and anxieties.[8] I maintain, to the contrary, that the fear generated by a witch-hunt, rather

Figure 9.2 During the witch-hunt years, civil and Episcopal authorities terrorized entire communities by means of systematic propaganda about Satan, his lethal unholy minions, and their clandestine and sinister activities. Francisco Goya's "*Conjuro*" [The Bewitching] (1794-5). By permission of Fundación Lázaro Galdeano Museo, Madrid.

than being an undesirable side-effect, was the force which both inspired and sustained the persecutions.

Cross-cultural and historical research has shown that terror and violence are often employed to serve the political needs of ruling authorities.[9] I submit that terror and violence, in the form of centrally-directed and officially sanctioned witch-hunts, torture, and executions, were used in Europe for the same purposes. The witch-hunts created a climate of terror and inculcated fear: fear of the Devil, fear of witches and werewolves, fear of being identified as a witch, and fear of the authorities, their torture chambers, and the stake. Fear is a vehicle of social control, and violence and torture are components of the machinery for producing fear.

Terror and violence, as forms of social control, operate under particular sociopolitical circumstances. Under conditions of minimal resistance, those in command of the coercive and judicial machinery tend to abstain from destructive methods of rule; real or perceived resistance escalates the probability of violence and terrorism.[10] Terror and violence, therefore, are a function of resistance, or potential resistance, and they are employed by regimes of terror to achieve two objectives: punishment and suppression; and the obstruction of potential resistance.

Regimes of terror, however, employ violence of a special kind. Violence used as an instrument of social control is limited, and is intended to instill fear and ultimately to suppress resistance. This kind of violence has been termed the "process of terror."[11] Unbounded violence, in contrast, becomes an end in itself, its purpose being destruction rather than pacification. Thus, violence against clearly identifiable resistance movements is like a surgical procedure, involving the systematic suppression of definite acts of resistance.[12] The terror process, on the other hand, can be compared to a chemical action, under which independent clusters of organized opposition dissolve in the medium of extreme fear, and the first steps leading to a confrontation with the forces of repression are never taken.[13]

The terror process involves an object for violence (the victim, or victims) and a target—the larger social group where terror is instilled—which is controlled. The desired outcome of rule by terror is not genocide, but rather the obliteration of a segment, class, group, or social category in order to instill fear among the

Figure 9.3 The infamous *Hexenhaus* of Johann Georg II in Bamberg. This special prison, which had numerous torture rooms, was built by the Prince-Bishop especially for witches. Here hundreds of people were brutally tortured, maimed, and killed. Judicial torture had one important objective: to deter opposition by setting pain and mutilation as the price of dissent. Courtesy of Historisches Museum, Bamberg.

remainder of society.[14] The condemnation of Doctor Fian, described in *Newes from Scotland*, points to this effect: "Upon great consideration therefore taken by the King's majesty and his Council, as well for the due execution of justice upon such detestable malefactors, as also *for example sake, to remain a terror to all others hereafter, that shall attempt to deal in the like wicked and ungodly actions, as witchcraft, sorcery, conjuration, and such like,* the said Doctor Fian was soon after arraigned, condemned, and adjudged by the law to die, and then to be burned according to the law of the land, and provided in that behalf."[15]

Bodin explained why witches had to be punished in the most horrible fashion possible: "Now, if there is any means to appease the wrath of God, to gain his blessing, *to strike awe into some by the punishment of others, to preserve some from being infected by others,* to diminish the number of evil-doers, to make secure the life of the well-disposed, and to punish the most detestable crimes of which the human mind can conceive, it is to punish with the utmost rigor the witches...."[16] Similarly Remy, the remorseless witch-slayer of Lorraine, concluded his *Daemonolatria* by emphasizing the desired effects of the merciless punishments of witches: "their lives are so notoriously befouled and polluted by so many blasphemies, sorceries, prodigious lusts and flagrant crimes, that I have no hesitation in saying that they are justly to be subjected to every torture and put to death in the flames; both that they may expiate their crimes with a fitting punishment, and that its very awfulness *may serve as an example and a warning to others.*"[17]

Such statements offer clear evidence that, in the minds of its engineers, a primary motive for witch-hunting was social control, achieved by terrorism. This, in fact, was the message of Innocent VIII's portentous bull, *Summis Desiderantes* (1484), in which he declared that the anti-witchcraft program and the ruthless prosecution of suspected witches was "to prevent the taint of heretical pravity and of other like evils from spreading their infection to the ruin of others who are innocent."[18]

The victim perishes, but the target reacts. While anyone can be the object of violence, the process of terror requires a steady flow of victims who are executed in a systematic fashion at a constant rate. In Europe, individuals accused of being witches perished, while the larger community reacted with fear, submission, and mutual distrust. The need for a constant supply of witches for burning resulted in waves of unrestrained attacks by governments upon citizens alleged to be aiding and abetting Satan in his quest to regain his lost empire. Thus, once the fires were ignited there could be no easy end to the witch-burnings.

Contemporary observers were astonished by the fact that the more vehemently the authorities sought witches, the more witches they seemed to uncover. As one eyewitness put it, "When the prosecution of witchcraft once begins it never remains still, but flies from person to person, from family to family, from village to village, from city to city. Hourly, daily, weekly, monthly the number grows of accused witches. The torturers and executioners have not enough wood ... to burn them, enough swords and halters to murder them."[19] Another observer wrote: "We see proceedings continued for years and the number of condemned increase until [entire] districts are consumed, with no result but to fill whole books with the names of others and no end of burnings in prospect until all the region is exhausted."[20]

Critics were appalled at the interminable persecutions and injustices and advised caution. "However, much Princes may burn," Spee lamented, "they cannot burn it out; they devastate the land more than any war and gain nothing; it is a thing to cause tears of blood."[21] The problem vexing demonologists, on the other hand, was that, despite all their efforts, witches were still multiplying at staggering rates. This was evident from the innumerable confessions, trials, and executions. "We see witches growing more audacious through impunity and untiringly adding to their numbers," Del Rio complained bitterly, "for there is nothing more ardently desired by the devil than that this cancer should infect all who as yet are clean. This has always provoked the wrath of God.... What hope remains for us now, when everyday there multiply defenders of these maleficent sorcerers in the councils of judges, consuls, fiscals, parliaments and even of princes themselves. I wish they would reflect on the past and see that to no prince, republic or province has sorcery been aught but destructive."[22]

Demonologists therefore demanded harsher punishments, greater zeal, swifter penalties, and death and destruction for Satan's minions. These they deemed necessary both to appease the wrath of God impending over the people, and to deter others from the path of darkness and iniquity.

The witch-hammerers seldom had difficulty detecting the personnel of the witches' clandestine conspiratorial organization they were bent on destroying. Indeed, the expert detectors-of-evil were so successful in snaring witches, that Spee remarked: "The inquisitors all cry that witchcraft is the most hidden of crimes. How can that be, if it is so easily discovered that there is in the world no crime in which so many guilty, as they think, have been dragged to light and are daily dragged?"[23] Witches were found everywhere in great numbers because the procedures used to find and prosecute people accused of witchcraft manufactured evidence and multiplied suspects and victims. But the fact that witches were being created by the very procedures employed to locate and obliterate them totally eluded the perplexed witch-hammerers. The demonic creatures conjured up in the torture chambers of Europe had acquired a life of their own, and they confronted their creators, the learned doctors and magistrates, with a frightening reality. The engineers and promoters of the witch-hunts were thus mystified by the very system they had help devise. The spiraling numbers of trials and executions served only to confirm their worst suspicions—order was being replaced by chaos, and the world was plummeting into wickedness.

The vain ravings of those who doubted the reality of witchcraft, therefore, had to be stifled and suppressed, and the witches purged at all costs. As the obdurate Binsfeld remarked, "many who are moved with too great compassion for this, the worst of the human races, ask when there is to be an end to the burning of sorcerers and witches, to which the answer is that punishment must continue as long as the crime."[24] As long as there are witches (*malefici*), enchanters (*sagae*), and sorcerers (*magi*), Binsfeld raged, the sentence must be uttered: "Fire for *malefici*, fire for *sagae*, fire for *magi*."[25]

Regimes of terror appear paradoxical—they are governments that destroy one portion of society in order to control the rest. This is precisely the reason why the witch-hunt years appear enigmatic and puzzling. Under a regime of terror, moreover, the segment being destroyed might be no different sociologically than the rest of society. Social identity, however, can be created in the torture chambers and by official propaganda. In the absence of a real conspiracy of witches, the rack, hot pincers, sharp needles, and psychotomimetic drugs served to reify the imaginary threat posed by the Devil's servants.

Normally, the objects of terror belong to the weakest and the most expendable and economically unimportant elements of society. Witches, as we have seen, were usually drawn from among the poor, the powerless, and particularly women, who, in the sixteenth and seventeenth centuries in Europe, fit both criteria.

Only when a witch-hunt got out of hand, or when the charges were politically motivated, as in the case of Dietrich Flade in Trier, the North Berwick witches in Scotland, or the legal proceedings against Urbain Grandier in Loudun, to name just a few examples, were members of the elite classes involved, and even then, only a small minority was ever punished or executed. Nevertheless, the victims themselves, the objects of terror, whether drawn from among the underprivileged or affluent classes, were seldom the sole targets of the persecutions which functioned to instill fear among communities as a whole.

The imposition of terror maintains the existing social order.[26] Historical evidence indicates that a social system can be stabilized by terror and violence for decades and even centuries.[27] The evidence examined in the previous chapters suggests that the witch-hunts may have indeed operated in this manner, as a form of government-sponsored, political terrorism involving the use of controlled violence directed against designated targets within the population. The witch-hunts were a function of political and economic instability, erosion of ecclesiastical authority, and sectarian rivalries, and were set in motion to punish and suppress, with the ultimate objective of undermining potential resistance and ensure compliance and conformity. This explains the sustained efforts of secular and ecclesiastical authorities to spread rather than allay the fear of witchcraft. It accounts, moreover, for the long duration of the witch-persecutions: rule by terror is stabilizing, and this very fact demands its continuation.

Notes

1. Del Rio (1599); Lea (1939:644).
2. Apologies to Purdum and Paredes. In their article, "Rituals of Death: Capital Punishment and Human Sacrifice," Purdum and Paredes (1989) argue that capital punishment in late-twentieth century United States and human sacrifice in pre-Columbian Mexico functioned in this manner. The witch executions could also be seen as a form of human sacrifice, intended to appease God and restore equilibrium and order in a world gone awry.
3. Spee (1631); Lea (1939:714).
4. See Harris (1975b:225-258); Blumer (1969:74).
5. See Kunze (1987) for a poignant account of the tragic fate of the Pappenheimers, a family of vagrants who fell victim to Duke Maximilian's law-and-order obsession.
6. For example, it has been suggested that the witch-hunts were an attempt by the elite (the godly) to reform "popular culture," and to impose their own ideology on the masses (Burke 1978:210–214). Catholics and Protestants, upholding a new moral rigorism, hunted witches not because of the harm they caused, Burke tells us, but because of their superstitious and false beliefs. Muchembled (1990) believes that the witch-persecutions represented the penetration of central authority into the heart of the village-level society of the countryside, during the conquest of rural Western Europe by the forces of law and order. Alternatively, it has been suggested that the witch-persecutions were an attempt to make women conform to male ideals of female behavior (Duerr 1985:56–57).
7. Meyfarth (1635); Lea (1939:731).
8. Midelfort (1972:196).
9. For example, Eugene Walter's important study *Terror and Resistance* (1969).
10. Walter (1969:15–16).
11. Walter (1969:15).
12. Walter (1969:26–27).
13. Walter (1969:27).
14. Walter (1969:15).
15. *Newes from Scotland* (1591:28), emphasis mine.
16. In Burr (1897:5), emphasis mine.
17. Remy (1930 [1595]:188), emphasis mine.
18. In Burr (1897:9).
19. Meyfarth (1635); Lea (1939:732–733).
20. Spee (1631); Lea (1939:699).
21. Spee (1631); Lea (1939:699).
22. Del Rio (1599); Lea (1939:644).
23. Spee (1631); Lea (1939:733).
24. Binsfeld (1623:i).
25. Binsfeld (1623:i).

26.   Walter (1969:14).
27.   Walter (1969:31).

Bibliography

Abrahams, Israel
1985   *Jewish Life in the Middle Ages.* Atheneum, NY: Temple.

Acha, Pedro N., and Boris Szyfres
1980   *Zoonoses and Communicable Diseases Common to Man And Animals.* Washington, D.C.: Pan American Health Organization.

Allen, A.
1979   "Toads: The Biochemistry of the Witches' Cauldron." *History Today* 29:265–268.

Ames, F.
1985   "Brain Dysfunction in Detainees." In *Detention and Security Legislation in South Africa: Proceedings of a Conference Held at the University of Natal, September 1982*, A. N. Bell and R. MacKie, eds. Durban, South Africa: University of Natal, Centre for Adult Education. Pp. 85–88.

Anglo, Sydney
1977a   "Evident Authority and Authoritative Evidence: *The Malleus Maleficarum*." In *The Damned Art: Essays in the Literature of Witchcraft*, Sydney Anglo, ed. London: Routledge and Kegan Paul. Pp. 1–31.

1977b   "Reginald Scot's Discoverie of Witchcraft: Skepticism, and Sadduceeism." In *The Damned Art: Essays in the Literature of Witchcraft*, Sydney Anglo, ed. London: Routledge and Kegan Paul. Pp. 106–139.

Anonymous
c. 1450 *Errores Gazariorum....* Savoy.

c. 1630 *Malleus Judicum....* n.p.

Arens, W.
1979   *The Man-Eating Myth: Anthropology and Anthropophagy.*
New York: Oxford University Press.

Aubin, Nicholas
1693   *Cruels effets de la vengeance du Cardinal de Richelie ou histoire
des diables de Loudun.* Amsterdam: Etienne Roger.

1703   (English translation) *The cheats and illusions of Romish priests
and exorcists. Discover'd in the history of the devils of Loudun
[being an account of the pretended possession of the Ursuline
nuns and of the condemnation and punishment of Urban
Grandier a parson of the same town..].* London: W. Turner.

Barber, Bernard
1967   *Drugs and Society.* New York: Russell Sage.

Barber, Malcolm
1978   *Trial of the Templars.* Cambridge: Cambridge University
Press.

Barger, George
1931   *Ergot and Ergotism: A Monograph Based an the Dohme
Lectures Delivered in Johns Hopkins University, Baltimore.*
London: Gurney and Jackson.

Baring-Gould, Sabine
1865   *The Book of Werewolves: Being an Account of a Terrible
Superstition.* London: Smith, Elder and Co.

Barnett, Bernard
1965a "Witchcraft, Psychopathology, and Hallucinations." *British
Journal of Psychiatry* 3:439–445.

1965b "Drugs of the Devil." *New Scientist* (27):222–225.

Barnett, Homer G.
1953 *Innovation: The Basis of Cultural Change.* New York: McGraw-Hill.

Baroja, Julio Caro
1964 *The World of Witches.* Chicago: University of Chicago Press.

1990 "Witchcraft and Catholic Theology." In *Early Modern European Witchcraft*, B. Ankarloo and G. Henningsen, eds. Oxford: Clarendon Press. Pp. 19–43.

Baron, Louis S.
1986 "Introduction." In *The Evil Eye: An Account of this Ancient and Widespread Superstition*, Frederick Thomas Elworthy. New York: Julian Press. Pp. v–xi.

Barthel, Manfred
1984 *The Jesuits: History and Legend of the Society of Jesus.* New York: William Morrow.

Baxter, Christopher
1977a "Jean Bodin's *De la Démonomanie des Sorciers*: The Logic of Persecution." In *The Damned Art: Essays In The Literature of Witchcraft*, Sydney Anglo, ed. London: Routledge and Kegan Paul. Pp. 76–103.

1977b "Johann Weyer's *De Praestigiis Daemonum*: Unsystematic Psychopathology." In *The Damned Art: Essays in the Literature of Witchcraft*, Sydney Anglo, ed. London: Routledge and Kegan Paul. Pp. 53–75.

Bean, J. M. W.
1982 "The Black Death: The Crisis and its Social and Economic Consequences." In *The Black Death: The Impact of the Fourteenth-Century Plague*, Daniel Williman, ed. Binghamton, NY: Center for Medieval and Early Renaissance Studies. Pp. 23–38.

Beattie, John
1964   *Other Cultures: Aims, Methods, and Achievements in Social Anthropology*. New York: Holt, Rinehart and Winston.

Beck, Felix
1951   *Russian Purge and the Extraction of Confession*. New York: Viking.

Beidleman, Thomas O.
1963   "Witchcraft in Ukaguru." In *Witchcraft and Sorcery in East Africa*, John Middleton and E. H. Winters, eds. London: Routledge and Kegan Paul. Pp. 57–78.

Benenson, Abram S.
1976   "Plague." In *Communicable and Infectious Diseases*, Franklin H. Top Sr. and Paule F. Wehrle, eds. Saint Louis: C.V. Mosby. Pp. 502–507.

Ben-Sasson, H. H.
1976   "Changes in the Legal Status and the Security of the Jews." In *A History of the Jewish People*, H. H. Ben-Sasson, ed. Cambridge: Harvard University Press. Pp. 477–489.

Bettelheim, Bruno
1959   "Feral Children and Autistic Children." *American Journal of Sociology* 64 (5):455–467.

Bexton, W. H., et al.
1954   "Effects of Decreased Variation in the Sensory Environment." *Canadian Journal of Psychology* 8:70–76.

Binsfeld, Peter
1623   *Tractus de Confessionibus Maleficorum et Sagarum*. Coloniae Agrippinae: Petri Henningij.

Birt, J.
1910   "Ergot and the Patellar Reflex." *The Lancet* 26:1580.

Blatty, William Peter.
1971   *The Exorcist.* New York: Harper.

Blum, Richard H., et al.
1964   *Utopiates: The Use and Users of LSD–25.* New York: Atherton.

1969   *Drugs and Society: Social and Cultural Observations.* San Francisco: Jossey-Bass.

Blumer, Herbert
1969   "Outline of Collective Behavior." In *Readings in Collective Behavior*, Robert Evans, ed. Chicago: Rand McNally. 65–88.

Boas, Franz
1938   "Introduction." In *General Anthropology*, F. Boas, ed. New York: D. C. Heath. Pp. 1–6.

Boccaccio, Giovanni
1903   *The Decameron of Giovanni Boccaccio.* London: J. M. Dent and Sons.

Bodin, Jean
1580   *De la démonomanie des sorciers.* Paris: I. Du Puys.

Boguet, Henri
1602   *Discours des sorciers.* Paris: D. Binet.

1929   (English translation) *An Examen of Witches* [*drawn from various trials of many of this sect in the district of Saint oyan de Joux, commonly known as Saint Claude, in the county of Burgundy, including the procedure necessary to a judge in trials for witchcraft*], M. Summers, ed. London: John Rodker.

Bossenbrook, William
1961   *The German Mind.* Detroit: Wayne State University Press.

Boulton, Richard
1715   *A Complete History of Magick, Sorcery, and Witchcraft.* London: E. Curll.

Bourguignon, Erika
1973   "Introduction: A Framework for the Comparative Study of Altered States of Consciousness." In *Religion, Altered States of Consciousness, and Social Change*, E. Bourguignon, ed. Columbus: Ohio State University Press. Pp. 3–35.

1974   "Cross-Cultural Perspectives on the Religious Uses of Altered States of Consciousness." In *Religious Movements in Contemporary America*, Irving Zaretsky and Mark Leone, eds. Princeton, NJ: Princeton University Press. Pp. 228–243.

1976   *Possession.* San Francisco: Chandler and Sharp.

Bove, Frank James
1970   *The Story of Ergot.* Basel, Switzerland: S. Karger.

Bovet, Richard
1684   *Pandaemonium [or, The devil's cloyster: being a further blow to modern sadduceism, proving the existence of witches and spirits, in a discourse deduced from the fall of the angels, the propagation of Satan's kingdom before the flood, the idolatry of the ages after greatly advancing diabolical confederacies, with an account of the lives and transactions of several notorious witches: also, a collection of several authentick relations of strange apparitions of daemons and spectres, and fascinations of witches, never before printed].* London: J. Wathoe.

Bradley, Leslie
1977   "Some Medical Aspects of Plague." In *The Plague Reconsidered: A New Look at its Origins and Effects in 16th and 17th Century England.* Derbyshire, England: Local Population Studies. Pp. 11–23.

Brady, Ivan
1982   "The Myth-Eating Man." *American Anthropologist* 84:595–611.

Brandt, Nicolaus
1622   *Disputatio de Legitima Maleficos et Sagas Investigandi et Convincendi Ratione.* Giessae Hassorum.

Brown, J. A. C.
1968   *Techniques of Persuasion: From Propaganda to Brainwashing.* Baltimore: Penguin.

Brown, Peter
1972   "Sorcery, Demons and the Rise of Christianity: From Late Antiquity to the Middle Ages." In *Religion and Society in the Age of Saint Augustine*, P. Brown, ed. London: Faber and Faber. Pp. 119–146.

Burke, Peter
1978   *Popular Culture in Early Modern Europe.* London:Temple Smith.

1990   "The Comparative Approach to European Witchcraft." In *Early Modern European Witchcraft*, B. Ankarloo and G. Henningsen, eds. Oxford: Clarendon Press. Pp.435–441.

Burr, George Lincoln
1939   "Introduction." In *Materials Toward a History of Witchcraft*, Henry Charles Lea. Philadelphia: University of Pennsylvania Press. Pp. xxi–xliii.

1943a   "On the Loos Manuscript." In *George Lincoln Burr: His Life; Selections from His Writings*, Lois Oliphant Gibbons, ed. Ithaca, NY: Cornell University Press. Pp. 147–155.

1943b   "The Literature of Witchcraft." In *George Lincoln Burr: His Life; Selections from His Writings*, Lois Oliphant Gibbons, ed. Ithaca, NY: Cornell University Press. Pp. 166–189.

Burr, George Lincoln, ed.
1897   "The Witch-Persecution." *Translations and Reprints from the Original Sources of European History*, vol. 3, no. 4. Philadelphia: Department of History, University of Pennsylvania.

Burton, Robert
1621   *Anatomy of Melancholy [what it is, with all the kindes, causes, symptomes, prognosticks and severall cures of it: in three maine partitions, with their seuerall sections, members, and subsections, philosophically, medicinally, historically opened and cut up]*. Oxford: John Lichfield and James Short.

Camporesi, Piero
1989   *Bread of Dreams: Food and Fantasy in Early Modern Europe*. Chicago: University of Chicago Press.

Caporael, Linnda R.
1976   "Ergotism: Satan Loosed in Salem?" *Science* 192:21–26.

Caras, Roger
1975   *Dangerous to Man: The Definitive Story of Wildlife's Reputed Dangers*. New York: Holt, Rinehart and Winston.

Cardozo, Rebecca A.
1970   "A Modern American Witch-Craze." In *Witchcraft and Sorcery: Selected Readings*, Max Marwick, ed. Middlesex, England: Penguin. Pp. 369–377.

Carmona, Michel
1988   *Les Diables de Loudun*. Paris: Fayard.

Carmichael, Ann G.
1986   *Plague and the Poor in Renaissance Florence*. Cambridge: Cambridge University Press.

Carpentier, Elisabeth
1971   "The Plague as a Recurrent Phenomena." In *The Black Death: A Turning Point in History?*, William M. Bowsky, ed. New York: Holt, Rinehart and Winston. Pp. 35–37.

Carpzov, Benedict
1670   *Practica Nova Imperialis Saxonica Rerum Criminalium.* Wittenberg: n.p.

Carr, Francis
1983   *Mozart & Constanze.* New York: Avon Books.

Carus, Paul
1900   *The History of the Devil and the Idea of Evil: From the Earliest Times to the Present.* Chicago: Open Court .

Certeau, Michel de
1970   *La Possession de Loudun.* Paris: Julliard.

Chagnon, Napoleon
1983   *Yanomamo: The Fierce People.* New York: Holt, Rinehart and Winston.

Christopherson, Victor A.
1971   "The Sociocultural Correlates of Pain Response." *Social Science* 46 (1):33–37.

Claridge, Gordon
1970   *Drugs and Human Behaviour.* London: Penguin.

Clark, A. J.
1971   "Flying Ointments." In *The Witch-Cult in Western Europe,* Margaret A. Murray. Oxford: Clarendon Press. Appendix V. Pp. 279–280.

Clark, Stuart
1977   "King James's *Daemonologie*: Witchcraft and Kingship." In *The Damned Art: Essays in the Literature of Witchcraft*, Sydney Anglo, ed. London: Routledge and Kegan Paul. Pp. 156–181.

Clarke, C. H. D.
1971   "The Beast of Gévaudan." *Natural History* 80 (4):44–51, 66–73.

Clarke, Samuel
1677   *A General Martyrology*. London: William Birch.

Cohen, Jeremy
1982   *The Friars and the Jews: The Evolution of Medieval Anti-Judaism*. Ithaca: Cornell University Press.

Cohn, Norman
1957   *The Pursuit of the Millennium: Revolutionary Millenarians and Mystical Anarchists of the Middle Ages*. London: Secker and Warburg.

1967   *Warrant for Genocide: The Myth of the Jewish World-Conspiracy and the Protocols of the Elders of Zion*. London: Penguin.

1970   "The Myth of Satan and His Human Servants." In *Witchcraft Confessions & Accusations*, Mary Douglas, ed. London: Tavistock. Pp. 3–16.

1975   *Europe's Inner Demons: An Enquiry Inspired by the Great Witch Hunt*. London: Sussex University Press.

Conklin, George N.
1958   "Alkaloids and the Witches' Sabbat." *American Journal of Pharmacy* 130:171–174.

Coulton, George Gordon
1929   *The Black Death*. London: Ernest Benn.

Crapanzano, Vincent
1977 "Introduction." In *Case Studies in Spirit Possession,* Vincent Crapanzano and Vivian Garrison, eds. New York: John Wiley and Sons. Pp.1–40.

Creighton, Charles
1965 *A History of Epidemics in Britain,* vol. 1. New York: Barnes and Noble. (Originally published, 1894.)

Crosby, Alfred W.
1976 "Virgin Soil Epidemics as a Factor in the Aboriginal Depopulation in American." *The William and Mary Quarterly* 23 (2):289–299.

1986 *Ecological Imperialism: The Biological Expansion of Europe, 900–1900.* New York: Cambridge University Press.

Crouch, Nathanial [pseudonym Richard Burton]
1688 *The Kingdom of Darkness [or The history of daemons, specters, witches, apparitions ... and other wonderful and supernatural delusions ... containing near fourscore memorable relations, forreign and domestick, both antient and modern. Collected from authentick records ... and asserted by authors of undoubted verity. Together with a preface obviating the common objections ... of the Sadduces and atheists of the age, who deny the being of spirits, witches, &...].* London: Printed for N. Crouch.

Damhouder, Josse [Joost de]
1601 *Praxis Rervm Criminalivm.* Antwerp: Ioan Belleri.

Davidson, Hilda E.
1978 *Patterns of Folklore.* Totowa, NJ: Rowman and Littlefield.

Davies, Reginald Trevor
1947 *Four Centuries of Witch-Beliefs: With Special Reference to the Great Rebellion.* London: Methuen.

Del Rio, Martin Antoine
1599   *Disquisitionum Magicarum*. Louvain: G. Rivius.

Des Niau
1634   *La véritable histoire [de Loudun]*. Paris.

1887   (English translation) *The History of the Devils of Loudun [the alleged possession of the Ursuline Nuns, and the trial and execution of Urbain Grandier, told by an eyewitness]*. Edinburgh: Private Print.

De Spina, Alphonsus
1489   *Fortalitium Fidei*. Lyon: Johanne de Romoys. (Originally published, 1467.)

Dioscorides Pedanius, of Anazarbos
1529   *De Medica Materia*. Argent: Apud Ioannem Schottum.

Dolgin, Janet L., et al.
1977   "As People Express their Lives, so they are .... " In *Symbolic Anthropology*, J. Dolgin, et al., eds. New York: Columbia University Press. Pp. 3–44.

Dols, M. W.
1977   *The Black Death in the Middle East*. Princeton: NJ: Princeton University Press.

Douglas, Mary
1966   *Purity and Danger*. London: Routledge and Kegan Paul.

1970   *Natural Symbols*. London: Cresset Press.

Duerr, Hans
1985   *Dreamtime: Concerning the Boundary Between Wilderness and Civilization*. Oxford: Basil Blackwell.

Durán, Fray Diego
1971   *Book of the Gods and Rites and the Ancient Calendar*. Norman, OK: University of Oklahoma Press.

Durant, Will
1957   *The Story of Civilization: The Reformation*, vol. 6. New York: Simon and Schuster.

Eisenstein, Elizabeth L.
1979   *The Printing Press as an Agent of Change: Communication and Cultural Transformations in Early-Modern Europe*. Cambridge: Cambridge University Press.

Eisler, Robert
1951   *Man into Wolf: An Anthropological Interpretation of Sadism, Masochism, and Lycanthropy*. London: Routledge and Kegan Paul.

Elich, Philipp Ludwig
1607   *Daemonomagia*. Frankfurt: W. Richteri.

Emboden, William J., Jr.
1979   *Narcotic Plants*. New York: Macmillan.

Estes, Leland C.
1983   "The Medical Origins of the European Witch Craze: A Hypothesis." *Journal of Social History* 17:271–84.

Etcheson, C.
1984   *The Rise and Demise of Democratic Kampuchea*. Boulder, CO: Westview.

Evans-Pritchard, E. E.
1935   "Witchcraft." *Africa* 8 (4):24–49.

1937   *Witchcraft, Oracles and Magic Among the Azande*. Oxford: Clarendon Press.

1970   "Preface." In *Witchcraft in Tudor and Stuart England: A Regional and Comparative Study*, Alan MacFarlane. London: Routledge and Kegan Paul. Pp. xv–xvii.

Ferckel, Siegbert
1979   "A Witches' Ointment and its Effects." In *Narcotic Plants of the Old World: Used in Rituals and Everyday Life,* Hedwig Schleiffer, ed. Monticello, NY: Lubrecht and Cramer. Pp. 15–17.

Fletcher, Robert
1896   "The Witches' Pharmacopoeia." *Bulletin of the Johns Hopkins Hospital* 7 (65):147–156.

1898   "A Tragedy of the Great Plague of Milan in 1630." *Bulletin of the Johns Hopkins Hospital* 9 (89):175–180.

Frankel, Charles
1960   "Philosophy and the Social Sciences." In *Both Human and Humane: Humanities and Social Sciences in Graduate Education,* Charles Boewe and R. F. Nichols, eds. Philadelphia: University of Pennsylvania Press. Pp. 94–117.

Frazer, James G.
1951   *The Golden Bough: A Study in Magic and Religion.* New York: Macmillan.

Fühner, H.
1930   "Los Estupefacientes." *Investigacion y Progreso* (4):37.

Fuller, J. G.
1968   *The Day of St. Anthony's Fire.* New York: Macmillan.

Furst, Peter T.
1982   *Hallucinogens and Culture.* San Francisco: Chandler and Sharp.

Garelik, Glenn
1986   "Exorcising a Damnable Disease." *Discover* 17 (12):74–82.

Garinet, Jules
1818   *Histoire de la magie en France....* Paris: Foulon et Compagnie.

Gasquet, Francis Aidan
1977   *The Black Death of 1348 and 1349*. New York: AMS Press.
        (Originally published, 1908.)

Gaule, John
1646   *Select Cases of Conscience Touching Witches and Witchcraft*.
        London: W. Wilson.

Geertz, Clifford
1973   *The Interpretation of Culture*. New York: Basic Books.

1977   "From the Natives Point of View: On the Nature of
        Anthropological Understanding." In *Symbolic
        Anthropology*, J. Dolgin, et al., eds. New York: Columbia
        University Press. Pp. 480–492.

Geiler von Kaysersberg, Johann
1517   *Die Emeis*. Strasbourg: Johannes Grieninger.

Ginzburg, Carlo
1983   *The Night Battles: Witchcraft and Agrarian Cults in the
        Sixteenth and Seventeenth Centuries*. Baltimore: The Johns
        Hopkins University Press.

1984   "The Witches' Sabbat: Popular Cult or Inquisitorial
        Stereotype?" In *Understanding Popular Culture: Europe from
        the Middle Ages to the Nineteenth Century*, Steven L. Kaplan
        ed. Berlin: Mouton. Pp. 39–51.

1990   "Deciphering the Sabbath." In *Early Modern European
        Witchcraft*, B. Ankarloo and G. Henningsen, eds. Oxford:
        Clarendon Press. Pp. 121–137.

1991   *Ecstasies: Deciphering the Witches' Sabbath*. New York:
        Pantheon.

Glanvill, Joseph
1689   *Saducismus Triumphatus* [*or, Full and plain evidence concerning witches and apparitions. In two parts. The first treating of their possibility, the second of their real existence ... With a letter of Dr. Henry More on the same subject. And an authentick, but wonderful story of certain Swedish witches*]. London: J. Collins and S. Lowndes.

Gluckman, Max
1955   "The Logic of African Science and Witchcraft." In *Readings in Anthropology*, E. Ademson Hoebel, et al., eds. New York: McGraw-Hill. Pp. 269–279.

Goodenough, Ward H.
1956   "Componential Analysis and the Study of Meaning." *Language* 32:195–216.

Gottfried, Robert S.
1983   *The Black Death: Natural and Human Disaster in Medieval Europe*. New York: The Free Press.

Gross, Daniel
1992   *Discovering Anthropology*. Mountain View, CA: Mayfield.

Guazzo, Francesco Maria
1608   *Compendium Maleficarum....* Milan: August Tradati.

1929   (English translation) *Compendium Maleficarum* [*collected in three books from many sources by brother Francesco Maria Guazzo, showing iniquitious and execrable operations of witches against the human race, and the divine remedies by which they may be frustrated*]. London: John Rodker.

Guerchberg, Séraphine
1964   "The Controversy Over the Alleged Sowers of the Black Death in Contemporary Treatises on the Plague." In *Change in Medieval Society: Europe North of the Alps, 1050–1500*, Sylvia L. Thrupp, ed. New York: Appleton-Century-Crofts. Pp. 209–224.

Haarstad, V. B.
1964 "Witchcraft: A Pharmacological Analysis." *Bulletin of the Tulane University Medical Faculty* 24:51–68.

Haggard, Howard W.
1929 *Devils, Drugs, and Doctors: The Story of the Science of Healing from Medicine-Man to Doctor*. New York: Blue Ribbon Books.

Hamel, Frank
1915 *Human Animals: Werewolves and other Transformations*. London: William Rider and Son.

Hansen, Harold A.
1978 *The Witch's Garden*. Santa Cruz: Unity Press.

Harner, Michael J.
1973 "The Role of Hallucinogenic Plants in European Witchcraft." In *Hallucinogens and Shamanism*, Michael Harner, ed. New York: Oxford University Press. Pp. 125–150.

Harris, Marvin
1975a *Culture, People, Nature: An Introduction to General Anthropology*. New York: Thomas Y. Crowell.

1975b *Cows, Pigs, Wars and Witches: Riddles of Culture*. New York: Vintage.

1976 "History and Significance of the Emic/Etic Distinction." *Annual Review of Anthropology* 5:329–350.

1979 *Cultural Materialism: The Struggle for a Science of Culture*. New York: Random House.

Hatch, Elvin
1973 *Theories of Man and Culture*. New York: Columbia University Press.

Hattwick, Michael A. W., and Michael B. Gregg
1975   "The Disease in Man." In *The Natural History of Rabies*, vol. 2, George M. Baer, ed. New York: Academic Press. Pp. 282–304.

Hays, H. R.
1964   *From Ape to Angel: An Informal History of Social Anthropology*. New York: Capricorn Books.

Hecker, Justus Friedrich Carl
1844   *The Epidemics of the Middle Ages*. London: G. Woodfall and Son.

Helleiner, Karl
1980   "The Population of Europe From the Black Death to the Eve of the Vital Revolution." In *The Cambridge Economic History of Europe*, vol. 4, E. E. Rich and C. H. Wilson, eds. Cambridge: Cambridge University Press. Pp.1–95.

Henningsen, Gustav
1980   *The Witches' Advocate: Basque Witchcraft and the Spanish Inquisition (1609–1614)*. Reno: University of Nevada Press.

Henningsen, G., et al. eds.
1986   *The Inquisition in Early Modern Europe: Studies on Sources and Methods*. Dekalb: Northern Illinois University Press.

Hesse, Erich
1946   *Narcotics and Drug Addiction*. New York: Philosophical Library.

Hirsch, August
1885   *Handbook of Geographical and Historical Pathology: Chronic Infective, Toxic, Parasitic, Septic and Constitutional Diseases*, vol. 2. London: The New Sydenham Society.

Hirst, L. Fabian
1953   *The Conquest of Plague: A Study of the Evolution of Epidemiology*. Oxford: Clarendon Press.

Hoffer, A.
1965   "D–Lysergic Acid Diethylamide (LSD): A Review of its Present Status." *Clinical Pharmacology and Therapeutics* 6:183–225.

Hoffer, A., and H. Osmond
1967   *The Hallucinogens*. New York: Macmillan.

Hofmann, Albert
1980   *LSD, My Problem Child*. New York: McGraw-Hill.

Hollister, Leo E.
1968   *Chemical Psychoses: LSD and Related Drugs*. Springfield, IL: Charles C. Thomas.

Hollyhock, W. M.
1965   "Weapons Against the Mind." *New Scientist* 26 (440):224–226.

Holmes, Ronald
1974   *Witchcraft in British History*. London: Frederick Muller.

Honigmann, John J.
1976   *The Development of Anthropological Ideas*. Homewood, IL: Dorsey Press.

Hopkins, Matthew
1647   *The Discovery of Witches [in answer to severall queries, lately delivered to the judges of Assize for the County of Norfolk and now published by Matthew Hopkins, witch-finder, for the benefit of the whole kingdom]*. London: n.p.

Horrox, Rosemary
1994   *The Black Death*. Manchester: Manchester University Press.

Howells, William
1962   *The Heathens: Primitive Man and His Religions*. Garden City, NY: American Museum of Natural History.

Hoyt, Charles Alva
1981   *Witchcraft*. Carbondale: Southern Illinois University Press.

Huxley, Aldous
1952   *The Devils of Loudun*. New York: Harper.

Illis, L.
1986   "On Porphyria and the Aetiology of Werewolves." In *A Lycanthropy Reader: Werewolves in Western Culture*, Charlotte F. Otten, ed. Syracuse, NY: Syracuse University Press. Pp. 295–299.

Itard, Jean Marc Gaspard
1932   *The Wild Boy of Aveyron*. New York: Century.

James VI (and I)
1597   *Daemonologie, in Forme of a Dialogue*.... Edinburgh: Printed by Robert Walde-graue, Printer to the King's Majestie.

Jones, William R.
1972   "Political Uses of Sorcery." *The Historian* 34:670–678.

Kamen, Henry
1985   *Inquisition and Society in Spain*. London: Weidenfeld and Nicolson.

Kaye, Sidney.
1954   *Handbook of Emergency Toxicology: A Guide for the Identification, Diagnosis and Treatment of Poisoning*. Springfield, IL: Charles C. Thomas.

Kieckhefer, Richard
1976   *European Witch Trials: Their Foundations in Popular and Learned Culture, 1300–1500*. Berkeley: University of California Press.

1979   *Repression of Heresy in Medieval Germany.* Philadelphia: University of Pennsylvania Press.

Kiesewetter, Karl
1895   *Die Geheimwissenschaften.* Leipzig: W. Friedrich.

1891   *Geschichte des Neueren Occultismus.* Leipzig: W. Friedrich.

Kittredge, George L.
1956   *Witchcraft in Old and New England.* New York: Russell and Russell.

Klaits, Joseph
1985   *Servants of Satan: The Age of the Witch Hunts.* Bloomington: Indiana University Press.

Kors, Alan C., and Edward Peters
1972   "Introduction." In *Witchcraft in Europe 1100–1700, A Documentary History,* A. Kors and E. Peters, eds. Philadelphia: University of Pennsylvania Press. Pp. 3–23.

Kors, Alan C., and Edward Peters, eds.
1972   *Witchcraft in Europe 1100–1700, A Documentary History.* Philadelphia: University of Pennsylvania Press.

Krader, Lawrence
1963   *Peoples of Central Asia.* The Hague: Mouton.

Kramer, Heinrich, and Jakob Sprenger.
1491   *Malleus Maleficarum.* Speyer [Germany]: Peter Drach. (Originally published, 1486.)

1928   (English translation) *Malleus Maleficarum.* London: John Rodker.

Krige, J. D.
1970   "The Social Functions of Witchcraft." In *Witchcraft and Sorcery: Selected Readings*, Max Marwick, ed. Middlesex, England: Penguin. Pp. 237–251.

Kunze, Michael
1987   *Highroad to the Stake: A Tale of Witchcraft.* Chicago: University of Chicago Press.

Lancre, Pierre de
1612   *Tableau de l'inconstance des mauvais anges et démons....* Paris: N. Bvon.

Langdon-Brown, Walter
1941   *From Witchcraft to Chemotherapy.* Cambridge: Cambridge University Press.

Langer, William
1964   "The Black Death." *Scientific American* 210 (2):114– 121.

1970   "Psychological Aspects of the Black Death." In *The Shaping of the Western Civilization*, Ludwig F. Schaefer, et al., eds. New York: Holt, Rienhart and Winston. Pp.370–372.

Larner, Christina.
1983   *Enemies of God: The Witch-Hunt in Scotland.* London: Basil Blackwell.

1987   *Witchcraft and Religion: The Politics of Popular Belief.* Oxford: Basil Blackwell.

Le Strange, Richard
1977   *A History of Herbal Plants.* London: Angus and Robertson Publishers.

Lea, Henry Charles
1878   *Superstition and Force: Essays on the Wager of Law—The Wager of Battle—The Ordeal—Torture.* Philadelphia: Collins.

1887   *The Inquisition of the Middle Ages: Its Organization and Operation*, vol. 3. New York: Macmillan.

1939   *Materials Toward a History of Witchcraft*, vols. 1–3. Philadelphia: University of Pennsylvania Press.

1961   *The Inquisition of the Middle Ages; Its Organization and Operation*. (Abridged). New York: Macmillan.

1973   *Torture*. Philadelphia: University of Pennsylvania Press.

Lerner, Robert E.
1982   "The Black Death and Western European Eschatological Mentalities." In *The Black Death: The Impact of the Fourteenth-Century Plague*, Daniel Williman, ed. Binghamton, NY: Center for Medieval and Early Renaissance Studies.

Lett, James
1987   *The Human Enterprise: A Critical Introduction to Anthropological Theory*. Boulder, CO: Westview.

Levack, Brian P.
1987   *The Witch-Hunt in Early Modern Europe*. London: Longman.

Levack, B. P., ed.
1992   *Articles on Witchcraft, Magic and Demonology: Witchcraft, Women and Society*, vol. 10. New York: Garland.

Levi-Strauss, Claude
1966   *The Savage Mind*. Chicago: University of Chicago Press.

Levine, Ruth R.
1973   *Pharmacology: Drug Actions and Reactions*. Boston: Little, Brown and Co.

Lewin, Lewis
1931   *Phantastica, Narcotic and Stimulating Drugs: Their Use and Abuse*. London: Kegan Paul, Trench, Trubner and Co.

Lienhardt, Godfrey
1951   "Some Notions of Witchcraft Among the Dinka." *Africa* 21:303–318.

Limborch, Philip van
1692   *Historia Inquisitionis*. Amsterdam: H. Wetstenium.

1816   (English translation) *The History of the Inquisition*. London: W. Simpkin and R. Marshall.

Lopez, Barry Holstun
1978   *Of Wolves and Men*. New York: Charles Scribner's Sons.

Luhrmann, Tanya
1989   *Persuasions of the Witch's Craft: Ritual Magic in Contemporary England*. Harvard: Harvard University Press.

Lütge, Friedrich.
1971   "Germany: The Black Death and a Structural Revolution in Socioeconomic History." In *The Black Death: A Turning Point in History?*, William M. Bowsky, ed. New York: Holt, Rinehart and Winston. Pp. 80–85.

MacCulloch, J. A.
1915   "Lycanthropy." In *Encyclopaedia of Religion and Ethics*, vol. 8, James Hastings, ed. Edinburgh: T. T. Clark. Pp. 206–220.

Macfarlane, A.
1970   *Witchcraft in Tudor and Stuart England*. New York: Harper and Row.

Mackay, Charles
1932   *Extraordinary Popular Delusions and the Madness of Crowds*. New York: Farrar, Straus, and Giroux. (Originally published, 1841.)

Madsen, William
1967 "Religious Syncretism." In *Handbook of Middle American Indians*, vol. 6, R. Wauchope, ed. Austin: University of Texas Press. Pp. 360–391.

Mair, Lucy
1970 *Witchcraft*. New York: McGraw-Hill.

Mannix, Daniel P.
1986 *The History of Torture*. New York: Dorset Press.

Masters, Robert Edward
1966 *Eros and Evil: The Sexual Psychopathology of Witchcraft*. New York: Matrix House.

Matossian, Mary K.
1982 "Ergot and the Salem Witchcraft Affair." *American Scientist* 70:355–357.

1989 *Poisons of the Past: Molds, Epidemics, and History*. New Haven: Yale University Press.

McElroy, Ann, and Patricia K. Townsend
1985 *Medical Anthropology in Ecological Perspective*. Boulder, CO: Westview Press.

McGinn, Bernard
1979 *Visions of the End: Apocalyptic Traditions in the Middle Ages*. New York: Columbia University Press.

McNeill, William Hardy
1976 *Plagues and Peoples*. Garden City: Anchor/ Doubleday.

Mejer, Ludwig
1882 *Die Periode der Hexenprocesse*. Hannover: Schmorl and von Seefeld.

Meyfarth, Johann Matthäus
1635 *Christliche Erinnerung....* Schleiszingen: Johann Birckners.

Michaelis, Sebastien
1613   *Histoire admirable de la possession et conversion d'vne pénitente....* Paris: Charles Chastellarbon.

1613   *The Admirable History of the Possession and Conversion of a Penitent Woman....* London: William Aspley.

Michelet, Jules
1862   *La sorcière.* Paris: Calmann-Levy.

Middleton, John
1967   "The Concept of 'Bewitching' in Lugbara." In *Magic, Witchcraft, and Curing,* John Middleton, ed. Garden City, NY: Natural History Press. Pp. 55–67.

Midelfort, H. C. Erik
1972   *Witch Hunting in Southwestern Germany, 1562–1684: The Social and Intellectual Foundations.* Stanford: Stanford University Press.

1981   "Heartland of the Witchcraze: Central and Northern Europe." *History Today* 31:27–31.

Mills, Henry Richmond.
1946   *The Reed and Donner Party; A Story of Starvation and Cannibalism in the California Mountains in the Winter of 1846-47.* Freedom, CA: n.p.

Mitchell, James, ed.
1982   *The Illustrated Reference Book of the Ages of Discovery.* Leicester, England: Winward.

Monter, E. William.
1967   *Calvin's Geneva.* New York: John Wiley and Sons.

1976   *Witchcraft in France and Switzerland: The Borderlands During the Reformation.* Ithaca: Cornell University Press.

1977   "The Pedestal and the Stake: Courtly Love and
        Witchcraft." In *Becoming Visible: Women in European
        History*. R. Bridenthal and C. Koonz, eds. Boston:
        Houghton Mifflin. Pp. 119–136.

Monter, E. William, ed.
1969   *European Witchcraft*. Ithaca: Cornell University Press.

Moody, Edward J.
1971   "Urban Witches." In Conformity and Conflict: Readings in
        Cultural Anthropology, James P. Spradley and David W.
        McCurdy, eds. Boston: Little, Brown and Co. Pp. 280–290.

Moore, Alexander
1992   *Cultural Anthropology: The Field Study of Human Beings*. San
        Diego: Collegiate Press.

Mora, George
1967   "History of Psychiatry." In *Comprehensive Textbook of
        Psychiatry*, Alfred Freedman, et al., eds. Baltimore:
        Williams and Wilkins. Pp. 2–34.

1991   "Weyer's Life and Work." In *Witches, Devils, and Doctors in
        the Renaissance: Johann Weyer, De Praestigiis Daemonum*,
        George Mora, ed. Binghamton, NY: Center for Medieval
        and Early Renaissance Studies. Pp.xxvii–xcii.

Muchembled, Robert
1990   "Satanic Myths and Cultural Reality." In *Early Modern
        European Witchcraft*, B. Ankarloo and G. Henningsen, eds.
        Oxford: Clarendon. Pp. 139–160.

Murray, Alexander
1976   "Medieval Origins of the Witch Hunt." *The Cambridge
        Quarterly* 7:63–74.

Murray, Margaret A.
1917   "Organisations of Witches in Great Britain." *Folk-Lore* 28
        (3):228–258.

1917-18 "The Devil of North Berwick." *Scottish Review* 15: 310–321.

1971   *The Witch-Cult in Western Europe*. Oxford: Clarendon. (Originally published, 1921.)

Nadel, S.F.
1952   "Witchcraft in Four African Societies: An Essay in Comparison." *American Anthropologist* 54 (1):18–29.

Newall, Venetia
1973   "The Jew as a Witch Figure." In *The Witch Figure*, Venetia Newall, ed. London: Routledge and Kegan Paul. Pp. 95–124.

Newes from Scotland: Declaring the DamnableLlife and Death of
1591   *Doctor Fian, A Notable Sorcerer Who was Burned at Edenbrough in January Last.* London: W. Wright.

Nider, Johannes
1480   *Formicarius.* Cologne: Johann Guldenschaff.

Nohl, Johannes
1969   *The Black Death: A Chronicle of the Plague.* New York: Harper and Row.

Noll, Richard
1992   *Vampires, Werewolves, and Demons: Twentieth Century Reports in the Psychiatric Literature.* New York: Brunner/Mazel.

Norman, H. J.
1933   "Witch Ointments." In *The Werewolf*, Montague Summers. London: Kegan Paul, Trench, and Trubner. Pp. 291–292.

Notestein, Wallace
1911   *A History of Witchcraft in England From 1558 to 1718.* Washington: The American Historical Association.

Nynauld, Jean de
1615   *De la lycanthropie, transformation, et extase des sorciers.* Paris:
        J. Millot.

O'Donnell, Elliot
1912   *Werewolves.* London: Methuen.

Oesterreich, Traugott Konstantin
1930   *Possession and Exorcism.* London: Kegan Paul, Trench and
        Trubner.

Olaus Magnus, Archbishop of Uppsala
1555   *Historia de Gentibus Septentrionalibus.* Rome: Ioannem
        Mariam de Viottis Parmensem.

1658   (English translation) *A Compendious History of the Goths,
        Swedes, & Vandals, and Other Northern Nations.* London: J.
        Streater.

Oldekop, Justus
1698   *Observationes Criminales Practicae.* Frankfurt-on-Oder: C.
        Zeitleri.

Otten, Charlotte
1986   "Introduction." In *A Lycanthropy Reader: Werewolves in
        Western Culture,* Charlotte F. Otten, ed. Syracuse: Syracuse
        University Press. Pp. 1–17.

Pandian, Jacob
1985   *Anthropology and the Western Tradition.* Prospect Heights,
        IL: Waveland Press.

Parrinder, Geoffrey
1958   *Witchcraft.* Harmondsworth, Middlesex: Penguin.

1973   "The Witch as Victim." In *The Witch Figure,* Venetia
        Newall, ed. London: Routledge and Kegan Paul. Pp. 125–
        138.

Parry, Martin L.
1978   *Climatic Change, Agriculture and Settlement.* Folkston, England: Dawson and Sons.

Perkins, William
1609   *A Discourse of the Damned Art of Witchcraft* [*so farre forth as it has been revealed in the Scriptures and manifested by true experiences*]. Cambridge: C. Legge.

Peters, Edward
1978   *The Magician, the Witch, and the Law.* Philadelphia: University of Pennsylvania Press.

Peuckert, Will-Erick
1951   *Geheim Kulte.* Heidelberg: Pfeffer.

Pirenne, Henry
1936   *Economic and Social History of Medieval Europe.* London: Kegan Paul, Trench, Trubner and Co.

Pitcairn, Robert
1833   *Ancient Criminal Trials in Scotland Compiled from the Original Records and Mss.,* vol. 1, part 3. Edinburgh: Maitland Club.

Pollard, John
1964   *Wolves and Werewolves.* London: Robert Hale.

Porta, Giovanni Della
1561   *Magiae Naturalis.* Antverpiae: Ex officina Christophori Plantini.

1658   (English translation) *Natural Magic.* London: Thomas Young and S. Speed.

Pratt, Antoinette Marie
1915   *The Attitude of the Catholic Church Toward Witchcraft and the Allied Practices of Sorcery and Magic.* Washington, DC: National Capital Press.

Prince, Raymond
1974 "Indigenous Yoruba Psychiatry." In *Magic, Faith and Healing: Studies in Primitive Psychiatry Today*, Ari Kiev, ed. New York: Free Press. Pp. 84–120.

Purdum, Elizabeth and J. Paredes
1989 "Rituals of Death: Capital Punishment and Human Sacrifice." In *Facing the Death Penalty: Essays on Cruel and Unusual Punishment*, Michael Radelet, ed. Philadelphia: Temple University Press. Pp.139–155.

Quaife, G. R.
1987 *Godly Zeal and Furious Rage: The Witch in Early Modern Europe*. Kent, England: Croomhelm.

Read, Piers Paul.
1993 *Alive: The Story of the Andes Survivors*. London: Mandarin.

Redfield, Robert
1941 *Folk Culture of Yucatan*. Chicago: University of Chicago Press.

Reitlinger, Gerald
1953 *The Final Solution: The Attempt to Exterminate the Jews of Europe, 1939-1945*. London: Sphere Books.

Remy, Nicholas
1595 *Daemonolatria*. Lyons: n.p.

1930 (English translation) *Demonolatry*. London: John Rodker.

Report on Torture
1975 Amnesty International. New York: Farrar, Straus and Giroux.

Risso, M., and W. Böker
1968 "Delusions of Witchcraft: A Cross Cultural Study." *British Journal of Psychiatry* 144: 963–972.

Rituale Romanum Pauli V. Pont. Max Iussu editum.
1614   Rome: Ex Typographia Reverendae Camerae Apostolicae.

Robbins, Rossell Hope
1981   *The Encyclopedia of Witchcraft and Demonology.* New York: Bonanza. (Originally published, 1959.)

Rose, Elliot
1962   *A Razor for a Goat: A Discussion of Certain Problems in the History of Witchcraft and Diabolism.* Toronto: University of Toronto Press.

Rosenstock, Harvey A., and Kenneth R. Vincent
1977   "A Case of Lycanthropy." *American Journal of Psychiatry* 134 (16):1142–1149.

Ross, Eric B.
1995   Syphilis, Misogyny, and Witchcraft in 16th-Century Europe. *Current Anthropology* 36(2):333–337.

Rothman, Theodore
1972   "De Laguna's Commentaries on Hallucinogenic Drugs and Witchcraft in Dioscorides' Materia Medica." *Bulletin of the History of Medicine* 46:562-567.

Roughead, William
1919   *The Riddle of the Ruthvens and other Studies.* Edinburgh: W. Green and Sons.

Rowland, Robert
1990   "'Fantasticall and Devilishe Persons:' European Witch-beliefs in Comparative Perspective." In *Early Modern European Witchcraft*, B. Ankarloo and G. Henningsen, eds. Oxford: Clarendon Press. Pp. 161–190.

Russell, Jeffrey Burton
1972   *Witchcraft in the Middle Ages.* Ithaca: Cornell University Press.

1980 *A History of Witchcraft, Sorcerers, Heretics, and Pagans.* London: Thames and Hudson.

1987 "Witchcraft." *The Encyclopedia of Religion,* vol. 15, Mircea Eliade, ed. New York: Macmillan. Pp. 415–423.

Russell, Josiah C.
1966 "Effects of Pestilence and Plague, 1315–1385." *Comparative Studies in Society and History* 8 (4): 464–473.

Russell, W. M. S., and Claire Russell
1978 "The Social Biology of Werewolves." In *Animals in Folklore,* J. R. Porter and W. M. S. Russell, eds. Totowa, NJ: Rowman and Littlefield. Pp. 143–182.

Sagan, Carl
1981 *Broca's Brain: Reflections on the Romance of Science.* New York: Ballantine.

Scarre, Geoffrey
1987 *Witchcraft and Magic in Sixteenth- and Seventeenth-Century Europe.* Atlantic Highlands, NJ: Humanities Press International.

Schenk, Gustav
1955 *The Book of Poisons.* New York: Rinehart.

Schlaadt, Richard G., and Peter T. Shannon
1982 *Drugs of Choice: Current Perspectives on Drug Use.* Englewood Cliffs, NJ: Prentice-Hall.

Schonfield, Hugh J.
1971 *The Passover Plot: A New Interpretation of the Life and Death of Jesus.* New York: Bantam.

Schultes, Richard Evans
1976 *Hallucinogenic Plants.* New York: Golden Press.

Schultes, Richard Evans, and Albert Hofmann
1979   *Plants of the Gods: Origins of Hallucinogenic Use.* New York: McGraw-Hill.

Schutz, Alfred
1967   *The Phenomenology of the Social World.* Evanston, IL: Northwestern University Press.

Scot, Reginald
1584   *The Discouerie of Witchcraft [wherein the lewde dealing of witches and witchmongers is notablie detected ... heerevnto is added a treatise vpon the nature and substance of spirits and diuels, etc].* London: William Brome.

Seligmann, Kurt
1948   *The Mirror of Magic.* New York: Pantheon.

Seymour, St. John Drelincourt
1973   *Irish Witchcraft and Demonology.* New York: Causeway Books. (Originally published, 1913.)

Shader, Richard I., and David J. Greenblatt
1972   "Belladonna Alkaloids and Synthetic Anticholinergics: Uses and Toxicity." In *Psychiatric Complications of Medical Drugs*, Richard I. Shader, ed. New York: Raven Press. Pp. 103–148.

Shumaker, Wayne
1972   *The Occult Sciences in the Renaissance: A Study in Intellectual Patterns.* Berkeley: University of California Press.

Sidky, H.
1990   Malang, Sufis, and Mystics: An Ethnographic and Historical Study of Shamanism in Afghanistan. *Asian Folklore Studies* 49 (2):275–301.

1994   Shamans and Mountain Spirits in Hunza. *Asian Folklore Studies* 53: 67–96.

Siegel, Ronald K.
1984 "The Natural History of Hallucinogens." In *Hallucinogens: Neurochemical, Behavioral, and Clinical Perspectives*, Barry L. Jacobs, ed. New York: Raven Press. Pp. 1–24.

Sigerist, Henry E.
1943 *Civilization and Disease*. Ithaca: Cornell University Press.

Singh, Joseph Amrito Lal, and Robert M. Zingg
1940 *Wolf-Children and Feral Man*. New York: Harper and Brothers.

Sinistrari, Ludovico Maria
1927 *Demoniality*, M. Summers, trans. London: The Fortune Press. (English translation of *De Daemonialitate et Incubis et Succubis*, c. 1690.)

Siraisi, Nancy
1982 "Introduction." In *The Black Death: The Impact of the Fourteenth-Century Plague*, Daniel Williman, ed. Binghamton, NY: Center for Medieval and Early Renaissance Studies. Pp. 9–22.

Sjoberg, Gideon
1962 "Disaster and Social Change." In *Man and Society in Disaster*, George Baker and Dwight Chapman, eds. New York: Basic Books. Pp. 356–384.

Smith, Geddes
1941 *Plague on Us*. New York: The Commonwealth Fund.

Society for the Diffusion of Useful Knowledge
1846 "Aqua Tofana." In *Supplement to the Penny Cyclopedia of the Society for the Diffusion of Useful Knowledge*, vol. 2. London: Charles Knight. Pp. 204, 443–444.

Sollmann, Torald H.
1936 *A Manual of Pharmacology and its Applications to Therapeutics and Toxicology*. Philadelphia: W. B. Saunders.

Soloman, P., et al.
1957   "Sensory Deprivation: A Review." *American Journal of Psychiatry* 114:357–363.

Spanos, Nicholas P., and Jack Gottlieb
1976   "Ergotism and the Salem Village Witch Trials." *Science* 194:1390–1394.

Spee, Friedrich von
1631   *Cautio Criminalis....* Rinthelii: Petrus Lucius.

Spiro, Melford
1986   "Cultural Relativism and the Future of Anthropology." *Cultural Anthropology* 1(3):259–286.

Spradley, James
1972   "Foundations of Cultural Knowledge." In *Culture and Cognition: Rules, Maps, and Plans*, J. Spradley, ed. San Francisco: Chandler. Pp. 3–38.

Stafford, Helen
1953   "Notes on Scottish Witchcraft Cases, 1590–91." In *Essays in Honor of Conyers Read*, Norton Downs, ed. Chicago: University of Chicago Press. Pp. 96–118.

Staub, Ervin
1989   *The Roots of Evil: The Origins of Genocide and Other Group Violence.* New York: Cambridge University Press.

1990   "The Psychology and Culture of Torture and Torturers." In *Psychology and Torture*, Peter Suedfeld, ed. New York: Hemisphere. Pp. 49–76.

Steadman, Lyle B.
1975   "Cannibal Witches Among the Hewa." *Oceania* 46:114–21.

Steadman, Lyle B., and Charles F. Merbs
1982   "Kuru and Cannibalism." *American Anthropologist* 84:611–627.

Steele, James H.
1975   "History of Rabies." In *The Natural History of Rabies,* vol. 1. George M. Baer, ed. New York: Academic Press. Pp. 1–29.

Stefansson, Vilhjalmer
1936   *Adventures in Error.* New York: Robert M. McBride.

Stewart, Caroline Taylor
1909   "Origins of the Werewolf Superstition." *University of Missouri Studies, Social Science Series* 2 (3):253-286.

Suedfeld, Peter
1990   "Torture: A Brief Overview." In *Psychology and Torture,* Peter Suedfeld, ed. New York: Hemisphere. Pp. 1–11.

Summers, Montague
1933   *The Werewolf.* London: Kegan Paul, Trench and Trubner.

1971   "Introduction." In *Malleus Maleficarum,* H. Kramer and J. Sprenger. New York: Dover Publications. Pp. xi–xvi.

1987   *The History of Witchcraft and Demonology.* New York: Dorset Press. (Originally published, 1926.)

Surawicz, Frida G., and Richard Banta
1975   "Lycanthropy Revisited." *Canadian Psychiatric Journal* 20 (7):537–42.

Szasz, Thomas S.
1967   *The Myth of Mental Illness: Foundations of a Theory of Personal Conduct.* New York: Dell Publishing Co.

Tanner, Adam
1629   *Tractatus Theologicus de Processu Adversus Crimina Excepta, ac Speciatim Adversus Crimen Veneficii.* Cologne: n.p.

Taube, Johann
1783   *Die Geschichte Der Kriebel-Krankheit.* Göttingen: n.p.

Taylor, Norman
1963   *Narcotics: Nature's Dangerous Gifts.* New York: Delta.

Tedeschi, John
1990   "Inquisitorial Law and the Witch." In *Early Modern European Witchcraft,* B. Ankarloo and G. Henningsen, eds. Oxford: Clarendon Press. Pp. 83–118.

Thienes, Clinton Hobart, and Thomas J. Haley
1955   *Clinical Toxicology.* Philadelphia: Lea and Febiger.

Thomas, Keith
1985   *Religion and the Decline of Magic: Studies in Popular Beliefs in Sixteenth- and Seventeenth-Century England.* Middlesex, England: Penguin. (Originally published, 1971.)

Thompson, Charles John Samuel
1934   *The Mystic Mandrake.* London: Rider and Co.

Thorndike, Lynn
1936   "Magic, Witchcraft, Astrology and Alchemy." In *The Close of the Middle Ages: Cambridge Medieval History,* vol. 8. C. W. Previte-Orton and Z. N. Brooke, eds. New York: Macmillan. Pp. 660–687.

1941   *A History of Magic and Experimental Science,* vol. 6. New York: Columbia University Press.

Thrupp, Sylvia L.
1966   "Plague Effects in Medieval Europe." *Comparative Studies in Society and History* 8 (4):474–483.

Thurston, Herbert
1912   "Witchcraft." In *The Catholic Encyclopedia,* vol. 15. New York: Robert Appleton. Pp. 674–677.

Tierkel, Ernest S.
1975   "Canine Rabies." In *The Natural History of Rabies*, vol. 2. George M. Baer, ed. New York: Academic Press. Pp. 123–154.

Tonkinson, Robert
1974   *The Jigalong Mob: Aboriginal Victors of the Desert Crusade.* Menlo Park, CA: Cummings.

Trachtenberg, Joshua
1987   *Jewish Magic and Superstition: A Study in Folk Religion.* New York: Atheneum. (Originally published, 1939.)

Trevor-Roper, H. R.
1959   "The Persecution of Witches." *Horizon* 2 (2):57–63.

1967   "The European Witch-Craze of the Sixteenth and Seventeenth Centuries." In *Religion, the Reformation and Social Change, and other Essays*, Trevor-Roper. London: Macmillan. Pp.101–108.

1988   *The European Witch-Craze of the 16th and 17th Centuries.* London: Penguin.

Trithemius, Johann
1555   *Antipalus Maleficorum.* Ingolstadt: n.p.

A True Discourse Declaring the Damnable Life and Death of one
1590   *Stubbe Peeter.* London.

Turner, Victor
1969   *The Ritual Process: Structure and Anti-Structure.* Chicago: Aldine.

Valle de Moura, Manuel
1620   *De Incantationibus seu Ensalmis....* Evora: L. Crasbeek.

Veith, Ilza
1965   *Hysteria: The History of a Disease.* Chicago: University of Chicago Press.

Verstegan, Richard
1605   *A Restitution of Decayed Intelligence [in antiquities concerning the most noble and renowned English nation].* Antwerp: Robert Bruney.

Walker, Daniel Pickering.
1981   *Unclean Spirits: Possession and Exorcism in France and England in the Late Sixteenth and Early Seventeenth Centuries.* Philadelphia: University of Pennsylvania Press.

Wallace, Anthony F. C.
1966   *Religion: An Anthropological View.* New York: Random House.

Walter, Eugene Victor
1969   *Terror and Resistance: A Study of Political Violence.* New York: Oxford University Press.

Walzel, Diana L.
1974   "Sources of Medieval Demonology." *Rice University Studies* 60:83–99.

Werner, Oswald
1973   "Structural Anthropology." In *Main Currents in Cultural Anthropology,* R. Naroll and F. Naroll, eds. Englewood Cliffs, NJ: Prentice Hall. Pp. 281–307.

West, L.
1985   "Effects of Isolation on the Evidence of Detainees." In *Detention and Security Legislation in South Africa: Proceedings of a Conference Held at the University of Natal, September 1982,* A. N. Bell and R. MacKie, eds. Durban, South Africa: University of Natal, Centre for Adult Education. Pp.69–84.

Weyer, Johann.
1568   *De Praestigiis Daemonum et Incantationibus ac Veneficiis.* Basileae: I. Oporinum.

1577   *De Lamiis.* Basileae: Ex Officina Oporiniana,.

1991   (English translation) *Witches, Devils, and Doctors in the Renaissance: Johann Weyer, De Praestigiis Daemonum*, George Mora, ed. Binghamton, NY: Center for Medieval and Early Renaissance Studies.

Williams, Harold L., et al.
1962   "Illusions, Hallucinations and Sleep Loss." In *Hallucinations*, Louis J. West, ed. New York: Grune and Stratton. Pp. 158–165.

Wilson, Monica H.
1951   "Witch-Beliefs and Social Structure." *The American Journal of Sociology* 56:307–313.

Wiltenburgh, Joy
1992   *Disorderly Women and Female Power in the Street Literature of Early Modern England and Germany.* Charlottesville: University Press of Virginia.

Witters, Weldon L., and Patricia Jones-Witters
1975   *Drugs and Sex.* New York: Macmillan.

Wolff, Harold G., and Stewart Wolf
1958   *Pain.* Springfield, IL: Charles C. Thomas.

Woodward, Ian
1979   *The Werewolf Delusion.* London: Paddington Press.

Ziegler, Philip
1969   *The Black Death.* New York: John Day .

Zilboorg, Gregory
1935   *The Medical Man and the Witch During the Renaissance.*
        Baltimore: Johns Hopkins University Press.

Zimen, Erik
1981   *The Wolf: A Species in Danger.* New York: Delacorte Press.

Index